APPLIED MARKETING RESEARCH

APPLIED MARKETING RESEARCH

DONALD SCIGLIMPAGLIA
SAN DIEGO STATE UNIVERSITY

THE DRYDEN PRESS
Chicago New York Philadelphia San Francisco Montreal Toronto London Sydney Tokyo Mexico City Rio de Janeiro Madrid

Acquisitions Editor: Anne Elizabeth Smith
Developmental Editor: Paul Psilos
Project Editor: B.L. Weber
Design Director: Alan Wendt
Production Manager: Mary Jarvis

Cover design by William Seabright

Address orders to:

383 Madison Avenue
New York, New York 10017

Address editorial correspondence to:

One Salt Creek Lane
Hinsdale, Illinois 60521

Library of Congress Catalog Number: 81-71833
ISBN: 0-03-057634-2
Printed in the United States of America
345-090-987654321

CBS College Publishing
The Dryden Press
Holt, Rinehart and Winston
Saunders College Publishing

THE DRYDEN PRESS SERIES IN MARKETING

Block and Roering
ESSENTIALS OF CONSUMER BEHAVIOR, 2nd ed.

Boone and Kurtz
CONTEMPORARY MARKETING, 3rd ed.

Churchill
MARKETING RESEARCH: METHODOLOGICAL FOUNDATIONS, 2nd ed.

Dunn and Barban
ADVERTISING: ITS ROLE IN MODERN MARKETING, 5th ed.

Engel and Blackwell
CONSUMER BEHAVIOR, 4th ed.

Futrell
SALES MANAGEMENT: BEHAVIOR, PRACTICE AND CASES

Futrell
CASES IN SALES MANAGEMENT

Green
ANALYZING MULTIVARIATE DATA

Hutt and Speh
INDUSTRIAL MARKETING MANAGEMENT

Kurtz and Boone
MARKETING

Marquardt, Makens, and Roe
RETAIL MANAGEMENT: SATISFACTION OF CONSUMER NEEDS, 2nd ed.

Rosenbloom
MARKETING CHANNELS: A MANAGEMENT VIEW

Sciglimpaglia
APPLIED MARKETING RESEARCH

Talarzyk
CASES FOR ANALYSIS IN MARKETING, 2nd ed.

Talarzyk
CONTEMPORARY CASES IN MARKETING, 2nd ed.

Terpstra
INTERNATIONAL MARKETING, 2nd ed.

Young and Mondy
PERSONAL SELLING: FUNCTION, THEORY AND PRACTICE, 2nd ed.

Zikmund
EXPLORING MARKETING RESEARCH

Zikmund, Lundstrum, and Sciglimpaglia
CASES IN MARKETING RESEARCH

CONTENTS

CONTENTS (Continued)

CONTENTS (Continued)

PREFACE

Marketing research is an extremely interesting field. One of the factors that make it so is that it is both creative and analytical at the same time. The creative part of marketing research is largely in the design of research projects to analyze various marketing problems. The analytical part deals with analysis and interpretation of the results of a project. In a way, marketing research projects are analogous to jig-saw puzzles. Each project situation, like each puzzle, is uniquely different from each other. Although each project may utilize steps or methods in common with other projects, each is its own creative situation waiting for a proper analytical approach.

Purpose

The purpose of this book is to give students of marketing research simulated research experience -- in both the creative and analytical areas. The book covers a broad range of research situations and firms or organizations. Nearly all of the situations described are based on real problems or actual happenings, although ficticious names have sometimes been utilized.

The book itself is organized along the lines of a typical research process. An overview of the areas covered are:

1. Problem definition
2. Secondary sources of information
3. Exploratory research and focus groups
4. Research design
5. Sampling methods
6. Data collection forms
7. Measurement and scaling
8. Data collection
9. Editing and coding
10. Data analysis
11. Reporting research results

To Students

This book was written for you. It is designed to give you simulated experience in actually doing marketing research. Most of the exercises in the book are based on "real world" events and firms. By working on the exercises you will gain valuable expertise in both applying research techniques in various situations and in analyzing results.

To Instructors

Applied Marketing Research is designed as a virtually self-contained marketing research laboratory covering major topics from problem identification to reporting results. The book can be used in conjunction with any major marketing research text. A wide variety of situations are available for you to choose from in most sections.

An instructor's manual and a computer card deck for the CONVIS case are available from the publisher. The computer deck includes both an S.P.S.S. program deck and 200 cases.

Acknowledgements

Many assisted in my preparation of this book. William Zikmund of Oklahoma State University and Roger Baran of DePaul University offered valuable suggestions in their reviews. A number of firms and organizations, notably San Diego Convention and Visitors Bureau, allowed me use of various research materials and results. Many past and present students helped in a variety of ways, particularly Lynn Bryant, Ginger Geist, Dave Chambers and Ken Parent. Special thanks go to Sher Brewer, who has performed superlative assistance on numerous consulting and professional manuscript tasks over the past four years. Lastly, I wish to acknowledge the very special people in my life, to whom I dedicate this book: Becky, Jeff and Marc.

Donald Sciglimpaglia
San Diego, California

CHAPTER 1

PROBLEM DEFINITION IN MARKETING RESEARCH

Perhaps the most difficult tasks of the research process are gaining a good understanding of what the problems are and deciding on the research objectives. In general, the researcher should start with a clear image of the problems which dictate the research project. Next, it is up to the researcher, often in consultation with the decision maker, to formulate a set of overall research objectives which pertain to these problems. A final step is to determine specifically what information is needed from the project in order to satisfy these objectives. These information needs are the researcher's attempts at operationalizing the research objectives and, thus, become the heart of the research project to follow. Presented in this section are six short case situations. In each, a series of questions follows this process from management problem to research objectives to information needs.

1.1 Carter's Komet Kites

The Komet Kite was the invention of Rufus Carter, an air conditioning mechanic. Carter had always been fascinated by kites and was also interested in "tinkering" with new ideas that he had.

The product that he subsequently developed was actually more of an airfoil than a kite. After much experimentation, he had perfected a design which he felt was unique. It was composed of two styrofoam disks attached at the centers by a plastic axle. A ring attachment at the center of the axle allowed the disk-axle assembly to rotate freely. Attached to the ring assembly were plastic streamers and the kite line. Notches were cut into the circumference of the disks. As the whole thing was launched, the rotation of the disks and the action of the airflow against the notches caused it to rise (much as a helicopter rotor creates lift).

After much work, Carter had perfected the kite to the point where it now was quite impressive in action. Highly reflective plastic foil covered the outer ends of the disks and made up the streamers. The kite could be launched with very little effort, needing only moderate wind. On fairly windy occasions, it would stay up almost indefinitely. As sunlight reflected from its shiny surfaces, it resembled a small, shiny comet with a shimmering silver tail.

Carter had produced these kites in his spare time and sold them to interested onlookers at the beach and at public parks. The kites cost Carter about $.75 each to make and he sold them for $3.00. On a good day he could sell twenty-five or thirty in about four hours.

Carter had heard success stories of other small inventors who had made it big with their inventions. Therefore, he approached a local marketing consultant with the kite and asked how to proceed with the idea of commercializing it. The consultant, who agreed to devote his time in exchange for a share of the proceeds, suggested that they needed to know such things as who currently made and sold kites, the current market for such products and whether any similar products were currently being sold. Carter was also startled to find out that, unless they sold the idea to another firm on a royalty basis, he would soon have to make decisions regarding distribution, pricing, promotion and other areas about which he currently knew little.

Name ______________________________

1. What specific information needs can you suggest for Carter and the consultant?

1.2 Industrial Dishwashers

Charles Finch and his son own and operate a medium sized firm which distributes materials-handling equipment manufactured by various companies. While most of its sales are to accounts in California, it sells throughout the western part of the United States. Its customers cover a broad range of industrial uses including distribution centers and food processing plants.

While attending a trade show a few years ago, Finch met Hans Busch, the president of a small German firm which manufactures industrial dishwashers. Industrial dishwashers are used in a wide variety of ways. For instance, these products are used to wash dishes and trays in large food service operations, to wash pallets and buckets in industrial production facilities, to sterilize jars and bottles before packaging and even to wash hams and other foods before processing. Although his product line has been successful in Europe, Busch had been unable to find a distributor in the United States.

Recently, Busch contacted Finch and inquired whether or not Finch's firm might be interested in becoming his distributor in the western part of the U.S. Busch also sent brochures concerning the product line and a good deal of information concerning sales and uses of industrial dishwashers in Europe. Also included were price and technical comparisons of Busch's line with competitive products sold in Europe.

Since Finch had never dealt with such a product before, he realized that much needed to be known before trying to enter such a venture. Busch was willing to make $5,000 available to commission a preliminary marketing research study to help generate the information that Finch thought would be necessary.

Name ______________________

1. Define the problems facing Finch.

Can be sell the product in U.S

2. If Finch commissions a research study, what specifically should the study investigate? (What are the information needs?)

1.3 Tom's Pizza Restaurant

Tom Sanders was a fairly successful franchisee of a nation-wide pizza restaurant in Virginia who moved to a new city when his wife was promoted in her job. Using the money he made when he sold his franchise rights, he decided to open his own restaurant. He felt that he was well prepared to run his own pizza restaurant based on the knowledge that he had gained from his franchise experience.

Sanders knew everything about the operational aspects of baking pizzas. He knew the proper proportions of ingredients, the right temperatures and times for cooking and the number of employees he would need at each time of the day or week. He even knew what types of people he wanted to hire. Sanders had an idea of how the ideal pizza restaurant should look, how many people it should seat, the kind of music to play, and even how the restaurant should smell when a customer walked in the door.

After getting several bids from local builders and locating an available building that wouldn't need too much renovation, Sanders started to develop the ideal pizza restaurant. Once the building was near completion, Sanders ordered the ingredients for his first two weeks of business using the customer volumes from his Virginia store as a guideline. He also used these volume guidelines for his pricing and breakeven analysis.

Finally, after weeks of preparation, Sanders was ready to promote his grand opening. Again, he used his previous experience in restaurant management to buy the advertising space for his grand opening.

Everything went well for Sanders during his first few months except for one thing -- his customer volume was so low that he was just barely breaking even. Although customers he served were apparently satisfied with the food and this good word of mouth helped somewhat, sales volume never did meet his goals.

One night Sanders was attending a cocktail party given by one of his wife's business associates. He found himself in a very interesting conversation with the president of a local marketing research firm. The researcher was describing one of his current projects for a national pizza chain. His expertise in site location and trade area analysis became immediately apparent. Finally, Sanders took the researcher into a corner where he could describe his problems with the pizza restaurant. As the conversation unfolded, the researcher found out that Sanders' restaurant was located in an area that he knew had a high average income, low traffic volumes and few activity generators. All of these the researcher knew were typically associated with low-volume pizza restaurants. He also thought he remembered several other pizza establishments in the area as well as many other types of restaurants.

The researcher told Sanders that he needed to determine whether there were ways to build his business at the present location to an acceptable level or whether he should just absorb the loss and move to a better location.

Name ______________________________

1. Define the problem that faces Sanders.

2. What specific information does Sanders need to know to help him in deciding on ways to increase business?

3. If Sanders elects to move to a new location, what kinds of information do you think he should gather in evaluating potential locations?

1.4 Old South Savings and Loan

Thomas Butler, President of Old South Savings and Loan in Birmingham, Alabama, is at lunch with Harry Weissman, the Chairman of the Board. Eventually the conversation comes around to the declining savings rate that their organization is currently experiencing. The problem has the President somewhat concerned as we see in the following conversation:

H.W.: Tom, I've been around this business a long time and I've seen savings withdrawal worse than this several times before. I don't know why you're so concerned this time.

T.B.: I know, Harry, that all banks and S&L's are experiencing lower savings rates due to the current economic conditions and I'm not eliminating that as part of the reason for our lower rates. But what concerns me is the possible shift in our predominant savers.

H.W.: What do you mean by that?

T.B.: Harry, you know that we're one of the oldest S&Ls in this area. We have come to be known as the "friendly neighborhood savings place" and everybody in the area knows us and trusts us. But for some time now, whether we like it or not, the majority of dollars in the area is coming from new businesses who would rather go to larger institutions for their loans and saving needs. In addition, most of the employees of these new businesses are new to the area so they too are more likely to use the larger institutions for their personal needs.

H.W.: Tom, what are you getting at? What do you think we can do about it, assuming you are right?

T.B.: I think if we step up our use of local advertising, possibly with some pamphlets and displays in the lobby, as well as a brief employee training session, we can create an image that would appeal both to the new local businesses and their employees without losing our current base of savers. I think it's important that we communicate our image to the Birmingham community so we are seen as equally competent to the larger institutions and not just a place to come and empty your cookie jar once a month.

H.W.: Hold on a minute Tom! I'm not so sure I like the idea of advertising. Now we haven't done too badly with our loyal clientele in the past and I think if we just pursue additional methods of saving which offer higher returns, our clientele won't be quite so anxious to shift their savings to other institutions. And we are only <u>assuming</u> that is where all our closed accounts are going. We may even be wrong about that! I'm also not so sure that we aren't getting our share of the new business in town. I think we should check on that before we do anything.

T.B.: I think that we need to know more about our customer base. Also we've never done any sort of research on former customers to see why they've closed out accounts at Old South or on potential customers to see why they don't have accounts with us.

Name ______________________________

1. What are the problems facing Old South?

loosing large & small accounts

2. What should be the overall ojbectives of the research suggested by Butler?

Why they are loosing customers

3. What are the specific information needs of the research study? (What specifically should the study address?)

Why they are leaving
What they are saying
what to do to keep them or get them back

1.5 Balboa Square Shopping Center

The management of twenty-year old Balboa Square Shopping Center has witnessed declining sales and increasing vacancy rates -- two major signs of a dying center. Though the center met the square footage requirements for classification as a regional center, trade area delineation studies showed that most of its customers were drawn from an average of only two miles away. Most regional centers pull customers from well over five miles while most community centers pull from a two mile radius.

To help identify and solve its problems, the shopping center management decided to hire an independent marketing research firm. After three months of research and contact with the merchants, the research firm identified the following problems as part of a preliminary report:

1. The center was built in three uncoordinated phases, about five years apart, with no common theme, storefront or traffic pattern. A street down the middle of the shopping center seemingly divided it into two separate centers, both visually and politically.

2. The center is two miles from the nearest freeway with no visibility possible. The city does not allow billboards or highrise signing, so this visibility problem cannot be easily overcome. To make the problem worse, independent merchants have been allowed to build their stores around the perimeter of the center so that visibility is blocked even for those in the immediate area.

3. Access to the center is blocked to the north by a major ravine and is limited to the west by the ocean, three and one half miles away.

4. Parking is limited and street access is very poor.

5. Three highly successful regional shopping centers lie within a five mile radius.

6. The center's advertising budget is very limited since none of the merchants' rents provide an advertising contribution. Instead, the advertising budget is made up from part of the dues paid by members of the Merchants Association.

7. Membership in the Association is not mandatory. Just over one half of the 80 merchants are members including none of the six major anchor stores. When asked to join, managers of the anchors decline, complaining about the inability of the board to get anything done since it is run by "small-minded mom and pop shop owners."

8. The tenant mix of the center resembles a community shopping center more than a regional center.

9. The part-time promotions director, who has worked for the center for years, feels that he alone knows what types of promotions work well for the center. His attitude has forced the major merchants to put on promotions independent of the center.

Now, the research firm is preparing to conduct a major consumer survey of households within the center's trade area. The major purpose of the survey will be to try to uncover ways that the center could increase its customer base and increase the average sales to customers.

Name ______________________

1. What are the major problems facing Balboa Square's management?

2. What should be the overall objectives of the consumer survey?

3. What are the specific information needs for the survey? (What should the research uncover?)

1.6 Brave Bull Steak House

Salfa Hotels, Inc. owns and operates several fine hotels and restaurants in South Florida. Salfa has experienced great success, for the most part, since the popularity of the area provides more than adequate numbers of vacationers and conventioners. One of its restaurants, a high-priced steak house called the Brave Bull, differs from its other restaurants in that it does not have a unique theme. Instead, it is a fine restaurant with low lighting, ample amounts of privacy for each booth, a dark wood interior and red tablecloths. It caters to the more affluent visitors and residents in the area.

In accordance with corporate policy, the manager of the restaurant, Robert (Bob) Nesmith, is directly responsible for the profitability of the unit. Unfortunately, he must have all of his major decisions cleared through the Board of Directors, thus losing partial authority over the restaurant's operations.

For some time, Nesmith has been witnessing a declining sales trend due to decreasing customer counts. Since the restaurant was first opened, many new restaurants competing for the same target market have opened. These large restaurants hold more customers than does the Brave Bull and offer the diner comparable or lower prices. In addition, they have taken advantage of the recent trend in using "a dining theme" when planning the restaurant. This type of planning integrates the menu, prices, decor, uniforms and music around a central theme that offers the diner a "total dining atmosphere" instead of simply a place to eat. Restaurants with such themes have been found to appeal to a wider market segment than non-theme restaurants.

Though the number of hotels and permanent residents in the area have also grown, Nesmith feels that the Brave Bull is losing market share because the newer restaurants are giving customers a more appropriate offering. He believes that if management would have approved his request for remodeling and repositioning the restaurant, long-term profitability would improve.

Since his first request two years ago, he has been forced to make numerous short-range cost cutting decisions in order to meet his compensation goals, which fluctuate with the restaurant's profitability. Since sales were declining, he has been forced to raise prices, cut advertising expenditures and to replace some of the high-paid senior employees (including the head chef) in order to keep the net income in line with upper management's expectations. Nesmith decided to recommend that Salfa conduct a research study to investiage the competitive position of the Brave Bull.

Name ________________________

1. What are the problems facing Nesmith and the Brave Bull?

2. What should be the overall objectives of the research study?

3. What are the specific information needs of the research study? (What specifically should the study address?)

CHAPTER 2

SECONDARY SOURCES OF INFORMATION

Secondary sources of information, information collected and tabulated by others, are often valuable but underutilized as marketing research resources.

Some of the major sources of secondary data include the U.S. government, state and local governments, trade associations, periodicals and syndicated publications (such as A.C. Neilsen's television ratings). Another source is information which has already been collected internally by the firm, such as sales and expense data.

Although secondary data provide a relatively quick and inexpensive source of information, the marketing researcher should be aware of some potential problems in their use. Below are some questions to keep in mind when using secondary sources:

1. Is the information current?

2. What information is available with respect to how the information was gathered? (What was the sample? What units of measurement were used? etc.)

3. Is the information accurate?

4. Is the source credible?

5. How consistent are estimates of the same information from different secondary sources?

6. How well do the sources of information fit the needs of a specific marketing problem?

Fortunately, a great wealth of secondary data, which may go far in solving part or all of a research problem, is located in many large public libraries. In fact, the information may be so vast and abundant for many projects that the beginning marketing researcher often has a difficult time knowing where to begin the search or how to proceed. As an aid in learning about how to use secondary sources, this section includes a guide to locating information and an exercise including an example.

The guide to secondary sources, the Marketing Research Factfinder, is a compilation of various sources of marketing-related information. It is organized by major topical area and progresses from very general sources to those which deal with more specific areas. You should find it useful for conducting research on assigned projects and as a future reference.

MARKETING RESEARCH FACTFINDER

by

Dr. Donald Sciglimpalia

MARKETING RESEARCH FACT FINDER*

This list should serve not only as a guide to free and inexpensive sources of management information for research and planning purposes, but also as an "eye-opener" to the wealth of available data that is yours for the asking. Effective utilization can save hours of time and provide useful information that might otherwise be missed.

I. General Sources

Obviously, the first place to look is the library. However, you can save yourself a great deal of time if you know what you are looking for. The first place to head is an indexing service.

A. Indexing Services

1. F & S Index of Corporations and Industries. (Cleveland: Predicasts, Inc., weekly, with quarterly and annual cumulations). Indexes company, product and industry information from over 750 business publications. Section One, covering products and industries, is arranged by SIC number. Section Two, covering individual companies, is in alphabetical order by company name.

2. Business Periodicals Index. An accumulated subject index covering approximately 170 periodicals in the fields of accounting, advertising, public relations, automation, banking, communications, economics, finance and investments, insurance, labor, management, marketing, taxation, and specific businesses, industries and trades.

3. Readers' Guide to Periodical Literature. Indexes the contents of the nation's general magazines.

4. Public Affairs Information Service Bulletin. A selective list of the latest books, pamphlets, government publications, reports of public and private agencies, and periodicals relating to

---

*Based in part on C.R. Goeldner and Laura Dirks, "Business Facts: Where to Find Them," MSU Business Topics (Summer 1976) and Kathleen Coleman, "Basic Sources on Marketing," unpublished manuscript, San Diego State University Library, 1977. The author gratefully acknowledges the permission to use these materials.

economic and social conditions, public administration and international relations.

5. Economic Abstracts. Semimonthly review of abstracts of books and reports on economics, finance, trade and industry, management and labor.

6. Applied Science and Technology Index. A cumulative subject index to periodicals in the fields of aeronautics, automation, chemistry, construction, electricity and electrical communication, engineering, geology and metallurgy, industrial and mechanical arts, physics, transportation, and related subjects.

7. The Wall Street Journal. An index listing all articles that have appeared in the publication.

   The New York Times Index, The Engineering Index, The Agricultural Index, Psychological Abstracts, Advertising Age Editorial Index and Sociological Abstracts are other illustrative examples of indexes.

B. Periodicals

Illustrative of business periodicals are

Business Week, Forbes, Foutune, Dun's Reviews, Nations Business, Newsfront, Harvard Business Review, Industrial Marketing, Advertising Age, Sales Management, Marketing/Communications, Journal of Marketing Research, Journal of Retailing, Journal of Marketing, Journal of Advertising Research, Media Scope, Distribution Age, Journal of Business, Journal of Finance, Modern Packaging and many others. In addition, there are hundreds of trade publications covering almost every field.

The sources of locating these are

1. Ulrich's International Periodicals Directory. (New York: R.R. Bowker Co.). Includes entries for over 40,000 in-print periodicals published throughout the world.

2. Ayer Directory of Publications. (Philadelphia: N.W. Ayer and Son, Inc. annual). Comprehensive listing of approximately 21,700 newspapers and periodicals.

3. Business Publications Rates and Data. (Skokie, Illinois: Standard Rate and Data Service, Inc., monthly). Also lists publications by trade or professional categories.

C. Trade Associations

Don't overlook trade sources. Many trade associations maintain research departments and collect basic data on sales, expenses, shipments, stock-turnover rates, bad-debt losses, collection ratios, returns and allowances, net operating profits, market share, consumer profiles and significant trends.

To locate trade associations, check

1. Judkins, Jay. Directory of National Associations of Businessmen. (Washington, D.C.: U.S. Department of Commerce).

2. Encyclopedia of Associations. (Detroit: Gale Research Co.)

3. National Trade and Professional Associations of U.S. 1970 (Washington, D.C.: Columbia Books, Inc.)

4. Directory of Trade and Professional Associations of the United States and Trade Unions.

D. Business Directories Company Info

1. Moody's Manual of Investments. (New York: Moody's Investors Service, Inc.). Contains a brief history of each company and its operations, description of products and plants, names of officers and five years of income accounts.

2. Standard and Poor's Register of Corporations, Directors, and Executives. (New York, annual, with three supplements).

   Lists 37,000 corporations. In three volumes: vol. 1, corporate listings indicating address, telephone numbers, officers, accountant, sales, number of employees, SIC number, products and subsidiaries; vol. 2, biographical register of executives; vol. 3, indexes.

3. Thomas' Register of American Manufacturers. (New York: Thomas Publishing Co., annual). Directory classifies manufacturers by product. Includes alphabetical list of trade name index. (In general gives information on companies incorporated for less than one million dollars.)

4. Reference Book of Dun and Bradstreet. (New York: Dun and Bradstreet, Inc., bimonthly). This reference book gives names, lines of business, Standard Industrial Classification code numbers, and credit and financial ratings of over 3 million business establishments in the United States and Canada. These are manufacturers, wholesalers, retailers and other businesses that buy on credit. Each listing contains five or more elements of information. The Reference Book is revised every two months. Sectional editions are also available.

5. Middle Market Directory. (New York: Dun and Bradstreet, annual).

   Lists corporations with a net worth of $500,000 to $999,000. Gives address, telephone number, sales, number of employees, names of officers or directors and line of business. In four sections; businesses alphabetically, businesses geographically, product classification and D-U-N-S number classification.

6. Million Dollar Directory. (New York: Dun and Bradstreet, annual).

   Lists firms with a net worth of $1,000,000 or more. Format and arrangement are like those of Middle Market Directory, except that Million Dollar Directory has an additional section listing top management personnel.

7. Directory of Corporate Affiliations. (Skokie, Ill.: National Register Publishing Co., annual).

   Lists approximately 3,400 parent companies with all divisions and subsidiaries. Index leads from name of division or subsidiary to parent corporation. Very useful when the name of a parent firm must be identified when only the name of the subsidiary is known.

E. Directories of Trade Names

Often the name of the firm is not known, only the product or trade name. In that case check

1. Crowley, Ellen T., ed. Trade Names Directory. (Detroit: Gale Research Co., 1976.)

   A guide to brand, product and other trade names for consumer products. Gives company names and addresses for brand names.

2. Television Sponsors Directory. (Everglades, Fla.: Everglades Publishing Co., quarterly).

Identifies the companies behind advertised products, and gives the addresses of parent companies.

Another useful source is the Standard Directory of Advertisers below.

F. Advertising Directories

1. Standard Directory of Advertisers. (Skokie, Ill.: National Register Publishing Co., annual, with monthly supplements).

Lists more than 17,000 firms advertising nationally or regionally. Includes firm name, address, telephone, officers, trade names of products, advertising agencies and media used, and amount of annual billings. Indexed by firm name, geographical location, trade names and products.

2. Standard Directory of Advertising Agencies. (Skokie, Ill.: National Register Publishing Co., three times annually, plus supplements).

Lists 4,000 U.S. and 400 foreign agencies, as well as media service organizations and sales promotion agencies. Gives, for each agency, name, address (including branch offices), telephone, personnel, major accounts, approximate annual billings and breakdown of billings by media.

G. Directories of Marketing Services

1. American Marketing Association. Directory of Marketing Services and Membership Roster. (Chicago: published irregularly).

Lists market research firms and describes their services; also lists individual and corporate AMA members.

2. Green Book; International Directory of Marketing Research Houses and Services. (New York: American Marketing Assn., annual).

Includes basic information, principal personnel, and a description of services for U.S. and international marketing firms.

3. _Bradford's Directory of Marketing Research Agencies and Management Consultants in the United States and the World_. (Fairfax, Va.: biennial).

   Gives name, address and services available for over 500 market research and management consultant firms in the U.S., Canada and abroad.

4. Weiner, Richard. _Professional's Guide to Public Relations Services_. (Englewood Cliffs, N.J.: Prentice Hall, 1971).

   Covers agencies managing prize contests, clipping bureaus, mailing services, celebrity agencies, television and radio work, skywriting and other types of publicity. Gives names, addresses and descriptions of services.

H. _Information Guides_

1. _Executives' Guide to Information Sources_. (Detroit: Gale Research Co.).

   This three-volume set guides librarians, businessmen and other information seekers to specialized information on 2,300 subjects. Each entry covers a specific business or business-related subject, and refers the reader quickly and accurately to the best sources of up-to-date information: encyclopedias, dictionaries, handbooks, bibliographies, yearbooks, abstract services, indexes, trade associations, professional societies, periodicals, directories, biographical sources, statistical sources, statistical yearbooks, regular statistical publications, price sources, almanacs, manuals, books of tables and financial ratios.

2. _Statistics Sources_. (Detroit: Gale Research Co.).

   This book is a comprehensive, up-to-date compilation of sources of government and nongovernment statistics on industries, products, states and foreign countries, etc., including a plenitude of data compiled by various U.S. Government agencies.

   Other useful publications of Gale Research Company include

   Accounting Information Sources.
   Building Construction Information Sources.
   Business Trends and Forecasting Information Sources.

Commercial Law Information Sources.
Computers and Data Processing Information Sources.
The Developing Nations Information Sources.
Electronic Industries Information Sources.
Government Regulation of Business Including Antitrust.
Food and Beverage Industries: A Bibliography and Guidebook.
International Business and Foreign Trade Information Sources.
Investment Information Sources.
Packaging.
Public Finance Information Sources.
Real Estate Information Sources.
Research in Transportation: Legal/Legislative and Economic Sources and Procedure.
Standards and Specifications Information Sources.
Systems and Procedures Including Office Management Information Sources.
Textile Industry Information Sources.
Transportation Information Sources.

3. Daniells, Lorna M. *Business Information Sources.* (Berkeley: University of California Press, 1976).

   This is an excellent source for a wide variety of marketing and business information.

4. Coman, Edwin T., Jr. *Sources of Business Information.* (New York: Prentice Hall, Inc.).

   Guide to reference materials in the fields of statistics, finance, real estate, insurance, accounting, management, marketing, advertising, etc. Lists for each field the principal bibliographies, periodicals, sources of statistics, business or professional association, handbook, etc.

5. *Encyclopedia of Business Information.* (Detroit: Gale Research Co.).

   A two-volume set which lists data and sources of information for management.

6. Johnson, H. Webster and McFarland, Stuart W. *How to Use the Business Library, with Sources of Business Information.* (Chicago: South-Western Publishing Co.).

   This manual is a guide for training in the use of a business library.

7. *American Statistics Index; a Comprehensive Guide and Index to the Statistical Publications of the U.S. Government.* (Washington: Congressional Information Service, monthly).

   Covers statistics in all U.S. government publications, including Congressional hearings. In two parts: an abstract volume, arranged by issuing agency, which describes the statistics available in each publication; and a detailed index.

8. Frank, Nathalie D. *Data Sources for Business and Market Analysis.* (Metuchen, N.J.: Scarecrow Press).

   An annotated guide to sources of business data, with emphasis on marketing. Includes research services and data bases, as well as publications.

II. Basic Statistical Sources

A. Census Data

The Bureau of the Census gathers and publishes vast quantities of data about the U.S.; much of this information can be used in making marketing decisions.

Areas in which the Bureau of the Census publishes series of reports are

Agriculture
Construction Industries
Government
Housing
Manufacturers
Mineral Industries
Population
Retail Trade
Selected Service Industries
Transportation
Wholesale Trade

Since each census is a multivolume set, approaching these statistics can be a formidable task. To acquaint yourself with census materials, consult

1. *A Student's Introduction to Accessing the 1970 Census.* (Washington: U.S. Government Printing Office).

   A publication of the Bureau of the Census which gives background information and exercises to familiarize users with Bureau of the Census publications and their organization.

For a comprehensive listing and description of census materials, use

2. Catalog of Publications. Has both subject and geographic indexes. Semiannual and annual supplements describe data files and special tabulations, as well as new publications.

Specifically for marketing uses, a useful introduction is

3. Measuring Markets; a Guide to the Use of Federal and State Statistical Data. (Washington: U.S. Government Printing Office, 1974).

   Shows how government statistics can be used in shaping a marketing program; and gives titles and information for federal and state statistical publications covering publication, income, employment, sales and taxes.

To locate information about population characteristics or area statistics, the basic sources are

4. Census of Population. (Washington: Bureau of Census). The results of the U.S. Census contains characteristics of population and reports on selected areas.

5. Census Tract Reports. Contains detailed information on population and housing by census tract.

To locate comprehensive population data on a large geographical area consult

6. County and City Data Book (196 statistical items for each county or county equivalent) or Congressional District Data Book (a variety of data organized around congressional districts).

7. Census of Housing. Broken down by volume to include: States and small areas, metropolitan housing, city blocks, inventory change, financing, rural housing and senior citizens.

Other useful sources which cover a broad spectrum of topics are

8. Social Indicators: Selected Statistics on Social Conditions and Trends in the U.S. (Washington: U.S. Government Printing Office). A publication of O.M.B. which presents statistics on health, safety, education, income, housing, population, leisure and recreation.

9. *Statistical Abstract of the United States.* (Washington, D.C.: U.S. Government Printing Office, annual). This volume is a standard summary of statistics on the social, political and economic organization of the United States; derived from public and private sources.

B. Business Census Data

1. *Census of Manufacturers.* (Washington D.C.: Government Printing Office).

   Provides summary statistics on such things as output, size and employment of firms by 450 categories.

2. *Census of Retail Trade.* Data compiled by geographical areas on retailing by kind of business. Data includes number of establishments, sales, payroll and personnel.

3. *Census of Wholesale Trade.* Data compiled by geographical areas on wholesalers by kind of business. Data are similar to census of retailing above.

4. *Census of Selected Services.* Similar to census of retailing but for hotels, motels, beauty parlors, barber shops and other service retailers.

For other business activities, check

Census of Transportation, Census of Construction Industries, or *Census of Mineral Industries.*

5. *Survey of Current Business.* (Washington: U.S. Government Printing Office).

   The statistical section in each issue is a very comprehensive collection of current business statistics. Areas covered include labor, earnings, finance, prices, major industries and general business indicators.

6. *Business Statistics: The Biennial Supplement to the Survey of Current Business.*

   Provides 30 years worth of historical data for the *Survey of Current Business.*

To locate business census information on a local area basis, use

7. *County Business Patterns.* (Washington: U.S. Government Printing Office, annual).

   One report is published for each state, giving employment and payroll statistics by county and by industry.

C. *Market Data*

1. *Rand Commercial Atlas and Marketing Guide.* (Chicago: Rand McNally and Company, annual, with monthly supplements on business conditions).

   This volume contains over 500 pages of statistics and maps covering every part of the world, together with indexes of over 100,000 cities and towns. Marketing tables present more than 400 statistical items for each U.S. county. Population figures appear for over 60,000 U.S. localities, the majority of which are available in no other publication.

2. *Sales Management and Marketing Magazine Survey of Buying Power.* (New York: Bill Communications, Inc., annual).

   This is an annual reference book that is a prime nongovernment authority for population, income and retail sales data for cities, counties, metropolitan areas, states, and the United States. It actually includes four annual issues known collectively as the "Survey of Buying Power":

   a. *Survey of Buying Power.*

      Part 1 (July) presents population, effective buying income, and retail sales by type of establishment in all U.S. consumer markets. Part 2 (October) gives projections for U.S. and Canadian metropolitan markets, as well as a survey of newspaper and television markets.

   b. *Survey of Industrial Purchasing Power.* (April).

      Gives number of plants, value of shipments and other data for major industries in all states and metropolitan areas.

c. <u>Survey of Selling Costs</u>. (February).

Presents data on sales costs for major industries in 79 U.S. markets, compensation of sales personnel and sales support activities.

Much of the data from the first two special issues is also published in

d. <u>The Survey of Buying Power Data Service</u>. (annual).

Presents market data in three sections: part 1, population and household characteristics, effective buying income and total retail sales for all counties in the U.S.; part 2, retail sales by store groups and merchandise lines; and part 3, television market data, and projections by SMSA for population, effective buying income and retail sales.

3. <u>Editor and Publisher Market Guide</u>. (New York: Editor and Publisher, annual).

This guide contains standardized surveys of over 1,500 daily newspaper markets, with data on transportation, population, automobile registrations, housing, banks, utilities, principal industries, number of wage earners, average weekly wages and principal paydays.

4. <u>Printers' Ink Marketing/Communications Guide to Marketing</u>. (New York: Decker Communications, Inc., published each fall).

Covers over 100 leading U.S. metropolitan markets, including important local trends and developments, population characteristics, industry and employment, financial activity, sales volume, major media and outlook for the future.

5. <u>Progressive Grocer's Marketing Guidebook</u>. (New York: Butterick Co.).

Gives market characteristics, statistical information and a directory of major food distribution centers for all U.S. market areas.

6. <u>Marketing Economics Guide</u>. (New York: Marketing Economics Institute Ltd., annual).

Presents market information for 1500 cities, as well as all U.S. counties and metropolitan areas.

Features detailed breakdowns of population, households, disposable income, type of economic base, and retail sales by type of store. Includes detailed maps.

A useful general guide is

7. A Guide to Consumer Markets. (New York: The Conference Board, annual).

   Presents fundamental statistics gathered from various sources on population, employment, income, expenditures for goods and services, production, distribution and prices.

D. Industry Data

In addition to trade associations and trade publications, check

1. Standard and Poor's Industry Surveys. (New York: Standard and Poor's Corp.). A current analysis of about 70 major industries which summarizes recent data and events.

   [Also check major financial brokerages for industry reviews.]

2. Current Industrial Reports. (Washington: U.S. Government Printing Office). Government reports on such items as sales and shipments by S.I.C. category.

3. U.S. Industrial Outlook. (Washington: U.S. Government Printing Office, annual).

   Gives both short- and long-term (ten year) outlooks in most major manufacturing industries, transportation, distribution, marketing, communications, and services.

E. Retailing Data

1. Fairchild's Financial Manual of Retail Stores. (New York: Fairchild Pubs., annual).

   Gives background and financial information for publicly-owned retail firms, including general merchandise, drug, food and specialty chains.

2. Expenses in Retail Business. (Dayton: National Cash Register Co., published irregularly).

   Gives operating ratios for 35 lines of retail business, as well as guidelines for such issues as markups and salesforce compensation.

3. Park, William R., and Sue Chapin-Park. _How to Succeed in Your Own Business_. (New York: Wiley, 1978).

   A practical guide to beginning and operating a small business. Appendix 1, "Characteristics of Selected Small Businesses," gives specific operating and financial data for 80 small businesses, primarily retail establishments. Includes a bibliography.

F. Advertising Data

1. _Standard Rate and Data Service_. (Skokie, Ill.)

   This series of publications gives personnel, commission, advertising rates and specifications, deadlines, circulation and other information for all types of media. Publications of the service include:

   Business Publication Rates and Data (monthly).
   Canadian Advertising Rates and Data (monthly).
   Consumer Magazine and Farm Publication Rates and Data (monthly).
   Direct Mail List Rates and Data (semiannual).
   Network Rates and Data (monthly).
   Newspaper Circulation Analysis (annual).
   Print Media Production Data (quarterly).
   Spot Radio Rates and Data (monthly).
   Spot Television Rates and Data (monthly).
   Transit Advertising Rates and Data (quarterly).
   Weekly Newspaper Rates and Data (semiannual).

2. _Leading National Advertisers_. (LNA, New York: quarterly)

   A three-volume service which analyzes advertsing expenditures of major corporations. The three parts are

   Company/Brand $. Expenditures in six media by company and brand.

   Class/Brand $. Expenditures by product category.

   Ad $ Summary. List of brands alphabetically with expenditures.

G. Comprehensive Consumer Survey Data

1. Consumer Expenditure Survey Series. (Washington: U.S. Government Printing Office, 1976). Includes: Interview Survey, 1972 and 1973, and Diary Survey, July 1973-June 1974.

   The surveys, done by the Bureau of Labor Statistics for a recent revision of the Consumer Price Index, present average expenditures of American families for products and services. Data is presented by family income, family size and composition; age, race, and education of family head; housing tenure, region and type of area.

2. Study of Selective Markets and the Media Reaching Them. (New York: W.R. Simmons Media Studies, annual).

   A thirty-six volume report giving the results of a nationwide consumer survey of approximately 15,000 adults. The annual survey explores demographic characteristics of consumers, readership/viewing/listening habits for advertising media, and use of 500 products and services.

3. Target Group Index. (New York: Axiom Market Research Bureau, annual).

   A series of fifty reports giving the result of a national product and media market research survey, doing in-depth interviewing of 20,000 adults per year. Classifies users of over 500 products and services by degree of use and brand loyalty. Covers use of all types of media, including a reader quality study for magazines. Gives both demographic and psychographic data for respondents.

H. International Statistics

1. Statistical Yearbook. (New York: United Nations Publications, annual). Compiles international statistics on population, agriculture, mining, manufacture, finance, trade, education, etc. The tables cover a number of years and references are given to the original sources.

2. Monthly Bulletin of Statistics. (New York: United Nations Publications, monthly). This is the current supplement to the United Nations Statistical Yearbook.

I. Forecasting Data and Area Economic Projections

1. Predicasts. (Cleveland: Predicasts, Inc., quarterly, with annual cumulations).

   Gives long- and short-term forecasts for all U.S. industries, according to SIC number, as well as composite forecasts of basic economic indicators. Data is gathered from both U.S. government sources and a large number of business periodicals. The annual Basebook provides annual statistics since 1960 in the following areas: general economics; agriculture, mining, and construction; manufacturing; transportation, communication and utilities; trade and financial services; services; and government.

2. U.S. Industrial Outlook. (Washington: U.S. Government Printing Office, annual).

   Gives both short- and long-term (ten year) outlooks in most major manufacturing industries, transportation, distribution, marketing, communications, and services.

3. Area Economic Projections, 1990. (Washington: U.S. Government Printing Office, 1975).

   A supplement to the Survey of Current Business giving projections of personal income, employment, and population for all areas of the U.S. in 1980 and 1990.

   1972 OBERS Projections: Regional Economic Activity in the U.S. (Washington: U.S. Government Printing Office, 1974).

   Projects GNP, employment, and industrial production by state, by SMSA's, and by other geographical division.

J. Trade Publications Statistical Issues

Many trade publications publish statistical summary issues. If not located in the library contact the publisher directly by consulting Standard Rate and Data Service Business Publications Rates and Data [F.1.]. These include:

1. Advertising Age. (Chicago: Crain Communications, Inc.) Journal issued weekly.

   "Marketing Profiles of the 100 Largest National Advertisers," issued the last week in August. This issue presents data on leading product lines, sales profits, advertising expenditures, and names of marketing personnel.

"Agency Billings," published the last week in February. This issue provides data on advertising agencies ranked by their billings for the year.

2. Appliance. (Elmhurst, Illinois: Dana Chase Publications, Inc.) Publication issues monthly.

   "Forecast Report," issued in February. An issue devoted to sales and other projections by products of the appliance producing industry for the coming year.

   "Annual Statistical Review," issued in April. A special issue reviewing the sales of appliances and fabricated metal products over several years.

3. Broadcasting. (Washington, D.C.: Broadcasting Publications, Inc.) Trade journal issued weekly.

   Broadcasting Yearbook, published in March or April. A fact book which compiles television and radio facts and figures.

   Cable Sourcebook, issued on October. A fact book providing facts and figures for cable television.

4. Business Week. (New York: McGraw-Hill, Inc.) Business magazine published weekly.

   "Liquor Sales," published in February or March. An issue which contains an annual survey of the liquor industry.

   "Cigarette Sales," reported in December. The issue presents annual statistics on cigarette trends in the United States.

5. Chain Store Age - Super Markets. (New York: Lebhar-Friedman Publications, Inc.) Trade journal published monthly with an extra issue in July.

   "Outlook," presented in January. An article which provides a general preview of the coming year for chain stores.

   "Annual Product Merchandising Report," printed in March. A report on the trends for product sections of chain store merchandising.

"Annual Sales Manual," published in July. A full issue providing a performance analysis of thirty-five product categories. Facts and charts are based on actual warehouse withdrawal data for stores that do $1 million or more annually.

"Annual Meat Study," issued in November. A feature article on the status and trends in meat sales.

6. Computerworld. (Newton, Massachusetts: Computerworld, Inc.) Journal published fifty-one times a year.

   "Review and Forecast," presented at the end of December. A section of the last issue of each year devoted to analysis of the industry's previous year and the outlook for the next year.

7. The Discount Merchandiser. (New York: McFadden-Bartell Publishing Company.) Journal issued monthly.

   "The True Look of the Discount Industry," published in May and June. Special annual issues which provide marketing and sales facts and figures on the $30 billion discount store industry.

8. Discount Store News. (New York: Lebhar-Friedman Publications, Inc.) Newspaper published every other week and monthly in December.

   "Statistical Issue," published in September. An issue devoted to presenting statistics on apparel, automotive products, health and beauty aids, hardware, housewares and sporting goods sales in discount stores.

9. Distribution Worldwide. (Radnor, Pennsylvania: Chilton Company.) Magazine published monthly.

   Distribution Guide, published in July. An annual issue compiling information on U.S. shipper associations, container carriers and lessors, a directory of top truckers, air container guide, a piggy-back guide, information for a world ports directory, and a guide to public warehouses.

10. Drug and Cosmetic Industry. (New York: Drug Markets, Inc.) Journal issued monthly.

    Drug and Cosmetic Catalog, published in July. A separate publication which provides an annual list of the manufacturers of drugs and cosmetics and their respective products.

11. Drug Topics. (Oradell, New Jersey: Litton Publications Corporation.) Journal published twice a month.

Red Book, published in November. A separate publication which lists all pharmaceutical products and their wholesale and retail prices.

12. Editor & Publisher. (New York: The Editor & Publisher Company, Inc.) Trade journal issued weekly.

Market Guide, published annually in January. A guide containing standardized surveys of over 1,500 daily newspaper markets in the United States and Canada, with data on automobiles, banks, gas meters, housing, principal industries, population, and transportation.

13. Forest Industries. (San Francisco: Miller Freeman Publications, Inc.) Trade journal published monthly, with an extra issue in May.

"Forest Industries Wood-Based Panel," published in March. An article devoted to a review of the production and sales figures for fiberboard, hardboard, particleboard, and plywood.

"Annual Lumber Review and Buyer's Guide," published in May. A special issue presenting a statistical review of the lumber industry including information on forestry and logging as well as the manufacture of hardboard, lumber, particleboard, plywood and other wood products.

14. Implement & Tractor. (Kansas City, Missouri: Intertec Publishing Corporation.) Magazine published twenty-four times a year.

"Red Book Issue," published the end of January. A special issue providing equipment specifications and operating data for farm and industrial equipment.

"Product File Issue," printed the end of March. An issue which serves as an annual directory and purchasing guide for the industry.

"Market Statistics Issue," presented in November. A special issue giving statistics on the farm industry, changes in farming, tractor usage, farm income, and equipment production and use.

15. Men's Wear. (New York: Fairchild Publications, Inc.) Magazine published twice monthly.

"MRA Annual Business Survey," issued in July. A summary of the Menswear Retailers of America annual survey which gives trends in sales, markups, markdowns, turnover ratios and breakdowns of stock classifications, by geographic region and for the total menswear industry.

16. Merchandising Week. (Cincinnati, Ohio: Billboard Publications, Inc.) Journal published weekly.

"Annual Statistical and Marketing Report," issued the end of February. A special issue which compiles ten-year sales data in units and dollars and household usage saturation for housewares, major appliances, and home electronic products.

"Annual Statistical and Marketing Forecast," printed in May. A special issue providing a survey of manufacturers' estimates for the year's sales performance of housewares, major appliances and home electronic products.

17. Modern Brewery Age. (Stamford, Connecticut: Business Journals, Inc.) Tabloid published weekly; magazine issued every other month.

"Review," published in February. Magazine section reviews sales and production figures for the brewery industry.

The Blue Book, issued in May. A separate publication which compiles sales and consumption figures by state for the brewery industry.

18. National Petroleum News. (New York: McGraw-Hill, Inc.) Magazine issued monthly and twice in May.

"Factbook Issue," published in mid-May. A special issue which compiles statistics on sales, consumption, distribution advertising, and marketing trends of fuel oils, gasoline, and related products by company, state, and nation categories.

19. Product Management. (Oradell, New Jersey: Litton Publications Corporation.) Formerly Drug Trade News. Journal issued monthly.

"Advertising Expenditures for Health and Beauty Aids," published in July. An annual survey of the advertising expenditures for the industry.

"Top Health and Beauty Aids Promotions" published quarterly. Articles reviewing the advertising, displays, packaging and other marketing promotions of top drug and cosmetic companies.

20. Progressive Grocer. (New York: Progressive Grocer, Inc.) Journal published monthly.

    "Annual Report," issued in April. A special issue reporting sales by size and type of store, industry trends and issues, and operating performance indicators for the grocery business.

21. Quick Frozen Foods. (New York: Harcourt, Brace, Jovanovich Publications.) Trade journal published monthly.

    "Frozen Food Almanac," issued in October. A special issue providing statistics on the frozen food industry by products.

22. VENDing Times. (New York: VENDing Times.) Journal published monthly with one extra issue in February and in June.

    "The Buyers Guide," issued in February. A special issue providing information for use by the industry.

    "The Census of the Industry," published in June. A special issue reporting statistics on the industry, including number of vending machines by type, best-selling brands and company operating patterns.

Name ______________________

2.1 Exercise on Secondary Sources

Below is a list of secondary sources from the Marketing Research Factfinder. Think of the kinds of uses to which each source could be put. From a marketing research or management perspective, what information needs or decision areas could the source satisfy? In the space provided, indicate a specific use or purpose for each source.

Secondary Source (information use)

1. Census of Retail Trade (II.B.2) -

   Example: This source would be useful for manufacturers or distributors in making distribution decisions. For example, it would be possible to determine the number of retail stores in a particular category (e.g., hardware stores) in the United States or in a specific market territory. Knowing sales volume and employee size would be helpful in determining the typical size of retail accounts.

2. Census of Population (II.A.4)

3. Social Indicators (II.A.8)

4. F&S Index of Corporations and Industries (I.A.1)

5. Applied Science and Technology Index (I.A.6)

12. <u>Survey of Industrial Purchasing Power</u> (II.C.2.b)

13. <u>U.S. Industrial Outlook</u> (II.D.3)

14. <u>Standard Rate and Data Service Business Publication Rates and Data</u> (II.F.1)

15. Leading National Advertisers (II.F.2)

16. Consumer Expenditure Survey (II.G.1)

17. Target Group Index (II.G.3)

18. Cable Sourcebook (II.J.3)

19. Drug Topics Red Book (II.J.11)

20. MRA Annual Business Survey (II.J.15)

2.2 Secondary Sources Research Study

Conduct a research study using only secondary sources on one of the following topics:

1. A brand of product (e.g., Heineken beer, Pepsi-Light, No-Nonsense pantyhose, Scope mouthwash, etc.)

2. A product category (light beers, sugar-free soft drinks, ten-speed bicycles, subcompact cars, etc.)

3. A product class (soft-drinks, tennis racquets, mouthwash, deodorants, etc.)

4. An industry (racquetball equipment, health spas, stereo equipment, beer, etc.)

5. A company or a product related division of a company (McDonald's, Coca-Cola, AMF's Head, Voit or Brunswick divisions, Pillsbury's Burger King division, etc.)

Your research report should deal with the market, the industry and the marketing programs utilized. An example of a typical topical outline is included in this section. This outline is merely a suggestion and should be used to stimulate your thinking with respect to the types of material to investigate. It includes more detail than you will probably elect to try to include in your report. The finished report should be limited to about five pages in length plus any tables or exhibits that are included. About two or three weeks should be allocated to complete the project.

An example, a brand profile on L'eggs hosiery, is also included. Again, this example should serve to stimulate your thinking as to how to go about this project. You may wish to emphasize other points or to organize your report differently.

AN EXAMPLE OUTLINE FOR SECONDARY SOURCES PROJECT

I. Introduction: the Brand or Product

II. The Company

(brief background, other products and/or divisions, financial resources)

III. The Market for the Product Class or Category

A. Market Segmentation (is the market segmented?)

1. By uses or users
2. By product types or characteristics
3. By customer characteristics

B. Market Profile for Product Category and Brand

1. Demographics
2. Geographical location
3. Usage
4. Loyalty
(and so forth)

C. Demand

1. Size of total market and past history
2. Significant trends within the total market

D. Major Factors Influencing Demand

1. Social trends
2. Technological trends
3. Economic trends
4. Legal or political trends

IV. The Industry

A. Recent trends affecting the industry (resources, prices, etc.)

B. Present and Recent Structure of Competition

1. Identification of number of and major competitors.
2. Market shares of major competitors.

C. Overview of current marketing programs of major competitors.

V. Product or Brand Target Market Strategy

(which market segments, how many market segments, etc.)

VI. Product or Brand Marketing Program

A. Product Strategy (product positioning, brand strategy, product line, product extensions, etc.)

B. Distribution Strategy (channels used, types of wholesalers and/or retailers, locations, distribution share, etc.)

C. Price Strategy (pricing objectives, price levels, discounts, margins, etc.)

D. Promotional Strategy (promotional mix, expenditures, media used, etc.)

VII. Summary

History. Before Hanes Hosiery introduced its inexpensive L'eggs brand of pantyhose in 1970, the women's hosiery market was so highly fragmented that leadership in the industry was nonexistent. Hundreds of companies sold nearly 600 brands of stockings and pantyhose. As a result, consumers generally failed to differentiate among these brands. Hosiery was viewed as a fashion item and was primarily sold in department and specialty stores. When L'eggs entered the industry a drastic change occurred. L'eggs was the first hosiery brand to both successfully achieve strong brand recognition and to establish pantyhose as a commodity item which the consumer could conveniently purchase in supermarket and drug stores. In fact, it was so successful that by 1971, L'eggs became the leader of the women's hosiery industry, capturing a 35% share of supermarket category sales and sending hosiery manufacturers into a mad panic [1:1].

Hanes introduced L'eggs brand hosiery as part of its shift from being an apparel company, which traditionally manufactures garments that are distributed through wholesalers; to being a consumer goods marketing company, which heavily promotes its own branded products directly to the consumer. The overwhelming success of L'eggs can be attributed to several factors associated with this consumer-goods orientation shift [2:9].

Marketing Research. First of all, Hanes invested heavily in researching L'eggs prior to its development. One thing which was observed was a strong sales surge in food, drug, and discount stores since women visited these more often than department stores. Furthermore, although hosiery had been introduced in supermarkets at the same time as health and beauty products, it exhibited a growth trend of only 12%, while the latter exhibited a growth trend of 50%. This indicated tremendous untapped potential. Hanes therefore spent $400,000 on marketing research to discover the potential of supermarket hosiery sales [3:96,97].

Research showed that supermarket hosiery sales accounted for 18% of total hosiery sales and were rapidly increasing [4:5]. There were, however, certain problems. Existing supermarket hosiery was primarily private label -- (i.e., there were no brand identities) -- and no brand was widely distributed. Both product consistency and good quality fit were lacking as women complained about never knowing what size they were getting from these private labels. Additionally, both retailers and women were unhappy with continual out-of-stock problems [1:1-10].

*Prepared by Giselle Geist, undergraduate marketing student, San Diego State University, 1979.

Marketing Strategy: Product. Hanes took these problems into account when developing the L'eggs product, marketing strategy, and advertising theme. With stretch yarns predominating the market, a high quality "one-size fits all" pantyhose was developed which fit 90% of all women [1:11]. The advertising slogan emphasizing this product attribute was then created: "Our L'eggs Fit Your Legs." Ads stressed quality instead of price as the product cost $1.30 while most pantyhose then sold in supermarkets and drug stores ran below $1.00 [3:96].

Packaging. To build brand awareness Hanes developed a brilliantly unique packaging--a white styrene egg which clearly served to set the product apart from all others. The L'eggs "eggs" were placed in attractively colorful displays in suppermarkets near the check out stand and had a tremendous appeal to the impulse shopper [5:48].

Promotion. To further create brand awareness, Hanes used heavy consumer advertising to support the L'eggs product. Ten million dollars were spent on introductory advertising, double the amount spent by the entire industry. Network and spot tlevision, newspapers, magazines, and Sunday supplements were utilized. The slogan "Our L'eggs Fit Your Legs" was continually repeated for the consumer's awareness in order to reinforce brand permanency. In addition, the point-of-purchase L'eggs egg displays were cleverly tied to most ads. An additional $5 million was spent on promotional advertising in the form of coupons. As is shown in Exhibit 1, L'eggs is still the leading advertiser in the hosiery industry [3:97]. In Exhibit 2, it can be seen that high levels of advertising as a per cent of sales have been maintained through the years [6:135], [7:144], [8:136], [9:138].

Distribution. Hanes' brilliantly devised and unique distribution method accounted for the rapid introduction of L'eggs into the supermarkets. To overcome the out-of-stock and service problems which hurt other manufacturers, Hanes decided to distribute directly to retailers. Their own representatives, women dressed in distinctive outfits, not only offered goods to retailers on consignment but performed all restocking and cleaning of the L'eggs display [5:48]. This offered tremendous incentive to the retailer, who did not have to invest in inventory or service costs -- he only had to supply L'eggs with 2.5 square feet for its display [3:98]. By 1973, L'eggs was distributed nationally in over 60,000 retail outlets and had achieved a total market share of hosiery sales of over 10% [7:144].

To monitor the inventory of each of these distribution outlets, an information gathering and control system was subsequently developed by a consulting firm [3:100]. The system enabled Hanes to have complete control of its product so that it could respond immediately to shifting consumer demands [4:6].

Product Extensions. L'eggs has managed to experience substantial growth in terms of both market share and sales (see Exhibit 3) as it has developed several new products in response to these shifting consumer preferences. L'eggs Queen Size pantyhose introduced in 1973, and both Sheer-Energy, a lightweight support pantyhose, and L'eggs Knee-Highs introduced in 1974 are leaders in their respective categories and have all contributed heavily to the brand's growth [7:144]. The newest additions to the L'eggs line of products are L'eggs Control Top pantyhose and Undie-Leggs, a pantyhose-panty combination, both introduced in 1977. A list of all L'eggs products is presented in Exhibit 4.

Pricing. Hanes has used a pricing policy of offering a constant 35% margin to retailers. Since the suggested retail price varies greatly by product, the retailer's gross profit also varies accordingly. Exhibit 5 details this pricing information for four product categories (1977 data).

Customer Profile. The most recent Target Group Index report available does not separate out pantyhose as a separate product category. However, insight can be gained from evaluating the consumer profile of the most comparable product in the report. T.G.I. estimates the following target market characteristics for "heavy buyers" (three or more purchases in year) for bras and undergarments:

age - 18 to 34
income - upper income households
education - high school graduate or some college
employment - not employed (homemaker) or employed part-time. If employed, clerical or sales worker.
marital status - single
race - Latino/Hispanic/Oriental or white.

A complete demographic profile is shown in Exhibit 6. To the degree that the consumers of these two product categories are similar, it is assumed that this profile is close to that of the pantyhose buyer.

Competition. Competition in the hosiery industry remains keen although the number of hosiery manufacturers has dropped from 574 in 1968 to 330 in 1977 to a projected 150 in the year 2000 [10:B51]. L'eggs' only real competition comes from Kayser Roth's No-Nonsense brand. Introduced in 1973, it is not only cheaper than L'eggs at $.99 but allows retailers a 45% margin as opposed to L'eggs' 35%. It is also of the same quality as L'eggs. When No-Nonsense entered the market its advertising stressed the fact that it represented an alternative to L'eggs at a cheaper price. Although L'eggs' share of supermarket sales was cut from 35% to

29%, Hanes refused to budge in price in order to reinforce its high quality image and allow it to maintain its high advertising levels [12:98]. The heavier advertising allocations supporting _L'eggs_ products and their highly innovative promotional schemes account for Kayser Roth's inability to break _L'eggs_ dominant position. The _No-Nonsense_ brand does, however, clearly ranks number two in the industry.

L'eggs has continued to develop promotional programs in order to maintain industry leadership. In response to the downward economic trends of 1975, Hanes developed several promotional items including a "Save $1 Four Pack" of pantyhose [7:144].

Outlook. The hosiery industry outlook looks more promising than it did in past years. The popularity of pants in the early 1970s caused total hosiery sales to decline 8.5% while the fashion shift in 1978 back to skirts and dresses saved the market. In 1978, sales increased 4.8% [13:2]. Industry production is expected to increase at the rate of 4.4% through 1991, although it only increased 1.9% in the last three years [14:B-60] [15:B-70].

The industry continues its trend away from nonsupport pantyhose into such categories as support and control top. Those segments of total pantyhose sales have increased 12.5% reflecting the growing number of women entering the work force on a full-time basis [16:B-65]. _L'eggs_ is the number one brand in both of these categories [2:13].

As is shown in Exhibit 7, the grocery, drugstore, and discount outlets have continued to grow while the department store segment of hosiery has declined [13:10]. This indicates the fact that _L'eggs_ should be able to continue to expand its present market share of 42% of food and drug outlets and 18% of total hosiery sales [17:11].

Exhibit 1

LEADING NATIONAL BRANDS
ADVERTISING EXPENDITURES

Hosiery Brands	Rank	6 Media Total $(000)
L'eggs*	1	9,782.7
No-Nonsense**	2	8,278.2
Hanes (other)	3	6,875.3
Undie-Leggs Panty'n Pantyhose*	4	4,895.0
Easy to be Me Panties & Hose**	5	4,733.6
Burlington Hosiery (Men & Women)	6	3,485.8
Underalls Panty Pantyhose*	7	2,565.3
Pennys Hosiery	8	2,513.7
Slender-Alls pantyhose*	9	2,038.4
Sheer Indulgence Pantyhose**	10	1,427.1
Top 10 Total		46,595.1
Class Total		55,649.6
Top 10% of Class Total		83.7

* Hanes brands
** Kayser Roth brands

Source: Leading National Advertisers [19]

Exhibit 2

L'EGGS ADVERTISING EXPENSES AS A PERCENT OF SALES

Year	Sales	Advertising	Percent
1973	$103,000,000	$21,000,000	20.3
1974	116,000,000	22,000,000	18.4
1975	130,000,000	12,037,000	9.4
1976	150,000,000	13,013,200	8.6
1977	156,000,000	16,502,000*	10.5
1978	190,000,000	9,782,700	5.0

*Introduced Undie-L'eggs and Control Top Pantyhose

Source: Advertising Age 1974, 1975, 1976, 1977, 1978, 1979

Exhibit 3

BRAND SHARE AND SALES RESULTS
L'EGGS BRAND SHARE OF TOTAL HOSIERY MARKET

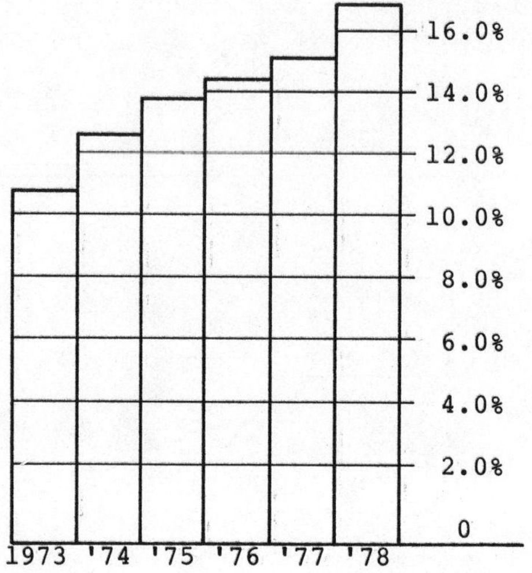

Source:
Hanes Annual Report '78

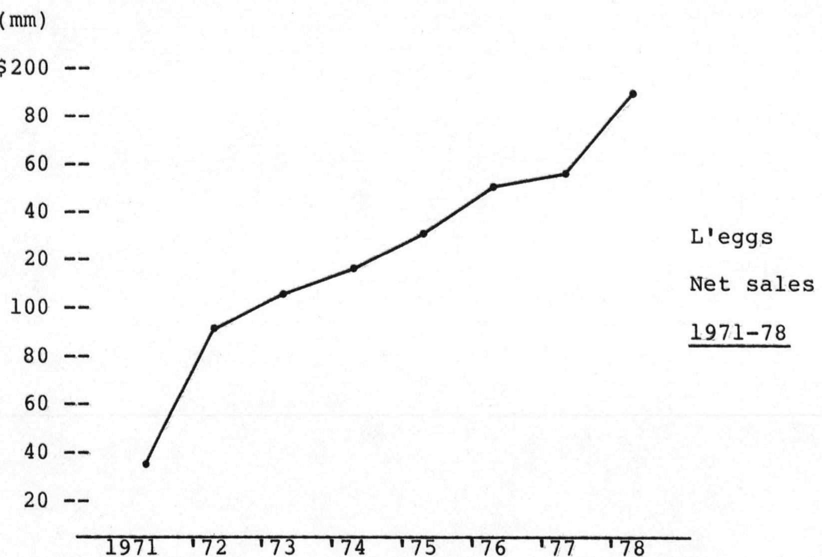

L'eggs

Net sales

1971-78

Exhibit 4

L'EGGS PRODUCTS

Product	Price
L'eggs Regular Pantyhose Sheer Toe	$1.59
L'eggs Regular Pantyhose Reinforced Toe	1.59
"Sheer Energy" Sheer Toe	2.09
"Sheer Energy" Reinforced Toe	2.09
"Undie-Leggs" Sheer Toe	1.89
"Undie-Leggs" Reinforced Toe	1.89
Queen Size Pantyhose Sheer Toe	1.59
Queen Size Pantyhose Reinforced Toe	1.59
Control Top Pantyhose Sheer Toe	2.09
Control Top Pantyhose Reinforced Toe	2.09
"Knee-Highs" Sheer Toe (2 pair pack)	1.49
"Knee-Highs" Reinforced Toe (2 pair pack)	1.49
"Sheer Energy Undie-L'eggs" Sheer Toe	3.29
"Sheer Energy Undie L'eggs" Reinforced Toe	3.29
Queen Size "Undie-L'eggs" Sheer Toe	1.89
Queen Size "Undie-L'eggs" Reinforced Toe	1.89
Queen Size Control Top Sheer Toe	2.09
Queen Size Control Top Reinforced Toe	2.09
"Sheer Energy Queen Size" Sheer Toe	2.09
"Sheer Energy Queen Size" Reinforced Toe	2.09
Promotional items:	
5 pairs of Knee-Highs	3.00
4 pairs of Regular Pantyhose	5.00

Source: Personal observation in grocery store

Exhibit 5

L'EGGS PRICE AND PROFIT DATA*

	Stockings	Regular Pantyhose	Queensize All Sheer Pantyhose	Sheer Energy Pantyhose
Retail/Pair	$ .89	$1.39	$1.49	$2.99
Cost/Pair	.58	.90	.97	1.94
Retail/Dozen	$10.68	$16.68	$17.88	$35.88
Wholesale Cost	6.94	10.84	11.62	23.32
Retail Gross Profit	3.74	5.84	6.26	12.56
Retail Margin	35%	35%	35%	35%
Payment Discount (2%)	.14	.22	.23	.47
Retail Gross Profit with Discount	$3.88	$6.06	$6.49	$13.03

*1977 Price and Cost Data

Exhibit 6

ASSUMED DEMOGRAPHIC PROFILES OF BUYERS AND HEAVY BUYERS OF PANTYHOSE

Demographic Characteristic	Buyers (purchase within past year)	Heavy Buyers (purchased 3 or more items)
Age:		
18-24	32.0%	18.6%
25-34	35.0	22.0
35-49	33.0	21.2
50-64	28.3	15.7
65 & over	17.5	6.6
Household income:		
less than $5,000	23.4	11.1
$5,000-7,999	30.5	16.9
$8,000-9,999	31.7	17.6
$10,000-14,999	30.9	18.4
$15,000-19,999	33.3	20.4
$20,000-24,999	31.3	21.5
$25,000 and over	31.3	21.2
Education:		
Did not graduate high school	24.2	12.5
High school graduate	35.6	22.4
Attended college	32.2	19.4
College graduate	27.2	15.6
Employment status:		
Not employed	34.8	19.1
Employed part-time	38.4	23.3
Employed full-time	24.7	15.3
Occupation:		
Professional/managerial	23.8	14.6
Clerical/sales	41.8	26.9
Blue collar	12.8	7.7
Other	24.4	14.6
Marital status:		
Single	22.4	19.0
Married	32.0	15.5
Race:		
White	31.3	18.1
Black	19.5	12.3
Other	29.3	22.1

Source: Target Group Index (1975)

Exhibit 7

TOTAL HOSIERY MARKET SHARE BY CLASS OF TRADE (percent)

	1970	1971	1972	1973	1974	1975	1976	1977	1978	1979
Food	16.3	18.2	19.8	21.3	22.1	22.6	23.9	22.0	22.0	22.6
Drug	6.0	5.7	6.2	6.8	6.9	7.3	8.1	9.0	9.2	9.2
Discount Variety	28.6	26.7	26.9	26.8	29.4	28.8	28.4	29.2	29.5	31.8
Department/ Specialty	27.2	27.2	24.8	24.6	22.4	20.4	20.8	19.5	18.8	18.7
Penneys/ Sears/Wards	14.3	14.0	13.9	14.5	14.0	14.2	13.9	12.5	12.5	12.5
Other	7.6	8.2	8.4	6.0	5.2	6.7	4.9	6.8	8.0	5.2

Percent of Industry Pantyhose Volume

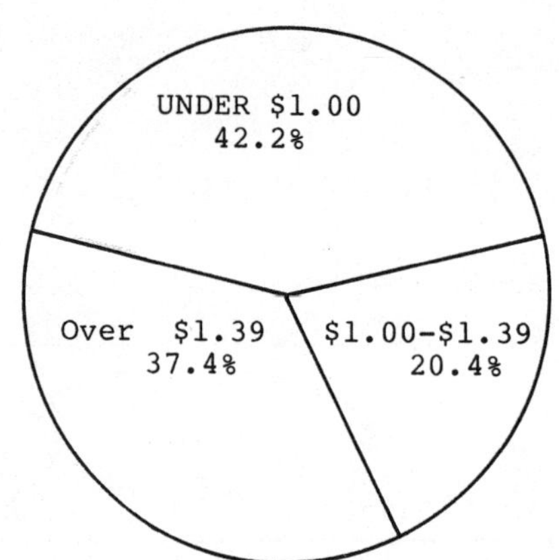

Source: Blue Book of the Hosiery Industry

SOURCES OF INFORMATION

1. "L'eggs-Hatching All Over," Advertising Age, 42:10-11, August 14, 1971.

2. Hanes Corporation Annual Report 1977, pp. 9-13.

3. "Our L'eggs Fit Your Legs," Business Week, March 25, 1972, pp. 96-100.

4. Interim Finncial Report Second Quarter 1979 and Report on the Merger of Hanes Corporation, published by Consolidated Foods, pp. 5-6.

5. "Hosiery Makers Skirmish In Supermarkets for a Bigger Share of Pantyhose Business," Wall Street Journal, November 20, 1973, p. 48.

6. "100 Largest National Advertisers," Advertising Age, 45:135-36, August 26, 1974.

7. "100 Largest National Advertisers," Advertising Age, 46:144, August 18, 1975.

8. "100 Largest National Advertisers," Advertising Age, 47:136, August 22, 1976.

9. "100 Largest National Advertisers," Advertising Age, 48:138, August 19, 1977.

10. Predicasts, Predicasts, Inc., 74:B-51, January 18, 1979.

11. "Textile Giants Slugging it Out in Pantyhose," New York Times, November 16, 1975, p.F3.

12 "The New Sag in Pantyhose," Business Week, December 14, 1974, p. 98.

13. The Blue Book of the Hosiery Industry, Published by L'eggs, p. 2.

14. Predicasts, Predicasts, Inc., 75:B-60, April 30, 1979.

15. Predicasts, Predicasts, Inc., 71:B-70, April 28, 1978.

16. Predicasts, Predicasts, Inc., 70:B-65, January 20, 1978.

17. Consolidated Foods Corporation Annual Report 1979, p. 11.

18. Million Dollar Directory, p. 368.

19. Leading National Advertisers, LNA, Inc., Vol. 5 #4, 1979.

20. Target Group Index, Axiom Market Research Bureau, Inc., Vol. 29, 1975.

CHAPTER 3

EXPLORATORY RESEARCH USING FOCUS GROUPS

Focus group studies are a commonly used marketing research technique, particularly for exploratory research. Rather than being used to generate definitive or quantitative results, focus groups are meant to evaluate consumer opinions or motivations in a qualitative sense. Such a process can be used for various purposes including the generation of hypotheses, the evaluation of proposed product concepts or promotional ideas, the elicitation of new ideas and the understanding of consumer motivations.

Focus groups are typically conducted in small group sessions, normally with between 10 and 12 participants. Careful screening must be done to insure that the group is composed of representative consumers for the areas to be explored. The focus group is led by a group moderator whose role is to lead the group discussion and to ask probing questions about areas which need added depth.

3.1 Air Pacific

Air Pacific is a regional airline serving destinations on the west coast. A good deal of its business is generated by business travelers who use Air Pacific as a commuter or short-haul carrier.

In an effort to improve its position among business travelers within the state of California, Air Pacific commissioned a series of focus group studies containing business persons who were frequent in-state fliers. Air Pacific wished to better understand their motivations for selecting airlines and their attitudes toward various carriers. Also Air Pacific wished to evaluate its California Sun Ship promotional theme and those of various competitors.

The outline used to lead the focus group interviews is shown below.

AIR PACIFIC FOCUS GROUP OUTLINE

I. Air Travel Experience

A. When was the last time you flew a commercial airline?

B. What was your destination?

C. How frequently do you fly within California?

II. Attitudes Toward Flying

A. For what reasons (occasions) do you fly?

B. How do you feel about flying?

[Do you look forward to a trip, see it as a means to an end (fastest form of travel), dislike it but see no other alternative?]

III. Attitudes Toward Airlines

A. Who actually makes your reservations?

B. How do you go about selecting the airline that you fly?

C. What do you look for in selecting the airline that you'll fly?

D. What would constitute an "ideal" airline?

E. Do you have preferences for any airlines?

F. Are there any airlines that you would prefer not to fly if given a choice?

G. What is it that you particularly like about airlines that you prefer? [probe]

H. What things do you particularly dislike about airlines? [probe]

IV. Awareness of Airlines and Airline Communications

A. What airlines operate within the state of California? [including interstate airlines]

B. Are you familiar with any of these messages of airlines currently flying in California:

"Our smiles aren't just painted on."	[P.S.A.]
"Fly the friendly skies."	[United]
"The California Sun Ship."	[Air Pacific]
"The Only way to fly."	[Western]
"The proud bird with the golden tail."	[Continental]
"The big yellow banana."	[Hughes Air West]
"The on-time airline."	[T.W.A.]

C. What do these messages mean to you? [impressions, believability, motivation]

D. Where [what media] are you most accustomed to seeing airline advertisements?

Name ______________________________

AIR PACIFIC

Refer to the Air Pacific focus group outline. What is the purpose behind asking each of the following questions?

1. Questions III.1, 2 and 3. (Who makes reservations? How is airline selected?)

2. Questions III.4, 5, 6, 7 and 8 (attitudes toward ideal airline and actual carriers).

3. Questions IV.2 (familiarity with promotional messages).

4. Questions IV.3 (meanings of promotional messages).

5. Comment on the length of the outline. How long do you think it will take to complete a focus group session?

3.2 Suncoast National Bank Olympics Promotion

Suncoast National Bank is a large multibranch bank on the west coast. The marketing department of Suncoast National was approached in 1979 with a novel promotional tie-in to the 1980 Olympics.

Long before President Carter's announcement of a boycott for the Moscow Olympics, roughly 60 firms in the U.S. were licensed to produce Olympics related products. As the symbol of the first Olympic games ever held in a communist country, the Russians had decided upon Misha the bear as the official mascot. Misha was a cute little animal with a build resembling an Olympic weight lifter. Around Misha's waist was a wide belt with a buckle made up of the five Olympic circles. R. Dakin Company, a San Francisco toymaker, had been awarded exclusive rights to market a stuffed Misha teddybear in the U.S.

Suncoast National had the exclusive rights to use the stuffed Misha bears for promotional purposes in its market area. The bears would cost the bank approximately five dollars apiece. A portion of this cost for each bear sold went directly to the U.S. Olympic Committee. Bob Redmund, the vice president of marketing at Suncoast National, was interested in using the bears as a promotional premium item in order to increase the number of savings accounts at the bank. Crocker National Bank, a Suncoast competitor, had recently seen great success with a similar program. Crocker had advertised that it would give away a Dakin-make "Crocker spaniel" to anyone putting at least $300 into new or existing saving accounts. Industry sources suggested that Crocker handed out nearly 125,000 stuffed toys in the first three weeks of the program. Redmund thought that the association with the upcoming Olympics would generate a good deal of interest in the promotion and that having exclusive rights to the stuffed bears in Suncoast's market area would be a real coup for the bank.

Research Questions. Redmund directed that his marketing research department conduct a study to determine whether or not Suncoast National should utilize the Misha premium. Redumund wanted to assess the appeal of the stuffed animal, the amount of money consumers would be willing to deposit to get a bear, whether this would be likely to be a new deposit and how mnay bears would be desired by consumers. Another thing that he was considering was possibly selling the bears at cost to savers who made a deposit. Lastly, Redmund was interested in whether or not consumers thought that it was appropriate for Suncoast National to engage in such a promotion (associated with the Olympics) and whether or not the fact that Misha was a Russian bear made any difference.

Focus Group Studies. Suncoast National commissioned Professional Interviewing, a local field interviewing company, to recruit for and conduct three focus group studies. All participants were adults who currently maintained savings accounts in the area. The group moderator for each session was Paula Jackson, the owner of Professional Interviewing.

Following is an excerpt from one of the focus group sessions containing ten participants. Participating were eight women (Carol, Mary, Molly, Maxine, Sheila, Jeanette, Louise and Sandy) and two men (Bob and Russell).

MISHA FOCUS GROUP

LEADER: Pick up the bears, look at them and pass them around so that each person can see them. I thank you all for coming here tonight. We're all here to talk about financial institutions and as you are passing these bears around, do you have any idea what kind of bear this is?

SEVERAL: The Olympics.

LEADER: What makes you think is has something to do with the Olympics?

CAROL: The insignia on the front. That's the Olympic thing.

LEADER: Some of you mentioned that these bears have something to do with the Olympics. Does this type of bear particularly have any meaning to you?

MARY: There's a beer that uses a bear in its advertising. It could be that one.

LEADER: A beer that advertises a bear?

CAROL: Yes - land of the sky blue waters.

MOLLY: It could be Hamms Beer.

LEADER: Hamms Beer?

MARY: Yes - uh huh.

CAROL: This is a cute teddy bear . .

BOB: It's a Russian bear.

MARY: I really don't know. His eyes are really sharp on the corners.

LEADER: Are they?

MARY: Uh huh. Very sharp. If a child were to play with it . . .there might be a problem.

BOB: It was made in San Francisco but the parts come from Korea.

LEADER: Oh, really? What does that mean to you? Does that have any special significance to you?

BOB: It means it was manufactured as cheap as possible but also the interior parts are not shredded foam; they're made out of shredded newspaper.

LEADER: Oh. Have you ever seen this particular type of bear before?

MAXINE: I never have.

BOB: Yes, I've seen it on television.

LEADER: You've seen it on television?

MOLLY: It reminds me a little of Smokey the Bear, too.

LEADER: You mentioned that you've seen it on television. How did you see it on TV?

BOB: I can't recall but I do remember it in connection with the upcoming Olympics.

LEADER: Really? What else did they say about it on television?

BOB: I don't recall. It's been some time ago.

LEADER: How long ago was it that you saw it on television?

BOB: In the last couple of months.

MAXINE: I can't stand stuffed animals but this one's not so bad.

LEADER: Why do you like it?

MAXINE: I can't stand them when they're really hard and everything. This one is soft and cuddly. A little kid could carry this around and hug it. I was surprised he said it had newspaper inside it instead of foam because some of them are so hard, you know.

MARY: I think it's cute and cuddly and ...

CAROL: Even a child would like to cuddle it.

LEADER: What kind of child do you think it would appeal to?

MARY: Even junior high kids might like it.

SHEILA: I think it appeals to teenagers.

JEANETTE: I have a 14-year old who would occasionally bring home some.

LOUISE: Our 19-year old ...

CAROL: I've got a 20-year old that would love it.

SANDY: I think the bear appeals to all ages.

LEADER: Did any of you notice the name of the bear?

SEVERAL: Misha.

LEADER: Misha is the name of the bear. You will be seeing this bear a lot in the future because it is the symbol for the 1980 Olympics. Some of you mentioned that you had seen it. Each time that one of these bears is sold a portion of the selling price goes toward the U.S. Olympics Team. Have you heard anything about that? This bear is completely handcrafted; it's washable and it meets all the federal and safety requirements. This bear cannot be purchased anywhere as of this time except by donating some funds to the Olympic Fund. What do you think of the bear as an item itself? For this particular purpose.

MARY: It depends on what age you're talking about. For a little tot, I think the eyes might be a problem.

SHEILA: I think overall it's a cute idea.

JEANETTE: I don't think the belt's really that sharp.

LOUISE: Oh, I do.

MARY: I would take it right off.

MOLLY: The belt?

MARY: Yes, it would be a problem with little ones.

BOB: I think it'll go over ... you can say, yea, gee I'd like to have a bear, you know, because I'm going to give it to my grandchild or keep the bear at the house when kids come over.

MARY: I think they'll like it just because of the symbol of the Olympics.

LEADER: At the very beginning you remember I said we were here tonight to talk about financial institutions and I might tell you that a financial institution might give away the bear for a minimum deposit to your own savings account or for a certificate of deposit. How much would you be willing to deposit to get a bear?

SHEILA: They're going to donate the money from the bear to the Olympics?

LEADER: Could be.

SHEILA: Are they going to donate what we put into the savings account?

LEADER: No, you would put your own money into your own savings account.

CAROL: You're using the bear as a promotional thing to open an account at the bank?

LEADER: Yes. How do you feel about that?

MARY: It wouldn't do it for me.

SHEILA: Oh, I think I would. I have a grandson that I think would really like that. I notice the savings and loan associations give away books and people just flock into those places to get that type of thing.

MARY: But they're free ...

SHEILA: Some things they give away if you deposit say a hundred dollars ...

LOUISE: To be honest, I think if someone in the family was dying to have that bear, I would open an account to get the bear. I would not change banks. They'd get my deposit to get that bear but that would probably be it.

MARY: But if I deposited money into their bank and they in turn matched me and deposited it into the Olympics, that's a tax write off for them but it isn't for you.

SHEILA: They're probably going to buy those for whatever they are sold for and that ...

CAROL: You know, Suncoast Bank had a TV thing not too long ago where they gave a TV set away. If you figured it out, you could go down to the store and buy the TV set and get it cheaper than what you had to open your savings account for. Of course, this one they'd probably set a limit of some kind. Most of the banks aren't even paying interest under a hundred dollars on a savings account anymore unless it's a child, so what it amounts to is that they're going to say, all right, you open it for a hundred dollars or more. They're going to have to have some kind of a limit on this. That bear's not worth a hundred dollars.

SHEILA: You're not giving up the money. You're putting it in a savings account.

LOUISE: Probably the bank would have to be very convenient for you. I assume that this would be a bank that would have branches all over the city.

LEADER: Maxine, how much would you be willing to deposit for the bear?

MAXINE: I think a hundred dollars.

LEADER: A hundred dollars? Carol, how about you?

CAROL: I would not go to another bank and switch for a hundred dollars for a bear, no. Not for this bear.

SHEILA: Fifty dollars if the bank were located conveniently for me, I think. If my daughter wanted the bear real bad, you know. I wouldn't go all the way downtown to do it.

LEADER: Given the bank were convenient to you where you live and you were given a bear for a deposit into a savings account, would you make the change or would you make a deposit to get a bear?

JEANETTE: I'd make a deposit to get a bear if it was located near me.

RUSSELL: I haven't any use for the bear to start with.

MAXINE: I think a lot of people would be banking by mail so of course if you're gonna get this bear you're going to have to go down and open up your account so it would probably have to be a bank that has a lot of branches ... a lot of people ... but I think around Christmas time people would do this. I know people who have opened bank accounts just to get free rent on their safe deposit box. Put a thousand dollars in the bank to do that ... so around Christmas time when people are thinking about presents for a grandchild or for children ...

LEADER: When you say you'd make a deposit to get the bear, would this be a new deposit or would you take this money from an existing account which you already have?

MAXINE: Well, either one. It could be a new account or add $100 to your account if you have an account with the bank that's giving it away. Is that what you're asking? Deposit $100 more, is that what you're asking?

LEADER: No, I'm not saying any specific limit at all, I'm just saying do you think you'd be interested in making a deposit in order to get this bear and what I'm trying to arrive at is whether you would make a new deposit or take the money from an existing account that you already have to start a new account to get this bear.

JEANNETTE: It really wouldn't matter where it came from though. I don't understand really what you're asking.

LEADER: If you had an existing account someplace and you saw an ad in the paper that this particular bank was giving away this bear for opening an account. Would you deposit new money into that account or would you take money out of an existing account?

SANDY: I would take $100 out of an existing account and put it into their bank.

LOUISE: It depends on how much money they want. If they want $20 or $30 deposit, you know, you might take it out of your pocket. But if they want $5000, $100, you know, it depends on what you have. I think it would be a nice keepsake for a lot of people.

SHEILA: Would it be just a new account? Like if I would do it, I'd want three bears. I have three children. I would want a bear for each child.

LOUISE: You would probably have to triple the minimum then.

MAXINE: You just get three friends to open an account.

LEADER: How do some of the rest of you feel about this? Would you prefer to start a new account with some new money or would you prefer to take some existing money in another account and switch it to start a new account with?

RUSSELL: I wouldn't do either one.

LEADER: Why not?

RUSSELL: I bank at a bank not for convenience but for business and I don't go in there for gimmicks to begin with. I've been banking the same place for over 20 years. Like the lady said a while ago something about calendars the bank would give out, that's true. In fact, I go there and I get that calendar and sometimes I call them because I'm with the youth organization and ask if I can get an extra calendar because of the big squares that people can write things in there. They said sure because they're advertisements. All right, but you don't have to open an account. The point being I still bank at the same place I have for 20 years. If they treat me wrong, I would change but

I wouldn't change banks for a bear or for a giraffe or an alligator or anything.

LEADER: What bank do you bank at?

RUSSELL: Coastal Bank. And there are banks that I'm quite sure could give me better service but for all the hassle of going through a change and everything else and when I fill out a form or an application or whatever it is, and how long did you bank here and I say 20 years - boy it don't take them a minute to give me my credit, see, I don't have all these problems because ... I don't hopscotch all over town. These people here don't have any credit as a rule.

MAXINE: Did you say this is a savings account or a checking account? Or either one. You said savings and I was thinking at first you said checking account and then when you shifted to savings account, I think the interest they pay would have to be competitive with other banks provided everything else was equal.

LOUISE: It depends also on the minimum amount of time you would have to leave your money in thre. That's another thing to think of.

LEADER: How do you feel about that? What type of time are you talking about?

LOUISE: Well, if you're just opening the account to get the bear obviously, you know, you're not thinking long term and it isn't my bank and I want my money back ...

MARY: If this is the official Olympics, everybody's gonna have the bear, so why should a bank have it?

LEADER: They cannot be purchased anywhere else.

CAROL: Even at a later date they will not come on the market? You know they start out with everything you cannot purchase and 6 months later you go into any store and buy it.

SANDY: The only thing denoting the Olympics is that little thing on the front there ...

LEADER: This bear has been specifically designed for the Olympics and it cannot be bought anywhere else. Sheila, you mentioned awhile back that you would want to open three accounts in order to get three bears.

SHEILA: No, I didn't say that I wanted to open three accounts. I'd like to open one account and get three bears. But I wouldn't shift all my money from my savings account now and put it all in; I would put in just the amount to get the bear and just leave it in there.

LEADER: How many deposits would you make and how many bears would you want to get?

JEANETTE: Just one.

LEADER: How about you Louise?

LOUISE: I probably would never do it. I happen to agree with Russell. I've banked at the same place for several years and I'm happy there. I don't believe in gimmicks in banking. Banking is business. I don't have a savings account at the bank; I have it at a savings and loan or the credit union. I could buy something similar to that at a store at a competitive price. It wouldn't appeal to me at all.

LEADER: Carol, what would you be willing to deposit to get a bear?

CAROL: I'm with Russell and Louise. I feel the very same way about a bank and I would not take any nonsense from a bank. I do too much business with them and I just won't. Like I said, I bank at Suncoast Bank. I have for 15 years. They had a new gimmick with the TV set. It did not interest me one bit.

LEADER: Molly, how about you?

MOLLY: I agree with all of them. The bear just doesn't motivate me to do anything.

LEADER: You wouldn't be willing to deposit any amount of money to get a bear?

MOLLY: Right. I've got all kinds of bears at home already. I've got frogs, turtles, and dogs too. Personally, my kids are old enough that I'm really not in the market for stuffed animals anymore.

LEADER: Sandy how about you? What would you be willing to deposit to get a bear?

SANDY: I don't think I'd be willing to go to the hassle of opening up an account at another bank. I think it would have to be really convenient to me. I wouldn't just put it in and take it out but I'd want to know the interest rate and if I tripled it, do I get three bears or whatever. There's too many things to it. It's not worth it. It's a waste of time.

LEADER: Say the bank was convenient to where you live and you were interested in making a deposit, how much would you be willing to deposit for a bear?

SANDY: I'm interested in finding a bank right now because I'm going to change mine. But I don't know, you know, I've no idea. I don't think I'd do it. If I went home and told my husband I was going to do something like that for a bear he'd probably laugh at me.

LEADER: But what if this bank was convenient to where you live?

SANDY: If there were three different banks on the block, would I go to the one with the bear? I'd have to check them all out but I doubt it because if they're busy doing this, they're not busy doing the other things.

CAROL: You know, I'd rather see a bank have the bear for sale for so much and have it go to the Olympics. You are saying that none of the money that we deposit goes to the Olympics.

LEADER: I didn't say that. I don't know.

CAROL: This would make the difference. If some of the money would go to the Olympics. Or if they matched your money.

LEADER: How about if they were willing to make a minimum deposit into the Olympics Fund for each deposit that you made. How would you feel about that?

SANDY: That would give me a lot more incentive.

MAXINE: They might have to.

LOUISE: Originally it was Olympic property. They evidently have to pay the Olympic people.

LEADER: What if the bear would be sold to you at the financial institution's cost of $5.00. How much would you be willing to deposit to buy a bear for $5.00? Would you be willing to make a deposit?

SHEILA: In other words, you're contributing to the Olympics.

MAXINE: Would the $5.00 go into the Olympics?

LEADER: Carol, how would you feel about making a deposit if you could buy that bear for $5.00?

CAROL: If the money was going for a good cause to the Olympics, then I would seriously consider it. I mean, I feel that we don't give much to our Olympics ... we should support them, I really do. I would really consider it then.

SANDY: Saying the Olympics, you mean our team?

LEADER: It would be the 1980 Olympics.

SANDY: You mean the United States.

LEADER: The United States, right.

SHEILA: It's the '84 Olympics that we're holding in this country that we have to worry about how to fund. And the '80 - the Russians are putting it on, aren't they?

SANDY: I don't care who's putting it on. Is it going to help our team or to help the Olympics, period?

LEADER: It's for the U.S. Olympic Team.

CAROL: I'd rather pay $15.98 for a bear if I knew that $4 or $5 was going to the Olympics, than to go and open an account.

LEADER: Why is that? If you could go and open a savings account and just pay $5 to get that bear, why would you want to do that?

CAROL: Because what if it was a bank I didn't like and there's a few I don't like. I won't have anything to do with. I wouldn't do it.

LEADER: What would a bank have to do to convince you that they had that bear for sale for $5?

CAROL: Well, it's the bank. It has to be the people that work in the bank; it has to be how they handle my money; if they know me when I come in to make a deposit and I don't have to go through all this hassle; if I want a loan, I can call up so-and-so and say, "Hey, such-and-such, I want this," "Fine, fill your papers out, come in and sign them." I don't have to go through all that hassle. In a new bank they wouldn't know you. I'd have to really consider all these things if I was going to transfer an account.

LOUISE: You don't have to transfer a whole account.

CAROL: Well, even just to open an account because if I'm going to deal with a bank, I'm going to do more than just put my money in.

MAXINE: If you only had to deposit a $100 in an account to get this bear, you really could go ahead and keep your banking relationship. You really wouldn't jeopardize that.

MARY: To me that's not worth it. I want to deal with the people at the bank.

LOUISE: I like things in order in my life and having an account here and an account there and an account here just would drive me crazy. I like it just simple and I like to know people and I like to know that I have an account there and everything and no gimmick in the world would get me to change. It's the service.

LEADER: Okay, getting back to the subject, where we asked how much would you be willing to deposit to buy a bear, how many bears would you buy, Maxine, for instance, if you were going to go to a bank, knowing that you could deposit some money and buy some bears, how many bears would you buy?

MAXINE: Probably only one.

LEADER: Only one?

MAXINE: I have a grandson that I might consider buying one for.

LEADER: Russell, how about you?

RUSSELL: Well, I've got some godsons. I don't know. If I went in I'd probably only buy one but if my wife went in, she'd probably come back with about six. That's the difference right there. She'd have to have one for all my godsons and close friends and all that jazz.

LEADER: Mary, how about you?

MARY: No. When I look at the bear, the only thing that I see is the logo thing can come off very easily and so that's the symbol of the Olympics and apart from that, it's just a bear.

LEADER: If the bank had this idea for the bear and they were going to charge you $5 if you opened a new savings account, that would not interest you at all, is that what you're saying?

MARY: Uh huh.

LOUISE: Chances are you'd have to take the belt off if you had a baby, anyway.

MARY: Well, we have two grandchildren who are small and that would come off right away. And they have lots of stuffed toys, so that would come off and so then you're left with just a bear. It would appeal I think to older children who want to put it on the shelf and display it as a souvenir rather than smaller children who would want to play with it.

LEADER: Now, I'm going to tell you that the financial institution thinking of offering Misha is Suncoast Bank. The bank is also thinking of using Misha as its symbol or mascot. What do you think of that?

SHEILA: I don't like the idea.

LEADER: Why not?

SANDY: Well, it would be just for one year like the bicentennial thing, like that. Just because they donated the money to the Olympics then they can use that.

LEADER: I'm really not aware of the entire situation but as far as them just using it as their mascot.....

RUSSELL: No, I don't like the idea at all.

LEADER: What are your reasons for feeling that way?

RUSSELL: Well, does a bank need a mascot? To me a bank is a place of business; why do they have to have a mascot?

MARY: I think ... that they are backing our Olympic Committee and they'd like your help so that could be a good reason to have it as a mascot. You know, we are doing this for our Olympic Committee.

RUSSELL: Well, if you know the bears are at the bank, they don't need it as a mascot. I just don't go for it at all.

BOB: The Olympics have it as their mascot, on their stationery advertising, so forth, that's one thing but if they're promoting the bank with it as a commercial venture, I think I just don't like that idea.

LEADER: Why not?

BOB: Well, I think it's devised for something else. It's devised to advertise the Olympics - to make money for the Olympics.

MAXINE: I think if they go very far with that they'll have the Olympic Committee down on them because I don't think they'd be allowed to.

MARY: If they just supported the Olympics in their advertisement and gave these away, they would be very patriotic and civic minded but if they used it as their mascot for their bank, it just doesn't seem right.

LEADER: How do you think it would affect their image?

SHEILA: Their image would be very good if they supported the Olympic team. Their image would look like fun and games if they used it just for themselves. Banking isn't fun and games.

LEADER: Carol, you said you have an account with the Suncoast Bank. How would this in your mind affect their image?

CAROL: I'm like her. I think it's dumb. For the Olympics, yes, I'm 100% for that. If I know that this bear and some of the money that I'm paying for this bear is going to the Olympics, yes, I'm 100% for it; but as far as just saying this bear represents Suncoast Bank for TV and stuff, I'm sorry, that's dumb. You know, I really don't like it.

LEADER: Molly, how do you feel about that, knowing now which bank it's for, as far as their image is concerned, how would it impress you?

MOLLY: It would depend on how they did it, like everybody's been saying. If they were using it as saying we're doing this for the Olympics and we're putting money - you know, the money for this goes towards the Olympics, I think that's great. But if they're trying to get your business by using your sentiment towards this bear and your feelings about that cause, I think it's tacky.

MARY: The bear does grow on you.

MOLLY: He is cute.

LEADER: Does it bring any other association to mind when you see it?

LOUISE: Can't you just see him skiing down the slopes in the Olympics? ...

MAXINE: And drinking a Hamms beer when he gets to the bottom ...

CAROL: ... on his way to make a deposit.

LEADER: Now, Misha is a Russian bear and it is the mascot for the 1980 Olympics in Moscow. The fact that this is a Russian bear, does this make any difference to you in your thoughts about the bear?

CAROL: No. Unless you read this card, you wouldn't know.

MARY: No, Misha's a cute name. If you read the card and if you didn't, you'd just think it was a cute bear.

SANDY: I think it's kind of a nice idea. It's a friendly competition thing rather than hard core "we're gonna get you guys" you know.

RUSSELL: Friendly competition? You're kidding?

SANDY: All right, I'm talking about ideals.

SHEILA: I'd like to think that there was no problems.

LEADER: Mary, how about you? The fact that it is a Russian bear, how does this affect you?

MARY: Nothing.

SHEILA: I really don't think they think about it being a Russian bear because a California bear is very brown ...

MARY: If I hadn't read the card, they wouldn't even think about it.

RUSSELL: The Russian bear idea, though, kind of works against me because I've seen so many cartoons in my lifetime portraying Russia as a big, old ugly looking bear.

MAXINE: It depends on the generation, then, because the kids would think of "Yogi."

LEADER: Do you think that using a Russian bear as a gift for making deposits will have any affect on Suncoast Bank's image?

MARY: Well, you noticed how we all wanted to know whether or not this money was going to one of the teams and that tells you.

SANDY: No, it didn't tell you because I said it. What I meant was did the money go to our team or was it going to the Olympics?

LEADER: It goes to the U.S. Olympic Team.

LOUISE: It doesn't matter where it's going ...

MARY: Yes, it would matter to me. I would want to support my own country's team.

MOLLY: I don't think we support a team anyway.

LEADER: Each country has to support their own team and the money from the sale of these bears will go to the U.S. Olympic Team.

MARY: We're not arguing that. We're just saying about the Russian bear, whether or not that will ... for my money I would absolutely want it to go to the American team.

RUSSELL: Why is it a Russian bear?

CAROL: That's where the Olympics are held; he's the symbol of the Olympic games.

MARY: The Olympics coming up pretty soon in Russia that we will bc going to.

SHEILA: Next summer - 1980.

LEADER: Do you think that using a Russian bear as a mascot will have any affect on the bank's image?

MOLLY: Why don't they just use an American bear?

LEADER: Well, because this is the symbol that has been drawn up for the Olympics.

MOLLY: I don't think really ... I didn't even realize it was a Russian bear until I read the card. You know, until you brought it up, I hadn't even thought about it.

MARY: Who's going to know the difference?

CAROL: We've got Russian bears at the zoo.

RUSSELL: I'm probably a minority but I for one belive in America 300% and the fact that Russia would be involved in it would be enough right there to turn me off, really.

LEADER: The fact that this is a Russian bear turns you off?

RUSSELL: Probably someday my son's going to have to go over there and fight. I'm just very funny this way. Like I said I'm probably a minority. A lot of people wouldn't feel this way but I'm very, very strong about it. Like when I take a vacation, I want to see the United States before I do anything else.

LEADER: Does anybody else feel this way?

SEVERAL: No.

MAXINE: The symbol is usually representative of the country. If it was Mexico, we have the sombrero. You know, the country is represented in the symbol each time.

RUSSELL: Well, there are other factors that I hadn't mentioned, like Russia owes us how many millions and billions of dollars they've never paid us; I just don't see why we should use any Russian symbol, period. If they'd paid their debts like they're supposed to have and everything, it might be a different story. But they owe us billions and billions of dollars from the Second World War, for crying out loud, plus everything after that they haven't paid. I see no reason why we ...

MAXINE: It's too bad the Olympics have to become political, though.

SANDY: What bothers me is we say that this is for the United States Olympic Team, right? But on this little bear here it says "organizing committee of the 1980 Olympic Games in Moscow." OK? Now, I want to now who they bought these from? If they bought them from the Russians, if so, then the money is not going to our American team.

LEADER: Well, all I can tell you is ...

SANDY: It might be propaganda. They might tell you that this is for the American team but it might be going over there. The Olympics need to be supported but who are we supporting here?

LEADER: We're supporting the U.S. Olympic Team.

SANDY: It does not say that on here.

RUSSELL: It says it on the card.

LEADER: It says it on your card here. It says, "Misha is the official mascot of the 1980 Moscow Olympic Games. A portion of the purchase price of Misha goes to the support of your country's Olympic Committee."

CAROL: OK, which country? These were probably sold to every country that participates in the Olympics.

MAXINE: The country that hosts the Olympics has the privilege of deciding what their mascot is going to be and as you were pointing out when it was in Mexico, they had something typical of Mexico. This year it's going to be in Moscow so the symbol is very typical of Russia and I think it's too bad when they let it become so political ...

JEANETTE: They have to get that money back to defray the cost of putting on the Olympic Games and we will have to get someting going like this in this country when they are held here.

SANDY: When will we have it here, 1984? Why don't they wait until 1984 and do something for the United States. Well, I don't feel that we're paying for the United States team; I feel that this is for the Olympics itself.

MOLLY: Remember those blazer badges that you could send $5 for? Every four years you get a blazer badge for the Olympic team. It's the same thing. You spend $5 to get a patch to put on your blazer or your coat.

MARY: Yea, but who gets that?

MOLLY: The American Olympic Team to buy their uniforms and defray the cost of keeping them there for the two weeks that they're there.

CAROL: Well, this is the same thing. The U.S. Olympic Team has bought these; that's what it amounts to ... from Moscow and they're trying to make money off it.

RUSSELL: Well, how come one bank has it then?

MAXINE: Because they want to support the Olympics.

LOUISE: Well, they got in first.

SANDY: How could they buy them from Moscow?

SHEILA: Probably the committee approached several financial institutions, manufacturing companies and large companies and asked them for their help and their support in this thing. I have no particular feelings about this bank. It's not mine but I rather imagine they wanted to support the Olympic Committee and said O.K., we will buy these and they want to get a little bit of return and figure how best they can use it to their benefit too.

LEADER: O.K., you as a nonuser of this particular bank, knowing that this bear may have some sort of affiliation with this particular bank, does that increase or decrease your feelings one way or the other as to your image of that bank? Or what they're trying to do?

SHEILA: I just get the impression that they want to help the Olympics or they wouldn't get involved in this in the first place. I think they're probably a little concerned about how their image is going to be concerned. That's why they're paying for this survey. My only impression is that they are trying to support the Olympics by buying these things in the first place.

LEADER: If they give these bears or sell them for $5 for opening a new savings account, would that increase your feelings about doing that in that particular bank one way or the other?

SHEILA: Well I think it might.

MOLLY: I do, too. I would rather have them give you the bear or let you buy the bear instead of having to open up an account.

LEADER: Well, those of you who do not have an account at this bank, if the bears were for sale at this particular bank, would you come in and buy these bears from this bank knowing that the money goes to the Olympic Team?

SHEILA: I would.

LOUISE: Yea.

LEADER: Sandy, how about you?

SANDY: I don't know if I would. I need to know where the money's going.

LEADER: Well, I'm telling you that it would go to the Olympic team.

SANDY: Would it go to the bank?

LEADER: No, it's not going to the bank.

SANDY: You're telling me that it's going to the Olympic team. I don't know if I would or not. Now, if the bank as an institution supported the making of these bears for the Olympics, like this lady over here said, fine. I'll go with it.

SANDY: I would go in the bank no matter what it was and buy one.

LEADER: How many would you buy?

SANDY: It depends on how much they were and how many kids I had at the time and you know. If I had one child, I'd buy one now. I'll have two in a short time. I'd probably buy two in a couple of months.

LEADER: O.K., now let's talk about if the bank said that they were going to sell you these for $5 or, first of all, they were going to give you these for opening a new account at their bank, would that increase your feelings about opening a new savings account at that bank?

SANDY: Not unless I was ready to do so at that time anyway.

JEANETTE: A children's account, maybe?

SHEILA: I would open an account. I like to think I'm getting something free. If I could go down and open an account for $100 and get one free, oh, I would be so happy. I don't know how many I'd go buy.

RUSSELL: If I could put five bucks in a child's account and put his name on there and it's his savings account, fine, give me the bear.

LEADER: But you would only be willing to deposit five dollars?

RUSSELL: Sure, the price of the bear.

LEADER: Let's say, what is the maximum amount you would be willing to deposit in order to get one of these bears free?

MOLLY: What interest do you get on $100?

MAXINE: 5-1/2 percent now - that is about $5 for a year. I would put $100 in their bank for a year. That's my deal - take it or leave it.

SANDY: Ok, but you're saying you'll make $5.25 a year on this $100?

MAXINE: Well isn't that right? My arithmetic isn't the best.

SANDY: Wait a minute. What if you took it out in six months. You'd lose money.

MAXINE: I said I would leave it in for a year and then somehow my brain would think that they're going to be paying me 5-1/2 percent on that $100 for the year. I got my interest and I got a $5 bear and I'd be very happy and I would give it to some child.

CAROL: And 90 percent of the people are just like that.

SANDY: Yes, they would probably do it if they said they got the bear free and the bank got to keep the interest, they'd probably still do it.

CAROL: No, the bank wouldn't keep your interest. They can't.

RUSSELL: They have hotels with bars on the windows for people who do things like that.

Name ______________________________

SUNCOAST NATIONAL BANK OLYMPICS PROMOTION

1. Would you say that the group leader (Paula Jackson) did a good job in moderating the focus group session? Why or why not?

Yes, she delved into several topics and got the heart

2. To what types of consumers would Misha most appeal?

housewives
students
teens
first time openers
not older people, because they have accounts

3. What do you conclude about the basic concept of a promotional tie-in with the Olympics?

good image builder

4. What can you conclude about how much consumers would be willing to deposit in order to get a stuffed animal?

50-100

5. Do you think that it makes the most sense to offer the bear free with a minimum deposit or to sell the bear at cost? Explain.

Free to new depositors, if sold no one would
Deposit, Depends on objectives:
1 Inc
2 New Deposits
if Inc sell
if Deposits give away

6. What do participants think about such a promotion being offered at Suncoast National?

O.k

7. Is the fact that Misha is a Russian bear of any concern?

no

8. Do you think that Redmund should utilize the Misha promotion?

Yes

CHAPTER 4

RESEARCH DESIGN

Commonly used marketing research designs include observation studies, experimental studies and surveys. Observation is often used to collect information concerning aspects of consumer behavior. In situations where other methods of data collection might prove difficult or might produce inaccurate results, observation is particularly useful.

Experimentation is used to test various components of the marketing effort. In either a field or simulated (lab) experimental study, the researcher attempts to assess the effect of a variable under control (such as level of advertising expenditure) on a related dependent variable (such as advertising recall).

Surveys are means of communicating with respondents. The survey may be an interview or may be self-administered. Survey techniques include mail surveys, telephone interview surveys and personal interview surveys. Often a research project may require a combination of techniques to achieve optimal results (e.g., personal contact to achieve cooperation but self-administered questionnaire to improve quality of responses to sensitive questions).

ANALYZING RESEARCH DESIGNS

4.1 La Quinta Motor Inns

La Quinta Motor Inns is a chain of motels targeted to business travelers. Situated at freeway locations in major commercial cities in eighteen states, the chain offers comfortable, clean, quiet rooms with color television and telephone service at a reasonable price. Except for a swimming pool, a La Quinta Motor Inn offers few amenities such as nightclubs or entertainment.

In an effort to evaluate the opinions of guests toward La Quinta and competitive chains, management conducted the following study. The marketing department generated a list of 250 guests from each of the chain's inns or a total of approximately 10,000. Each selected guest was mailed a short survey questionnaire with a letter from the Director of Marketing requesting participation and a twenty-five cent piece as an incentive. Overall, the return rate was roughly 56%.

Name ______________________________

1. What type of research design was used in this project?

2. Are there any potential problems or sources of error to be aware of?

4.2 Army ROTC

The regional directors of the U.S. Army's Reserve Officer Training Corps (ROTC) programs at colleges and universities were recently directed to conduct research on various campuses concerning attitudes toward the program. A survey instrument was constructed which dealt with cadet opinions of the program, motivations for joining ROTC, and cadets' perceptions of non-ROTC students' attitudes toward the program.

Since many of the questions were open-ended, the survey was designed as a personal interview allowing each cadet the opportunity to state his/her opinions as completely as necessary. At the designated campuses cadets were selected by the local commanding officers. Each was scheduled for a specific appointment and was interviewed by a member of the staff. Responses were forwarded to Washington D.C. for analysis.

Name ______________________________

1. What type of research design was used in this study?

2. Are there any potential problems or sources of error to be aware of in this research?

3. How might the research design be improved?

4.3 Aim Toothpaste

Aim toothpaste was designed as a competitor to Procter and Gamble's Crest brand, the leader in the stannous flouride (cavity prevention) segment of the toothpaste market. Lever Brothers, the makers of Aim, developed the product as a good tasting gel rather than a paste (such as Crest). The fact that it was good tasting would hopefully encourage children to adopt better brushing habits. Being a gel made the product low in abrasion and gave it a faster "dispersal rate," allowing the stannous flouride to spread rapidly in the normal brushing time.

In the course of product development for Aim, research was conducted to verify the assumptions concerning children's reaction to the taste of the product and its cavity preventative properities. Three separate studies were conducted. In blind taste tests with the two leading stannous flouride brands, Aim's taste was preferred. In two long-term tests (roughly three years long), Aim was compared to Crest in actual in-home use. No significant differences were found between Aim and Crest in reducing cavities, while both were significantly better than a placebo toothpaste (nonflouride) used as a control product for comparison. Roughly 3,000 children in different geographical locations participated in the clinical studies.

Name ____________________

1. How would you describe the research design(s) used in this project?

2. Are there any potential problems or sources of error to be aware of?

4.4 *Encore* Magazine

Encore Magazine is a publication associated with the performing arts in Denver Colorado. The magazine contains articles concerning the arts in the Denver area, schedules of future events and a substantial amount of advertising. Typically, the magazine is sold at musical and theatrical performances as a program (with a center insert included for the specific performance). Roughly ninety percent of the sales of the magazine are generated in this manner, with the remainder by subscription.

The publisher of *Encore* wished to develop an audience profile for use in *soliciting* new advertising. A marketing research firm was contracted to perform the study. The research firm developed a survey instrument which evaluated, among other things, the following demographic and lifestyle information:

1. attendance of performing arts events.
2. frequency of dining out.
3. leisure activities.
4. travel behavior.
5. car buying and ownership.
6. home buying and ownership.
7. education.
8. income.
9. age.

The research firm elected to include the self-administered questionnaire in copies of *Encore* distributed at various performances. Readers were *asked* on the form to complete it and turn it in upon leaving the theater. After two months, 1514 returns were collected in this fashion.

Name ______________________________

1. What type of research design was used in this study?

2. Are there any potential problems or sources of error to be aware of?

3. How might the research design be improved?

4.5 Los Angeles Gasoline Shortage Survey

During the late winter and early spring 1979, reports of a shortage of gasoline supplies in California and long lines at gasoline stations had begun to be carried by the news media. Immediately following the Easter weekend, many motels, hotels and attractions in the southern California area began reporting lower than expected occupancy rates and attendance. Particularly affected were visitor industry businesses in the San Diego area, which are heavily dependent on day trip, overnight or weekend visits from the Los Angeles area, approximately one-hundred miles to the north.

Consequently, a San Diego visitor and tourism group felt it necessary to research the extent to which gas shortages had altered the intent to travel to San Diego by Los Angeles area households. A marketing research firm was selected to conduct such a study. The firm constructed a telephone interview questionnaire and randomly selected 405 L.A. area households for the interview. Heads of households were selected in each case and asked questions about travel to San Diego in the previous year, travel in the current year and intent to travel for the remainder of the year. Respondents were also asked questions concerning knowledge and opinion of the gasoline shortage and if concern over the situation had influenced travel plans.

Name ______________________

1. What type of research design was used in this study?

2. Are there any potential problems or sources of error to be aware of in this research?

3. Should the interviews have been conducted with only heads of households?

4.6 Allergy Action

The makers of Allergy Action, a long lasting antihistamine product, were preparing the initial advertising copy for the product's introduction. Allergy Action was formulated to contain chlorpheniramine, a pharmaceutical product proven superior to all other antihistamines available for over the counter (OTC) sale. This ingredient had, until recently, been available only by prescription. Allergy Action was to be made available in a timed-release capsule offering relief up to 12 hours.

In addition to making a statement concerning the product's effectiveness, the advertising copy writer wanted to be able to include another statement regarding physicians' recommendations. Data were obtained for all prescription antihistamines from a government-approved industry source. This information was generated from a rotating national panel of pharmacies which kept track of prescriptions filled. Over the past year, products containing Allergy Action's major ingredient were prescribed most for allergies. The copy writers therefore included a statement that Allergy Action contained the antihistamine doctors recommend most.

Name ______________________

1. What type of research design was used in this study?

2. Are there any potential problems or sources of error to be aware of in this research?

4.7 Accountemps

Accountemps is a temporary employment contractor specializing in accounting, bookkeeping, auditing, tax work and related financial services. With 58 offices nationwide, it is thought to be the biggest such agency in the country.

Recently it has been using the phrase "...largest specialized accounting and financial temporary employment agency in the United States" in its Yellow Pages advertising. Prompted by a call by an Accountemps competitor, a Bell System representative has asked that Accountemps verify the claim or discontinue its use.

Name ______________________________

1. How would you attempt to verify the advertising claim?

2. Are there any things to be particularly cautious about in conducting this research?

4.8. Crest Distributing Company

Crest Distributing is a local distributor of Coors beer products. Coors is a brand of beer distributed mainly in the western part of the U.S. Until recently, Coors had enjoyed leadership positions in many geographical markets. However, union problems, boycotts by special interest groups and increased competition from other brands have seriously affected Coors sales in recent years. The introduction of new products, notably a light beer and a superpremium (now in test in Crest's area), along with increased advertising expenditures, have attempted to stem these sales declines.

Jim Merideth, the general manager of Crest, faces a specific problem. He would like to improve the Coors position among college age students and has decided to pay particular attention to the college relations program in his area. The aim of the college program, through special events and product contribution to social and university organizations, is to increase trial of Coors products and to establish brand loyalty. Merideth would like to determine what proportion of students of selected colleges in his area are Coors consumers and what the attitudes of students are toward Coors and other brands. Out of twenty-three colleges and universities in his area, Merideth is interested in a total of six. He estimates that there are about 50,000 students enrolled at these six schools, the major colleges in his area.

Name ______________________________

1. How should Merideth conduct the research? Be specific.

4.9 University Floral Shop

University Floral, located in Lawrence, Kansas, has recently been purchased by Chad Lawton. Lawton, a local attorney with a background in business, thought that the shop was available at a good price and that, with good management, it could end up being a very profitable investment for him. Lawton's plan was to provide the capital necessary and any legal or managerial advice that he could offer, but to have the shop "run itself" under the direction of the experienced florist he had just hired as manager.

Recently the shop had been only marginally profitable. As one of six floral shops in Lawrence, University Floral faced strong competition. But in a college town of 60,000, Lawton felt that there was sufficient demand for floral products to allow University Floral to grow and prosper.

Recognizing the value of research, Lawton elected to conduct a marketing study to help determine the changes that would be needed to be made at the shop and to guide his promotional efforts. With the aid of an outside consultant he identified the following questions:

1. What motivations or occasions are associated with flower buying?

2. What market segments are there in Lawrence for floral sales?

3. What characteristics are important to people in choosing a floral shop?

4. What (if any) advertising media do consumers use in selecting a florist?

5. What do customers (past and present) think of University Floral and of its services and products?

Name ______________________________

1. What research design do you suggest? Be specific.

2. Are there other questions that Lawton should consider in his research?

4.10 CalPIRG Nuclear Power Study

California Public Interest Research Group (CalPIRG) is a consumer research and advocacy organization associated with Ralph Nader's consumer interest groups. As part of its research program involving energy use and practices of public utilities in the Southern California area, CalPIRG was preparing to initiate a public opinion survey to determine attitudes related to nuclear power.

Of particular importance were public opinions regarding two new nuclear power plants scheduled to be approved soon by the Nuclear Regulatory Commission (NRC). CalPIRG hoped to make information available to the NRC regarding any public concerns related to such issues as overall safety, disposal of waste, evacuation procedures and the public's perceived risks of a nuclear accident. Care must be taken, therefore, to make the survey as free from criticism as possible on methodological grounds.

CalPIRG staff would like to have responses from about 400 households to be drawn from San Diego County. The budget for the project is limited however, and volunteer help is to be used wherever possible.

Name ______________________________

1. Assuming that CalPIRG's budget is limited, what research design do you suggest? Be specific.

2. Recognizing that critics may question the validity of the results, what steps should CalPIRG take to avoid criticism of the research?

4.11 McDonald's Corporation

Corporate marketing management at McDonald's would like to develop a system for tracking fast food restaurant usage, McDonald's share of market, awareness of fast food advertising, and attitudes toward McDonald's and competitive chains. Studies would be conducted four times yearly.

The Albuquerque, N.M. market has been selected as an initial test area to be used to develop the methodology. In that market area major competitors are

McDonald's.
Blake's Lot-A-Burger.
Wendy's.

Other competitors include

Der Wienerschnitzel.
What-A-Burger.
Dairy Queen.
Burger Chef.
Burger King.
Jack-in-the-Dox.
Shoney's.
Vip's Big Boy.

A decision was made by the research project director to collect data from 1600 consumers in the Albuquerque area. Respondents would have to be age 18 or older and would have to had eaten at a fast food restaurant within the past 30 days. Stan Bellows, a recently hired junior research analyst, was given the job of designing the pilot study.

Name ________________________________

1. What should Bellows propose as the research method for this pilot study? Be specific.

4.12 Memphis Transit Company

Memphis Transit operates bus transportation in the greater Memphis area. Prompted by the desire to encourage greater bus ridership, it launched a novel program in 1977 to appeal to bicyclists. On three of the system's thirty-five routes, buses are equipped with bike racks on the outside rear of each bus. The racks can hold up to five bicycles and are designed so that the bicycles could be easily attached and removed.

The three routes were chosen because they serviced major colleges and universities in the city as well as parks and other recreational areas. The company's management had hoped that more people would now use these routes who otherwise would have driven by car (such as a student who could now take the bus and travel around campus by bicycle). Another target market was the person who might be encouraged to commute by bicycle if the total travel distance by bike could be reduced.

Unfortunately, use of the bike racks has been modest at best. Weekday use per route is now about twelve bicycles. The average per weekend day is about twenty per route. High maintenance costs and problems associated with upkeep and replacement of the racks have created a serious problem for the company. With diminishing government subsidies, management is now questioning whether to do away with the program (which will probably cause a public relations problem) or whether it might be possible to somehow increase usage of the bike rack system.

A decision was made to conduct a research study to try to uncover reasons for the low usage levels. One approach suggested was to survey bus riders who might be encouraged to use the bike racks. Another idea suggested was to survey bicycle owners in areas served by the three bike rack routes to investigate their knowledge of and attitude toward the program.

Name ______________________

1. Do you favor researching current bus riders or researching bicycle owners in areas served by the bike rack routes? Why?

2. How should the company carry out the research approach you favor? Be specific.

4.13 Standard Paper Company

Phyllis North, the product manager in charge of writing paper products at Standard Paper, was contemplating a problem concerning the retail price of a new product. Standard Paper had been on an aggressive product development campaign in recent years and had introduced many new consumer paper products within the past decade. The product under consideration was to be a line of stationery and notes to be sold in drug stores, supermarkets and other mass merchandisers. The line would be targeted at women between the ages of 18 and 35 who were looking for writing paper and casual notes with contemporary themes and style, but who were also price sensitive. The stationery products were designed to be sold using a self-supporting point of purchase display stand and were to carry a manufacturer's suggested retail price.

Based on cost data and on competitive prices of other lines, North had decided on three potential price levels for the line. All were lower than the prices typically charged for similar products, but they ranged from a price of about 10 percent below to one of nearly 40 percent below competitive retail prices. Standard could make a profit at each of these prices with reasonable volume, but North wondered about how well the line would be received at the different price levels. She therefore asked the marketing research department to conduct a small study to help her in the decision.

Name ____________________

1. What research should be conducted to answer the pricing question? Be specific.

CHAPTER 5

SAMPLING

Sampling is that part of the research process involved with selecting individuals or other entities from some large population in order to draw inferences about it. In general, the sampling process involves the following typical steps:

1. definition of the population.
2. identification of the sampling frame (if any).
3. determination of the sampling method to be used.
4. determination of sample size.
5. selection of the sample.
6. estimation of population parameters based on sample results.

The population is that group about which the inferences will be made. Often, the population will be defined by various characteristics which make it more finite. An example would be a population defined as "all persons of voting age residing within the city limits of San Francisco who are registered and eligible to vote in the next San Francisco city election." Such a definition would be superior to a population defined as "San Francisco voters." Sometimes, a sample will be drawn of sampling units (such as households) which may be different than the elements which make up the population (such as voters or residents).

The sampling frame is the operational listing of the population. Examples include a telephone directory, a class list and a list of credit account customers. In certain cases no sampling frame as such exists. These are instances where the sample might be selected using screening criteria or other methods.

The <u>sampling method</u> is the procedure used to actually select the sample. These are normally divided into probability and nonprobability methods. Commonly used sampling methods include:

<u>Probability methods</u>

1. simple random sample.

2. stratified random sample.

3. systematic sample (cluster sample).

4. area sample (cluster sample).

<u>Nonprobability methods</u>

1. convenience sample.

2. judgment sample.

3. quota sample.

The <u>sample size</u> can often be determined statistically. In other cases the size of sample selected is based on judgment.

Based on the sample results, it is possible in many cases to make statistical inferences about the population. This is referred to as the process of statistical estimation using sample data.

SAMPLING METHODS

In this section, a number of research studies are illustrated with regard to the sampling plan used for each. Considering the material presented previously concerning sampling and the material in your textbook, you should analyze each study according to the following points:

1. What was the major objective as it pertains to sampling?

2. What population was explicitly or implicitly involved?

3. What (if any) sampling frame was used?

4. What sampling method (e.g., systematic, quota, simple random, etc.) was used?

5. What was the sample size (if given)?

6. Comment on the sampling plan with respect to such things as possible errors in the process, adequacy of sample size and ability to meet the research objectives.

An example is provided below.

Ski Magazine performs an annual readership profile study to help identify its readers and as an aid to potential advertisers. Since its readership is primarily by subscription, the sample is drawn by taking every "n^{th}" name from the subscription list. This sampling interval is adjusted to generate a total of approximately 1,600 names. A mail questionnaire is then sent to each subscriber selected.

Objective

-- to draw a sample which is representative of Ski Magazine readers.

Population

-- current readers of Ski Magazine.

Frame

-- current subscribers of Ski Magazine.

Sampling Method

-- systematic sample drawn from subscription list.

Sample Size

-- 1,600 selected (number responding will be less).

Comments on Sampling Plan

-- sampling process would miss nonsubscription purchasers of Ski Magazine and pass-along readers. Completed sample size for this descriptive study is dependent on response rate.

Name ______________________________

5.1. CASH Study

The publisher of The Chicago Tribune, one of that area's major newspapers, conducts an annual study of the preferences and shopping habits of grocery store customers in the Chicago area. This study is known as the CASH (Continuing Analysis of Shopping Habits) report.

In doing the survey, an outside interviewing firm developed a list of telephone numbers using a two-stage method. First, a complete list of the valid first-three digit numbers in the market area (i.e., residential telephone "bank" numbers) and their relative frequency of occurrence was developed. The last four digits were generated from a table of random numbers. The final seven digit numbers were allocated by taking the first numbers in proportion to their relative frequency in the area. Obvious blocks of unused or commercial numbers were avoided. A total of 2400 households were interviewed.

Objective

Population

Frame

Sampling Method

Sample Size

Comments on Sampling Plan

Name ______________________________

5.2. Endless Summer Pools

The management of Endless Summer Pools is considering whether or not to add solar pool heating equipment to its line of swimming pools and pool equipment. Management decided to conduct a survey of owners of pools with and without solar heating to help make the decision. Telephone calls were made to households in areas where swimming pools were likely to be located. The callers asked if the family had a pool and whether or not the pool was solar heated. This process continued until 100 solar-heated and 100 nonsolar pool owners were identified.

Objective

Population

Frame

Sampling Method

Sample Size

Comments on Sampling Plan

Name ______________________________

5.3 U.S. News & World Report

U.S. News and World Report regularly performs a research project to study buyers of new automobiles in the U.S. Among the questions asked is, of course, which magazines the buyers of various automobiles types read.

To do the study, a commercial list broker, R. L. Polk & Co., is used to develop a comprehensive listing of buyers of new autombiles within the past year. That list is derived from license plate registration and title application records received from 39 states and the District of Columbia. It is refined by deleting truck registration, firm names, government, transient and nonmailable addresses. In a recent study, for example, that list totaled 545,858 new car buyers.

The total list is sorted by automobile category (e.g., compacts vs. subcompacts) using a computer. From within each category, one of every 136 names was selected, resulting in a total of 4,014 buyer names.

Objective

Population

Frame

Sampling Method

Sample Size

Comments on Sampling Plan

Name ______________________________

5.4 Red Candle Steakhouse

Atlas Hotels, Inc. operates a number of hotels, motels and restaurants, including the Red Candle Steakhouse. The management of Atlas Hotels was interested in knowing what types of customers the Red Candle attracted and how they viewed the restaurant with respect to such factors as price, service, menu, decor and convenience.

A personal interview questionnaire was developed and an interviewer worked every lunch and dinner period for an entire week (except for Sunday brunch). An attempt was made to interview one adult out of every party, intercepting the potential respondent on the way out of the restaurant. The researcher had hoped for at least 100 customer interviews; 116 were completed over the week.

Objective

Population

Frame

Sampling Method

Sample Size

Comments on Sampling Plan

Name ______________________________

5.5. Boulder Parks and Recreation Department

The city of Boulder, Colorado conducts periodic surveys of its citizens concerning civic issues. Among these surveys is a study designed to sample leisure behavior and opinions of Boulder residents in order to better plan city programs designed to enrich local recreation.

Opinions were obtained from 400 households sampled in the following way:

1. The city was divided into areas corresponding to voting precincts.

2. The voting precinct areas were combined into six major areas representing different geographical locales.

3. The number of households in each area was estimated from census data.

4. The 400 households to be sampled were allocated to these six areas relative to their population.

5. Within each major area, the number of households on each census block was estimated. Census blocks were then selected within each area such that larger blocks were more likely to be selected than smaller blocks.

6. Interviewers were sent to the northwest corner of each chosen census block and were instructed to count a specified number of dwelling units in a clockwise direction.

7. From that point, every n^{th} house on the census block was selected until four interviews from the block were completed. (The interval was large for big blocks and small for little blocks so that every household on the block would have an equal chance of being selected.)

Objective

Population

Frame

Sampling Method

Sample Size

Comments on Sampling Plan

Name ______________________________

5.6. Gentlemen's Choice Restaurant

Gentlemen's Choice is a relatively new limited menu restaurant specializing in prime rib, steak and fish dishes. Opened by a marketing graduate from the local state university, the target market of this establishment is defined as families and senior citizens interested in good food value for the money. In 1979, its menu offerings ranged from $5.95 to $7.95 for a complete meal. Geographically, it is located in San Marcos, a small residential and retirement area, about 25 minutes from the nearest large community, Escondido. Management knew that patrons came from the local San Marcos area and from as far as 30-40 miles away. In a typical week, approximately 1,500 meals are served.

Management was interested in having a study conducted in order to do a marketing audit of the restaurant. Of principal concern were consumers' evaluations of the menu and service and their reactions to some proposed changes.

In order to compile a list of customers, an outside consultant suggested that a 3"x5" card be printed requesting "survey" information (previous visits, number in party, driving time) along with the respondent's name and telephone number. As a dinner party was seated, a card was given to one adult member of the group to complete in exchange for a complimentary glass of wine. A total of nearly 600 completed cards was collected at various times over a two-week period. These names were then used to conduct a telephone survey.

Objective

Population

Frame

Sampling Method

Sample Size

Comments on Sampling Plan

Name ______________________________

5.7. Outdoor Equipment Industry Association

Manufacturers' distributors and retailers of backpacking equipment have an established trade association, the Outdoor Equipment Industry Association (OEIA). Most of its members are involved in the marketing of tents, sleeping bags, packs, frames, footwear, clothing and hardware designed for the backpacking enthusiast.

As an annual research project, OEIA conducts a study to estimate the size of the backpacking market, to determine product category shares and to understand what types of retail outlets are most heavily used for each type of product.

A list of stores selling backpacking equipment was compiled using the Yellow Pages of telephone directories in all major U.S. markets. This list was supplemented by lists provided by two manufacturer members and by a list purchased from a trade publication. In all, a total of over 10,000 stores was identified. Ten percent of that list was used to identify an initial listing of sample stores. That list was purged so that a final listing was representative of geographic location and retail store type (sporting goods stores, ski shops, etc.). The final, resultant list contained 730 store names.

Objective

Population

Frame

Sampling Method

Sample Size

Comments on Sampling Plan

SAMPLE DESIGN

In this section you will be required to design the sampling plan necessary for a number of research studies. Although similar to the previous exercise on sampling methods, this section allows you to determine how the sample should be selected and which sampling procedure should be used.

Name ______________________________

5.8 Adult Life Resources Center (A)

The Adult Life Resources Center is operated by the University of Kansas to provide career, self-development, and self-enrichment courses and seminars to adults beyond the traditional college environment. In essence, it offers education and training to help people progress through the adult life cycle - from recent college graduates looking for their first jobs to retired adults looking for self-fulfillment activities.

Historically, most participants in the Center's programs have come from the Kansas City metropolitan area, approximately one hour away from the university by car. To better understand what programs to offer, when to offer them, how much to charge and where they should be offered, the Center's director decided to conduct a mail survey of Kansas City area households.

The Kansas City metropolitan area is made up of four major geographical sub-areas: (1) Wyandotte County, Kansas - a working class district including Kansas City, Kansas; (2) Leavenworth County, Kansas - a working class area surrounding Ft. Leavenworth; (3) Johnson County, Missouri - a upper-middle class suburban area; and (4) Douglas County, Missouri - a middle class suburban area.

Based on recent census data, the number of households in these four areas was found to be

Wyandotte County, Kansas -	186,560
Leavenworth County, Kansas -	51,267
Johnson County, Missouri -	243,938
Douglas County, Missouri -	60,592
S.M.S.A. total households -	542,357

1. What is the objective of sampling in this study?

2. Define the implicit population.

3. What frame could be used?

4. What sampling method do you suggest? Explain.

Name ______________________________

5.9 Allied Science Company

Allied Science Company is in the business of distributing scientific equipment and supplies to laboratories throughout the United States. All of its sales are generated through direct order catalogs which are updated and mailed annually.

The marketing manager is interested in knowing more about Allied's customer base. Specifically, he would like to know their opinions of Allied's catalog, how long the catalog is kept on hand after arrival, ways that the catalog could be improved and whether or not the catalogs were being mailed to those who made buying decisions in the labs.

Allied has a mailing list of all those who were sent a catalog in the past year. The list is segregated by geographical area (by state). In all, there are 12,365 names on the mailing list. Since catalogs were often sent to different individuals at a specific laboratory, Allied's computer system could also sort the mailing list so that it could be segregated by firms.

1. What is the objective of sampling in this study?

2. Define the population to be used.

3. What sampling method do you suggest? Explain.

Name ______________________________

5.10 Pilgrim Bank and Trust

Pilgrim Bank and Trust is one of several banks in the Providence, Rhode Island area. Recently, Pilgrim Bank has invested heavily in an advertising campaign designed to improve the image and visibility of the bank. To assess the effects of this campaign, the advertising director would like to conduct a telephone survey in the area to track awareness of advertising and to gauge Pilgrim's relative position among other area banks. The telephone survey would be conducted with Providence area residents who currently maintained an account with a local bank or savings and loan.

1. What is the objective of sampling in this study?

2. Define the population.

3. What (if any) frame could be used?

4. What sampling method do you suggest? Explain.

SAMPLE SIZE DETERMINATION

How big must the size of the sample be for a given marketing research project? Many factors are involved in this decision. Due to costs involved in sampling and data collection, difficulty in sample identification and time requirements, many marketing research studies use relatively small samples (100-200). In situations where statistical accuracy is more important, sample sizes in the range of 400 to 1,600 are more common. While every sampling situation is unique, it is possible to determine the sample size necessary to yield a specified level of statistical accuracy.

The general formula used to determine sample size in a sampling for attributes (characteristics) case is:

$$n = \frac{(Z^2)(s^2)}{(E^2)}$$

n = sample size

Z = critical value associated with degree of confidence

s^2 = estimate of population variance

E = minimum acceptable tolerance (precision) or allowable error

Basically, the marketing researcher must determine what the minimum acceptable tolerance or resulting probable error (E) can be for the project. For example, in a study to determine the average outstanding balance of credit card customers, one researcher may require tolerance to be within $\pm$ \$10, while another researcher may demand $\pm$ \$5. This is obviously a judgmental decision. The estimate of population variance of the variable in question (e.g., credit card balance) is usually based on past historical data, on the sample variance (s^2) of a pilot study, or on the researcher's personal estimate.

To illustrate this process using the credit card balance example, suppose we want to be able to estimate the average outstanding balance to within $\pm$ \$2. Historical data indicate that the standard deviation of credit balances is \$25 and we want to be at least 95 percent confident of our results. Notationally, we can summarize these figures as:

E = 2.0

s = 25

Z = 1.96 (critical value associated with 95% confidence)

$$n = \frac{(1.96)^2(25)^2}{(2.0)^2} = 600.25 \text{ or } 600 \text{ customers}$$

In sampling for proportions, the formula differs in that we must estimate the likely population proportion (e.g., 0.60). Where no reasonable estimate can be made, it's often best to use 0.50 as a conservative estimate of the population proportion. Because of this latter rule, the sample size for surveys which estimate many and varied population variables is estimated using a proportion estimate of 0.50.

The formula in this case is:

$$n = \frac{(Z^2)(p)(1-p)}{(E^2)}$$

n = sample size

Z = critical value

p = estimate of population proportion

E = minimum acceptable tolerance or allowable error (in percent)

As an illustration, suppose an FM radio station wanted to estimate the proportion of listeners it attracted in a given geographical area. Past studies indicated that it drew an audience of about 20 percent of households. The station manager wanted a new estimate which would be accurate to within $\pm$ 2.5 percent at 95 percent confidence. Notationally, this would be

$E = 0.025$

$p = 0.20$

$Z = 1.96$

$$n = \frac{(1.96)^2(.20)(1-.20)}{(0.025)^2} = 983.45 = 983 \text{ households.}$$

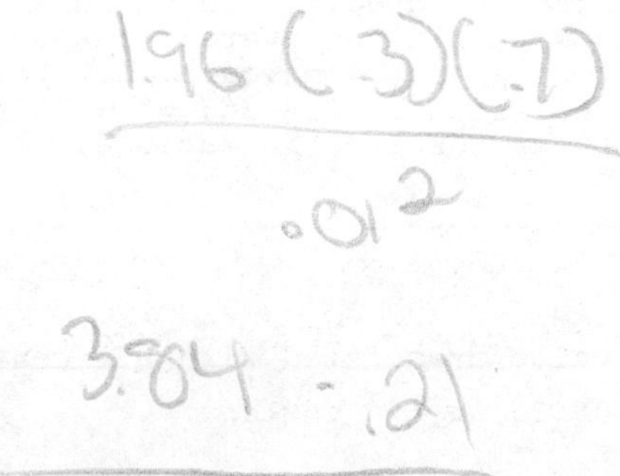

Name ______________________________

5.11 WTVT News

WTVT is a local television station in the Tampa-St. Petersburg area. Since a good deal of advertising revenues are generated from local news programs, WTVT's station manager would like to get an accurate estimate of its share of local news viewers and then conduct interviews to determine viewer's likes and dislikes concerning the station's news programming. It is estimated that WTVT's audience share is roughly 30 percent and that the results should be accurate to within ± 1 percent of audience. Furthermore, the station manager wishes to be able to state that the estimate is accurate within "95 percent probability of being correct."

1. What sample size is required for this problem?

2. Assume that we only wanted to be accurate to within ± 2.5 percent (at 95 percent confidence). What sample size would be required?

3. Assume we wanted to increase the "probability of being correct" to 99 percent and that the estimate was to be accurate to within ± 1 percent. What sample size would be required?

Name ______________________________

5.12 Personal Care Products Corporation

Personal Care Products Corporation manufactures and markets a variety of small household appliances, mainly hair care and personal appearance products. Management would like to estimate how often the average hair dryer is used, since hairdryers have caused numerous warranty and consumer complaint problems. From the original warranty registration information, Personal Care can develop a comprehensive list of owners of its hair dryers.

The firm would like to estimate the average number of times per month that the typical hair dryer is used. The estimate should be accurate to within $\pm$ 0.5 times per month at the 95 percent level. A best estimate of the standard deviation of number of uses per month is 5.

1. What sample size is required for this situation?

Name ______________________________

5.13 Adult Life Resources Center (B)

The director of the Adult Life Resources Center would like to conduct a mail survey of Kansas City area households. This metorpolitan area is made up of four counties - Wyandotte County, Kansas (186,560 households); Leavenworth County, Kansas (51,267); Johnson County, Missouri (243,938); and Douglas County, Missouri (60,592). Fundamentally, the survey would try to determine the degree of interest that adults in the Kansas City area would have in various programs which the center might offer.

The center director would like to estimate the percentage of adults who find each proposed program to be personally interesting. As such, it is assumed that some programs will be of high interest and some much lower. The estimates should be accurate to within ± 5 percent at the 95 percent level of confidence.

Since a mail survey is proposed, a pilot study was conducted to estimate response rate. Based on the pilot study it is assumed that approximately 20 percent of those surveyed will return a completed questionnaire.

1. What sample size (returned) is required for this project?

2. How many questionnaires should be mailed out for this survey? In other words, what is the size of the original sample which needs to be drawn?

3. How should the total mail-out sample be allocated among the three counties? What major assumption must the researcher make in this case?

POPULATION ESTIMATION BASED ON SAMPLING

With a probability sampling plan, such as simple random sampling, a confidence interval can be built around the sample results (point estimate). For instance, if 60 percent of voters sampled indicated that they planned to vote in the next election, we would want to be able to say with some statistical confidence (maybe 95 percent) that if we took a census of all voters that the real proportion is probably not less than some number or greater than another.

The ability to construct a confidence interval is based on the logic of statistical sampling and is discussed in most marketing research textbooks. Generally, we have to consider two cases: 1) sampling for a population proportion (as above); and 2) sampling for a population attributes (such as expenditure figures, or average age of consumers).

<u>Sampling for Proportions.</u> The general formula to determine the confidence interval when sampling for proportions is

$$C.I. = p \pm (Z)\sqrt{\frac{(p)(1-p)}{n}}$$

where

C.I. = confidence interval

p = sample percentage

n = sample size

Z = critical value associated with degree of confidence

To illustrate, suppose that we have just taken a sample of n = 400 and found that 65 percent of those sampled own a stereo system of some sort. Assume that we want an interval associated with the 95 percent level of confidence. Our best (point) estimate of those owning a stereo system is 65 percent. But, the interval estimate would be:

$$.65 \pm 1.96\sqrt{\frac{(.65)(.35)}{400}} = .65 \pm 1.96\sqrt{(.00057)}$$

or about $.65 \pm .05$

An interpretation would be: "our best estimate is 65 percent, but we're 95 percent sure that the true proportion is no less than 60 percent and no greater than 70 percent."

Sampling for Attributes. The general formula for this case is

$$C.I. = \overline{x} \pm (Z) \frac{s}{\sqrt{n}}$$

where
C.I. = confidence interval
$\overline{x}$ = sample mean
s = sample standard deviation
n = sample size
Z = critical value associated with degree of confidence

As an example, suppose that in the sample of 400 above we also asked how much money was spent per month on stereo albums and found x (the average amount in the sample) to be \$10.64 with s = 1.20. Again, our best point estimate is the sample mean, but an interval estimate (with 95 percent confidence) would be

$$\$10.64 \pm (1.96) \frac{(1.20)}{\sqrt{400}} =$$

$$\$10.64 \pm (1.96) \quad (.0.03) =$$

$$\$10.64 \pm (0.11)$$

An interpretation would be "Our best estimate is \$10.64, but we're 95 percent sure that the true amount spent is no less than \$10.53 or greater than \$10.75."

Name ______________________

5.14 Who Buys What in Chicago

A Chicago newspaper performs an annual study of the Chicago S.M.S.A. to audit consumer shopping habits. In a recent publication of the resulting report Who Buys What in Chicago, based on a sample of 2,507 households, it is reported that 6.7 percent of all households buy cat litter, 50.0 percent buy butter and 91.1 percent buy white bread.

1. At the 95 percent level of confidence, compute the confidence level for the percentage of population buying each product.

   a. percentage buying cat litter

   b. percentage buying butter

   c. percentage buying white bread.

Compute the confidence intervals as above.

2. For the percentage buying <u>butter</u>, change the confidence level to 90 percent and then 99 percent. What conclusion do you make about the effect of changing the level of confidence?

a. <u>90 percent confidence</u>

b. <u>99 percent confidence</u>

c. <u>conclusion</u>

Name ______________________

5.15 Kansas City Trust and Savings Bank

Kansas City Trust and Savings Bank is a long-established, multiple-branch bank serving the greater Kansas City metropolitan area. Recently, it has installed a number of 24-hour automatic teller machines called "Buttons" in bank advertising. "Buttons" acts as a cash dispensing machine and also allows the customer to make a limited number of other transactions, such as transferring funds from a savings to a checking account. Kansas City Trust was the first bank in that area to offer 24-hour automatic banking.

A study was conducted by the bank's marketing research department to determine characteristics of the typical "Buttons" user. A sample of 2,000 holders of automatic teller passcard accounts was drawn. A total of 1,312 responded to the survey yielding the following information:

	Mean	Standard Deviation
age of card holder	26.3 years	0.9
household income	$19,219	523
transactions per month	9.7	1.3

1. At the 95 percent level of confidence, compute the confidence interval for each characteristic of "Buttons" users.

   a. age

   b. income

   c. transactions

2. Interpret all three characteristics of account holders in a brief memo to the Vice President of Marketing of the bank.

CHAPTER 6

DATA COLLECTION FORMS

All types of primary research require the construction of data collection forms to collect the required information. Most typically this implies the design of a research questionnaire, although data collection forms are also necessary for observation and experimental studies.

Questionnaire design is a combination of art and science. In the overview that follows, some general guidelines to follow and questions to consider are presented. Following are an exercise on questionnaire design and two actual questionnaires which you will be asked to analyze.

OVERVIEW OF QUESTIONNAIRE DESIGN

Questionnaire Content and Sequence.

1. What information is really required?
2. How should the questionnaire be arranged?
   a. Consider use of classification or screening questions.
   b. Simple or interesting opening question first

      "Overall, can you tell me what you like most about ____?"
   c. General questions next.
   d. Most difficult questions follow.
   e. Demographic or sensitive questions last.
3. Arrange in logical (to respondent) order.
4. Develop a flowchart of question sequence.

How Should Each Question Be Asked?

1. Open-ended response question - respondent answers in own words:

   "What do you think about McDonald's restaurants? ______"

2. Dichotomous response -- only appropriate when there are only two responses. That is, responses must be truly dichotomous:

   "sex of respondent: ___M ___F"

   As opposed to situations where respondents could have more than two possible responses or want more latitude of response than possible with two categories:

   "This beer is ___ sweet ___bitter"

3. Multiple resonse -- response alternatives should cover all possible alternatives (should be exhaustive) and categories should not overlap (alternatives should be mutually exclusive):

   Respondent's Age:
   ___ 25-30
   ___ 30-35 (incorrect)
   ___ 35-40
   ___ 40-45

Question Writing.

1. Make questions as easy as possible to answer.

2. Allow for conditional answers:

   "Do you intend to buy or lease that equipment?"
   1. buy 2. lease 3. depends (specify) ___________

3. The meaning of all questions must be obvious and be the same to all respondents.

Some Rules for Individual Question Wording.

1. Keep wording simple - Avoid stilted or complicated wording.

2. Keep wording clear - Avoid ambiguous phrasing.

   "How often do you read *Time* magazine?
   __ regularly __ often __ sometimes __ irregularly

3. Avoid biased or leading questions.

   "Don't you think that foreign imports should be reduced so that there will be more jobs for loyal Americans?"

4. Where possible, avoid estimates.

   "How much money did you spend on soft drinks this year?"

   When necessary, have respondents estimate smaller quantities, more recent events or typical occurrences:

   "On the average, how many 12 ounce soft drinks do you consume in a week?" or

   "How many 12 ounce soft drinks do you think you consumed last week?"

5. Avoid double questions.

   "Should Richard Nixon have been impeached and sent to prison?"

6. Avoid questions without explicit alternatives.

   "Should taxes be reduced?" vs.

   "Should taxes be reduced even if it means a reduction in public services?"

7. Avoid asking the obvious - word questions to avoid bandwagon responses:

   "How important is quality of food in choosing a fast food restaurant?" vs.

   "How important is quality of food for the price you pay?"

Data Processing Considerations.

1. Consider how each question will be coded -- open-ended responses may require development of codes after seeing responses and will, therefore, be more difficult.

2. Consider whether or not to include numerical codes on questionnaire.

3. Consider whether or not to also include computer card column on questionnaire ("edge coding").

QUESTION SEQUENCE

A useful starting point in developing the questionnaire is to determine the logical order in which questions should be asked. This order should conform to the comments on question sequence discussed earlier. Next, develop a flow chart of question order. This is extremely important when certain questions will be asked of only some respondents (usually based on their previous answers).

Suppose a study was to investigate beer drinking behavior and brand choice for light beers and for imports. A sample of consumers is to be selected and asked about the following:

1. Does the respondent drink beer? (If not, only demographic questions will be asked.)

2. Have any "light" beers been consumed in the last week?

3. If yes, what brands were consumed and what is the favorite brand?

4. Have any "import" beers been consumed in the past week?

5. If yes, what brands were consumed and what is the favorite brand?

6. What is the age and income level of the respondent?

A flowchart of the question sequence would be as follows:

FLOWCHART OF QUESTION SEQUENCE

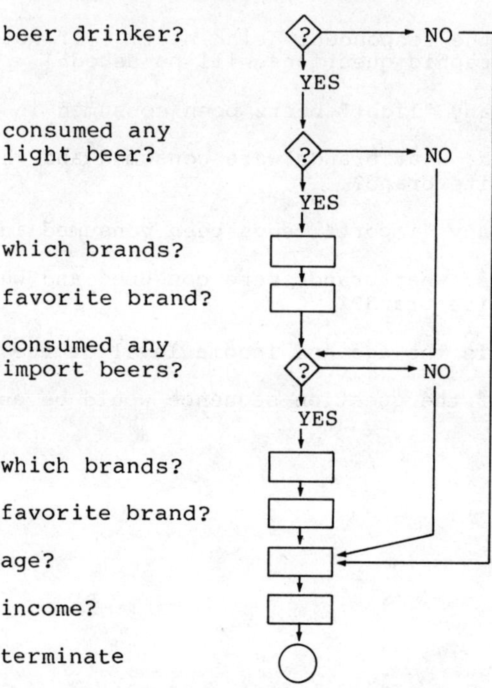

Name ______________________________

6.1 Exercise on Question Sequence

Arrange the following information needs in a logical order considering the basic rules of questionnaire construction.

(Asked of all:) Household income

(All:) Do you buy milk in a store or have it delivered to your home?

(Dairy users only:) Which dairy? Satisfaction with service?

(All:) How much milk consumed per week in household?

(Store users only:) Type of store?

(Convenience store users only:) Name of convenience store?

(All:) Household size

2. Develop a flow chart of the question sequence.

QUESTIONNAIRE EVALUATION

For each of the two examples included (Screen Actors Guild and Foothills Fashion Mall) you should analyze the questionnaires used in relation to the points discussed in the introduction to this chapter. It would also be useful to review the material in your textbook on data collection instruments.

Since the questionnaire cannot be evaluated without also considering the purpose of the research and the data collection methods used, you should also analyze the methodology employed in these studies.

6.2 Screen Actors Guild*

The Screen Actors Guild shares with all unions the goal of assuring its 29,000 members a living wage and job security. But lately the SAG has become increasingly interested, as well, in the accuracy and honesty of its members' roles. A driving force behind this trend is Kathleen North, SAG first vice president and national chairperson of its Women's Conference Committee. Last year Ms. North appeared before the F.C.C. and a meeting of television network producers to argue such issues as the media image of women and minorities, TV reruns, the prime-time access rule, and the "Family Viewing Time" rule. Now the committee, under Ms. North's leadership, has launched a national survey of television viewers' opinions. Although it is particularly concerned with how women are portrayed on television, the survey is also designed to touch on other areas where the public has not been given a chance to express itself.

"This is not just a question of women's image," Ms. North stated. "We want to be able to go before the F.C.C. and network producers and studio people and writers--especially the writers--and say that X amount of people in this or that area like this or don't like that. We can't go on feelings--we need facts, and input from around the country, in order to perform a better service as entertainers. It's a matter of projecting truth."

An attitude questionnaire was designed. Newspaper, Sunday magazine and television editors in 192 communities were asked to publish it. Readers were invited to complete the questionnaire, adding any personal comments, and then to send it directly to SAG (the address was to be provided when the questionnaire was published).

---

*Based on comments accompanying questionnaire appearing in Sunday Denver Post March 24, 1974.

SCREEN ACTORS GUILD ATTITUDES QUESTIONNAIRE

Occupation ________________________________ Male ___ Female ___

City and State: ____

Age Level: Under 12 ___
Under 18 ___
Under 25 ___
Under 35 ___
Under 45 ___
Under 55 ___
55 & over ___

Education:

Grade School Level ___
High School Level ___
Some Graduate ___
College Graduate ___

1. Do you think television influences the way you live your own life?

   a. Mode of dress ___ Yes ___ No ___ Undecided
   b. Mode of conduct ___ Yes ___ No ___ Undecided
   c. Products you buy ___ Yes ___ No ___ Undecided
   d. Attitudes about minorities ___ Yes ___ No ___ Undecided
   e. Attitudes about women ___ Yes ___ No ___ Undecided

2. Do you think that the images of women presented on TV are truthful and believable? ___ Yes ___ No ___ Undecided

   a. Do you identify with them? ___ Yes ___ No ___ Undecided

3. Do you like women you see on TV? ___ Yes ___ No ___ Undecided

4. Do you feel that women are abused and ridiculed by media more often than not? ___ Yes ___ No ___ Undecided

5. Do you feel the relationships and roles on TV shows mirror women's life-styles? ___ Yes ___ No ___ Undecided

6. Do you feel that the media encourages young girls to aspire to a useful and meaningful role in society?
___ Yes ___ No ___ Undecided

7. Do you identify with the women in daytime soap operas?
___ Yes ___ No ___ Undecided

8. Do you think there is hostility between women as portrayed in TV commercials? ___ Yes ___ No ___ Undecided

9. Do you think commercials portray women's total identity and happiness as dependent on the use of the product?
___ Yes ___ No ___ Undecided

10. Do you think sex is overused to sell products?
___ Yes ___ No ___ Undecided

11. Do you feel that women's news items are given equal time and serious consideration? ___ Yes ___ No ___ Undecided

12. Would you like to see more women in leading roles on TV

programs other than comedies, variety and talk shows?
___ Yes ___ No ___ Undecided

13. Are you aware of the small number of women appearing in dramatic shows? ___ Yes ___ No ___ Undecided

14. Would you like to see a woman appearing on TV in a position of authority? ___ Yes ___ No ___ Undecided

    a. Presenting National News? ___ Yes ___ No ___ Undecided
    b. Moderators of game shows? ___ Yes ___ No ___ Undecided
    c. Hosts of talk shows and children's programs?
    ___ Yes ___ No ___ Undecided
    d. Spokeswomen for national products?
    ___ Yes ___ No ___ Undecided
    e. Voiceovers (the voice you hear off camera)?
    ___ Yes ___ No ___ Undecided
    f. Narrators of documentaries?
    ___ Yes ___ No ___ Undecided
    g. Actresses portraying women in professions?
    ___ Yes ___ No ___ Undecided

15. Do you see any change in minority representation?

    a. Black ___ Yes ___ No ___ Undecided
    b. Mexican ___ Yes ___ No ___ Undecided
    c. Asian ___ Yes ___ No ___ Undecided
    d. Indian ___ Yes ___ No ___ Undecided
    e. Other ___ Yes ___ No ___ Undecided

16. Do you feel the image of minorities is accurately represented?
___ Yes ___ No ___ Undecided

17. What is your preference for prime-time evening programming? Mark in order of preference:

    Drama ___
    Documentaries ___
    Variety ___
    Comedy ___
    Game Shows ___
    Sports ___

18. Do you feel television generally is fantasy or fact?
Fantasy ___ Fact ___

19. Regarding reruns of TV series in prime time, do you think there are ___ Too few ___ Too many ___ Just enough ___ Undecided

20. Do you think the public should have some say in how many shows are reruns? ___ Yes ___ No ___ Undecided

Name ______________________________

SCREEN ACTORS GUILD

1. What is the stated objective of the study?

2 How would you describe the sampling procedure used in this study?

3. How would you describe the data collection procedure? How appropriate was it?

4. Analyze the sequence and order of the questionnaire.

5. Consider each question in the questionnaire and indicate any problem or weakness(es) that you observe.

Question	Weakness or Problem
Demographics	______________________________
	______________________________
No. 1	______________________________
	______________________________
No. 2	______________________________
	______________________________
No. 3	______________________________
	______________________________
No. 4	______________________________
	______________________________
No. 5	______________________________
	______________________________
No. 6	______________________________
	______________________________
No. 7	______________________________
	______________________________
No. 8	______________________________
	______________________________
No. 9	______________________________
	______________________________
No. 10	______________________________
	______________________________
No. 11	______________________________
	______________________________

No. 12 ______________________________

____

No. 13 ______________________________

____

No. 14 ______________________________

____

No. 15 ______________________________

____

No. 16 ______________________________

____

No. 17 ______________________________

____

No. 18 ______________________________

____

No. 19 ______________________________

____

No. 20 ______________________________

____

6.3 Foothills Fashion Mall (A)

Foothills Fashion Mall is a large, covered shopping mall in Ft. Collins, Colorado, a city about 60 miles north of Denver and home of Colorado State University. Containing about fifty shops and four major retailers (J. C. Penney, Wards, May D&F, and the Denver), it drew its customers from a wide geographical area including most of the eastern slope of Colorado north of the Denver-Boulder metropolitan area, and most of the eastern slope of Wyoming.

The Foothills Merchants Association was interested in gathering information on Mall shoppers to help its members make better decisions concerning such things as advertising media and scheduling. In addition, the association was interested in trying to assess overall attitudes toward shopping at the Mall and attitudes toward special promotions designed to increase patronage.

A questionnaire was designed by the manager of one of the Mall's clothing stores, who happened to be a recent business school graduate. She suggested that the questionnaire be handed to shoppers as they entered the main entrance of the Mall. The shoppers could then be asked to complete the questionnaire and drop the completed form in a box located in the lobby.

FOOTHILLS FASHION MALL

This is a customer profile study for the Foothills Fashion Mall. Through this study we hope to better know you, our customer, so that all the merchants in the mall can better serve your needs.

Thank you very much for your cooperation in filling out this questionnaire.

1. Male _____, Female _____,

2. Stage in the Family Life Cycle:

___ Single, not living at home.
___ Married, no children.
___ Married couple, with youngest child under six.
___ Married couple, with dependent children over six.
___ Married couple, children living away from home. Household head in labor force.
___ Married couple, children living away from home. Household head retired.

3. My occupation: ______________________

Spouse's occupation: ______________________

4. Family Income Bracket:

___ $5,000 - $9,999
___ $10,000 - $14,999
___ $15,000 - $19,999
___ $20,000 - $24,999
___ $25,000 - or over

5. Do you rent ___, or own ___ your own home?

6. Where is your place of residence?

___ Fort Collins
___ Loveland
___ Greeley
___ Cheyenne
___ Laramie
___ Other ________________________________

7. What is your favorite day to shop? Mark in order of preference.
___ Monday, ___ Tuesday, ___ Wednesday, ___ Thursday,
___ Friday, ___ Saturday, ___ Sunday.

8. Are the hours that the Foothills Fashion Mall is open (10:00a.m. - 9:00p.m. Monday through Saturday, and 12:00 - 5:00pm Sunday) satisfactory for you? Yes ___, No ___.

   If no, what hours would be better? _________________

9. How often do you shop at the Foothills Fashion Mall?

   ___ more than once a week, ___ once a week,
   ___ twice a month, ___ once a month, ___ other.

10. Do you shop the Mall for Advertised Sales? Yes ___, No ___.

11. How did you hear about Sale Promotions at the Mall?

   ___ Mail received at your home
   ___ Radio: What station? _______
   ___ Newspaper

12. Which of the following newspapers do you <u>read</u> regularly? (You may check more than one)

   ___ Denver Post
   ___ Fort Collins Coloradoan
   ___ First Wednesday
   ___ The Rocky Mountain News
   ___ Triangle Review
   ___ The CSU Collegian
   ___ Other: _____________________

Questions 13-20 refer to your feelings toward the mall itself in relation to the various items mentioned. Please place a check-mark in the spot that best expresses your opinion.

	VERY GOOD		ACCEPTABLE		BELOW STANDARD
13. Availability of Fashion or Quality Merchandise.......	___	___	___	___	___
14. Selection and Variety of Merchandise.......	___	___	___	___	___
15. Price Appeal (lower prices, good bargains and good values)....	___	___	___	___	___
16. Sales Clerk Service..	___	___	___	___	___
17. Access Routes to the Mall................	___	___	___	___	___
18. Parking Availability on arrival..........	___	___	___	___	___
19. Satisfaction with Returns and Adjustments......	___	___	___	___	___
20. Mall Events......	___	___	___	___	___

21. What percentage of purchases for clothes are made at the Foothills Fashion Mall?

___0-25%, ___25-50%, ___50-75%, ___75-100%.

22. Do you have any comments on anything in particular that you like or dislike about the mall? ______________________________

____

23. What were your favorite mall events? ______________________

____

____

Name ______________________________

FOOTHILLS FASHION MALL

1. What do you think the research objectives were (or should have been) in this study?

2. How would you describe the sampling procedure? How appropriate was the sampling method?

3. How would you describe the data collection procedure? How appropriate was it?

4. Analyze the sequence and order of the questionnaire.

5. Consider each question in the questionnaire and indicate any weakness(es) that you observe.

Question	Weakness or Problem
No. 1	________________________
	________________________
No. 2	________________________
	________________________
No. 3	________________________
	________________________
No. 4	________________________
	________________________
No. 5	________________________
	________________________
No. 6	________________________
	________________________
No. 7	________________________
	________________________
No. 8	________________________
	________________________
No. 9	________________________
	________________________
No. 10	________________________
	________________________
No. 11	________________________
	________________________
No. 12	________________________
	________________________

No. 13 ____________________

____

No. 14 ____________________

____

No. 15 ____________________

____

No. 16 ____________________

____

No. 17 ____________________

____

No. 18 ____________________

____

No. 19 ____________________

____

No. 20 ____________________

____

No. 21 ____________________

____

No. 22 ____________________

____

No. 23 ____________________

____

CHAPTER 7

MEASUREMENT AND SCALING

Measurement can be defined as the process of assigning numbers to characteristics of attributes of objects according to a set of standard rules or conventions. In marketing research, this translates into the researcher's attempts at quantifying various kinds of information which might be the subject of a research study. Examples would include attempts to "measure" a consumer demographic characteristic (e.g., age), a consumer behavior (frequency of shopping at a particular store) or attitude (evaluation of the store). The measurement process is most critical when the information to be gathered is to be distilled into a numerical score so that it may be entered into a data file.

Another prevalent aspect of measurement is the attempt to measure and scale consumer attitudes. Attitudes form an integral part of the consumer's orientation and intention regarding an organization and the products or services it markets. The evaluation of these attitudes is, therefore, often an important issue in research studies.

MEASUREMENT SCALES

Scales of measurement belong to a hierarchy (from lowest to highest):

1. nominal scales.
2. ordinal scales.
3. interval scales.
4. ratio scales.

These classifications are defined by properties of the measurement system. In this regard, two components must be considered:

1. What are the scale properties of the attribute that is being evaluated (i.e., the underlying scale)?

2. What are the properties of the scale used to quantify the attribute (i.e., the measurement scale)?

The measurement scale must always be equal to or lower in order than the underlying scale.

The scale hierarchy is determined by four characteristics of measurement:

1. The ability to uniquely classify into categories

2. The ability to preserve order or ranking

3. The equality of intervals between scale positions

4. The possession of a natural zero point

The correspondence between these scale characteristics and the scale hierarchy is as follows:

	Uniquely classifies	Preserves order	Equal intervals	Natural zero
nominal scale	X			
ordinal scale	X	X		
interval scale	X	X	X	
ratio scale	X	X	X	X

Name ______________________

7.1 Measurement Scales Exercise (A)

The measurement scale used can never exceed the underlying scale properties of the attributes that we wish to measure. A useful rule is to always first consider the natural properties of the attribute or construct in question and then consider the properties of the measurement scale.

In the exercise below, indicate the highest order of measurement that would be appropriate for each situation. In other words, what is the underlying scale property in each case?

Attribute	Underlying Scale
1. Age of head of household	Example: ratio scale
2. Current balance in your savings account	______________
3. Individual's preference ordering of three brands of soft drinks	______________
4. Whether or not a respondent owns a stereo system	______________
5. Type of transportation used by respondent	______________
6. Distance traveled to school/place of employment	______________
7. College class standing (freshman, sophomore, etc.)	______________
8. Place of birth	______________
9. Consumer's overall attitude toward fast food restaurants (from positive to negative)	______________
10. Amount of money spent on new autombile	______________

Now, consider how the following attributes were actually measured. In each case indicate the order of the measurement scale which was used (nominal, ordinal, interval, or ratio):

Measurement	Scale Used
1. Sex: Male (1) Female (2)	Example: nominal
2. Income: below $15,000 (1) $15,000 or above (2)	______
3. Income: below $10,000 (1) $10,001-20,000 (2) $20,001-30,000 (3) above $30,000 (4)	______
4. What is your total household income? _____(record exact amount)	______
5. Indicate the brand that you like <u>best</u> by placing a "1" beside it. Indicate the one you like next best by placing a "2" beside it and so forth until all brands and ranked.	______
6. Circle the number corresponding to the brand of cola drink that you prefer: 1. Coca-Cola 2. Pepsi-Cola 3. R.C. Cola 4. Other	______
7. On the average, how many times a week do you eat at a fast food restaurant? _____(record exact amount)	______
8. How often do you eat fast food? rarely or never (1) about once a month (2) about once a week (3) more than once a week (4)	______

9. Would you say that you're very satisfied, somewhat satisfied or not very satisfied with the performance of your hair dryer?

very satisfied	(1)
not very satisfied	(2)
somewhat satisfied	(3)

____

10. How many times in the last year did you travel on a commercial airline?

did not travel	(1)
1-2 times	(2)
3-4 times	(3)
5-10 times	(4)
10+ times	(5)

____

Name ______________________

7.2 Manuel's Mexican Food

Manuel's is a small chain of Mexican food restaurants in the Dallas area. The average monthly sales and location of three of the restaurants are summarized below:

	Location	Average Monthly Sales
Store 3	Ft. Worth	$36,000
Store 6	Ft. Worth	18,000
Store 7	North Dallas	45,000

In each space below, assign a set of numbers to either location or sales which is appropriate for the type of measurement scale indicated. Also, write a short statement for each regarding the stores which is consistent with the characteristics of scale of measurement used.

a. Nominal Measurement (example)

Store 3 1

Store 6 1

Store 7 2

Measures (check one):

✓ location

___ sales

Statement: Stores 3 and 6 are in the same location (Ft. Worth) and are assigned the number 1. The number 2 is assigned to Store 7 since it is in a different location (North Dallas). Thus, the numbers 1 and 2 measure the store locations.

b. Ordinal Measurement

Store 3 ___

Store 6 ___

Store 7 ___

Measures (check one):

___ location

___ sales

Statement:

c. Interval Measurement

Store 3 ___ Measures (check one):

Store 6 ___ ___ location

Store 7 ___ ___ sales

Statement:

d. Ratio Measurement

Store 3 ___ Measures (check one):

Store 6 ___ ___ location

Store 7 ___ ___ sales

Statement:

PAIRED COMPARISONS

The method of paired comparisons is a technique used to develop an ordinal scale from a series of choices regarding pairs of objects (e.g., different brands or products). Respondents are asked to select one of two possible choices from each pair of choices. This process is continued until all possible pairs of choices have been evaluated. From this series of choice decisions an ordinal scale representing the ranking or preference order can be inferred.

An example illustrates this method. Suppose that a researcher wanted to develop the overall preference ordering among consumers of the following brands of cola drinks:

1. Coca-Cola
2. Pepsi-Cola
3. R.C. Cola
4. King Cola

All possible pairs of these brands are:

1. Coca-Cola vs. Pepsi-Cola
2. Coca-Cola vs. R.C. Cola
3. Coca-Cola vs. King Cola
4. Pepsi-Cola vs. R.C. Cola
5. Pepsi-Cola vs. King Cola
6. R.C. Cola vs. King Cola

These six pairs are evaluated by asking a sample of consumers to select which brand in the pair is preferred (e.g., Coke or Pepsi) for all pairs. Suppose that the results for this example were:

	Percent of Sample Prefering	
1.	Coke (52)	Pepsi (48)
2.	Coke (60)	R.C. (40)
3.	Coke (80)	King (20)
4.	Pepsi (63)	R.C. (37)
5.	Pepsi (75)	King (25)
6.	R.C. (55)	King (45)

These results can be transferred to a matrix showing the percentage preferring the brand in a column to the one in a row:

	Coke	Pepsi	R.C.	King
Coke	--	.48	.40	.20
Pepsi	.52	--	.37	.25
R.C.	.60	.63	--	.45
King	.80	.75	.55	--

The ordinal scale can be inferred by constructing another matrix (a dominance matrix) to show how many times each column brand "dominates" the row brand. A score of "1" is assigned to each pair which is dominated by the column brand and then these scores are summed. The sums (from highest to lowest) indicate the ordinal scale.

	Coke	Pepsi	R.C.	King
Coke	--	0	0	0
Pepsi	1	--	0	0
R.C.	1	1	--	0
King	1	1	1	--
Sum	3	2	1	0

In this example the preference scale would be

Coke > Pepsi > R.C. > King

Name ______________________________

PAIRED COMPARISONS

7.3 Jack-in-the-Box

Jack-in-the-Box Restaurants is a regional chain of fast food restaurants owned by the Ralston Purina Co. Recently, corporate management wished to evaluate a number of promotional ideas which had been suggested by area managers. The list of ideas was reduced to the following:

A - a sweepstakes giveaway promotion.

B - a free food item with coupon redemption.

C - a free glass with beverage purchase.

D - two for the price of one on selected items.

E - a free poster with a food purchase.

To evaluate the ideas, the marketing research department commissioned a research project in which consumers were shown mock-ups of each of the promotions. Respondents evaluated every possible pair of promotions (e.g., sweepstakes vs. free poster) and selected the one which they liked better for each of the pairs. The results are shown below:

Pair	Preference (percent of sample preferring each)	
A-B	A (68)	B (32)
A-C	A (74)	C (26)
A-D	A (54)	D (46)
A-E	A (60)	E (40)
B-C	B (48)	C (52)
B-D	B (57)	D (43)
B-E	B (54)	E (46)
C-D	C (83)	D (17)
C-E	C (63)	E (37)
D-E	D (51)	E (49)

How should the marketing research department rank the five promotional ideas?

1. Complete the paired comparison matrix below:

	A	B	C	D	E
A	---	( )	( )	( )	( )
B	( )	---	( )	( )	( )
C	( )	( )	---	( )	( )
D	( )	( )	( )	---	( )
E	( )	( )	( )	( )	---

2. Determine the dominance matrix below:

	A	B	C	D	E
A	---	( )	( )	( )	( )
B	( )	---	( )	( )	( )
C	( )	( )	---	( )	( )
D	( )	( )	( )	---	( )
E	( )	( )	( )	( )	---
Total	( )	( )	( )	( )	( )

3. What is the order of preference of the five promotions?

( ) > ( ) > ( ) > ( ) > ( )

ATTITUDE SCALING

Most marketing research studies typically include at least some attempt to evaluate or measure attitudes. Typically, we consider a consumer's attitude structure to be composed of three components:

affect - the overall evaluation
cognition - beliefs or opinions
behavioral intention - feelings toward future action

Attitude measurement may attempt to evaluate any or all of these.

Commonly used attitude scaling techniques include the following:

1. Likert scale items (for example)

   Budweiser beer is a high quality beer.

strongly disagree	disagree	neither agree nor disagree	agree	strongly agree

2. Semantic differential scale items (for example)

   What is your rating of Budweiser beer?

   poor quality _ _ _ _ _ good quality

3. Staple scale items (for example)

   Rate Suncoast Bank on the following dimensions:

   +5
   +4
   +3
   +2
   +1
   convenience of 0 locations
   -1
   -2
   -3
   -4
   -5

4. Graphic rating scales (for example)

   Place a mark on the scale below which best describes your opinion of the Alpha Co.

   very unfavorable ____________________ very favorable

When using attitude rating scales, a number of questions or issues should be addressed by the researcher in constructing the scales. These include:

1. How many categories should the scale contain?

2. Should the researcher use an odd or even number of categories?

3. Should the scale be balanced or unbalanced?

(unbalanced scale)	___ extremely likely	___ very likely	___ somewhat likely	___ unlikely

4. How much verbal description should each scale item category have?

Attitude scale items are typically treated as interval data. However, for this to be true, the respondent must be assumed to treat the scale intervally (the perceptual difference between categories is equal).

7.5 Foothills Fashion Mall (B)

The questionnaire used by Foothills Fashion Mall (exercise 6.3) contained the following attitude scale questions and instructions:

Questions 13-20 refer to your feelings toward the mall itself in relation to the various items mentioned. Please place a check-mark in the spot that best expresses your opinion.

	VERY GOOD		ACCEPTABLE		BELOW STANDARD
13. Availability of Fashion or Quality Merchandise.......	___	___	___	___	___
14. Selection and Variey of Merchandise......	___	___	___	___	___
15. Price Appeal (lower prices, good bargains and good values)	___	___	___	___	___
16. Sales Clerk Service ..	___	___	___	___	___
17. Access Routes to the Mall	___	___	___	___	___
18. Parking Availability on Arrival	___	___	___	___	___
19. Satisfaction with Returns and Adjustments	___	___	___	___	___
20. Mall Events	___	___	___	___	___

Name ______________________________

1. What major dimensions of the mall are being evaluated by the scale?

2. Evaluate the rating scale used.

3. Are there any problems with any of the statements (e.g., availability of fashion or quality merchandise)

7.6 Student Course Evaluation (A)

Many colleges and universities have a program of student ratings of courses and instructors. As an example, consider the student evaluation form below:

STUDENT EVALUATION OF FACULTY

Compared to other courses and instructors at this university, rate the following aspects of this course:

		Below Average		Average		Above Average
1.	Open communication is encouraged in the classroom.	1	2	3	4	5
2.	The professor is enthusiastic about the subject being taught.	1	2	3	4	5
3.	Ideas are supported with examples, comparisons and facts.	1	2	3	4	5
4.	Students are encouraged to think for themselves.	1	2	3	4	5
5.	Concepts presented in class are explained clearly.	1	2	3	4	5
6.	Useful feedback on progress in the course is provided.	1	2	3	4	5
7.	The professor evidences a broad, accurate, up-to-date knowledge of the subject.	1	2	3	4	5
8.	The professor motivates me to do my best work.	1	2	3	4	5

Name ______________________________

Evaluate this student evaluation form as an attitude scale.

1. What major dimensions of attitude toward the course are being evaluated with this scale?

2. Evaluate the comparative rating system used in this scale. Consider such things as whether an adequate number of categories is used, whether the scale should use an odd or even number of categories and whether the verbal descriptions for the scale categories are adequate. Also, are there any other aspects of this scaling method which should be considered or questioned?

3. What assumptions must be made for the results of this scale to qualify as interval data?

Name ______________________

7.7 Student Course Evaluation (B)

Construct your own scale to be used for evaluating courses and instructors. Conduct a few exploratory interviews with other students to help determine what factors to include in your scale. Try to obtain copies of rating forms already in use at your school. Once you have decided on the factors to include, determine the scaling method (e.g., Likert scale) and the rating system to be used.

Instructions and Scale:

CHAPTER 8

DATA COLLECTION

Most marketing research projects utilize data collected by surveys or from observation studies. The purpose of this section is to provide some experience with different form of data collection.

Name ______________________________

8.1 Fast Food Survey

On the following pages are twelve copies of a questionnaire for conducting a telephone survey about fast food restaurants. The questionnaire is a combination of open-ended and closed response questions. Some of the open-ended questions are precoded for the interviewer.

1. Conduct ten telephone interviews with respondents selected at random. You may use a telephone directory or random digit dialing. Keep track of the number of refusals, terminations and not-at-homes below.

	Number	Percent
Completed interview	______	______
Not-at-home	______	______
Refused interview	______	______
Terminated/other	______	______
Total Contacted	( )	100%

2. Estimate the total time it took you to complete the ten interviews. If another interviewer were working at the same speed, approximately how many interviews could be completed per hour?

3. Are there any questions which respondents found difficult or which you think could be improved? Explain.

Name ______________________

FAST FOOD SURVEY

Questionnaire Number ___1___
Phone Number Called: ________
Date/Time: ______________

HELLO, MY NAME IS ________. I'M A STUDENT AT ___________ AND I'M CONDUCTING AN OPINION SURVEY ABOUT RESTAURANTS IN OUR AREA. IT WILL ONLY TAKE A FEW MINUTES OF YOUR TIME. WOULD YOU MIND IF I ASK YOU A FEW QUESTIONS?

[wait for response]

	Circle:
Yes -- Terminate and record	1
No -- Continue	2

MANY PEOPLE USE THE TERM FAST FOOD TO DESCRIBE CERTAIN RESTAURANTS.

1. FIRST OF ALL, WHAT DO THE WORDS FAST FOOD, AS IN FAST FOOD RESTAURANT, MEAN TO YOU? [probe]

____

____

2. DURING A TYPICAL MONTH ABOUT HOW OFTEN DO YOU VISIT A FAST FOOD RESTAURANT? [do not read]

never (skip to Q.7)	1
less than once a month (skip to Q.7)	2
1-2 times (continue)	3
3-4 times (continue)	4
5-9 times (continue)	5
10 or more (continue)	6

3. AT WHICH FAST FOOD RESTAURANT DO YOU EAT MOST FREQUENTLY?

____

4. CAN YOU TELL ME IF YOU RECALL SEEING OR HEARING ANY ADS FOR ANY FAST FOOD RESTAURANTS WITHIN THE PAST TWO WEEKS?

No (skip to Q.6)	1
Yes (continue)	2

5. CAN YOU TELL ME WHICH RESTAURANT YOU RECALL SEEING OR HEARING THE ADS FOR? ...... ANY OTHERS? [check if don't recall____]

first mention: ______________________

second mention: ______________________

third mention: ______________________

6. NOW, I WOULD LIKE YOU TO THINK OF ONLY FAST FOOD RESTAURANTS THAT SPECIALIZE IN HAMBURGERS. CONSIDERING ALL OF THE HAMBURGER RESTAURANTS WHICH YOU'VE RECENTLY VISITED, WOULD YOU SAY THAT THE (insert first item) AT THESE RESTAURANTS IS (ARE) EXCELLENT, GOOD, FAIR, OR POOR? [repeat items]

[rotate order of reading items]	Excellent	Good	Fair	Poor	Don't Know
a. FOOD QUALITY	1	2	3	4	5
b. SPEED OF SERVICE	1	2	3	4	5
c. CLEANLINESS OF THE RESTAURANT	1	2	3	4	5
d. VALUE FOR THE MONEY	1	2	3	4	5
e. COURTESY OF EMPLOYEES	1	2	3	4	5
f. PRICES	1	2	3	4	5

7. NOW, I'D LIKE TO ASK YOU JUST A FEW QUESTIONS ABOUT YOU AND YOUR HOUSEHOLD TO HELP US CLASSIFY YOUR ANSWERS.

ARE THERE ANY CHILDREN AGE 15 OR UNDER LIVING IN YOUR HOME?

Yes	1
No	2

8. INTO WHAT AGE GROUP DO YOU FALL? [read categories]

18 AND UNDER	1
19-24	2
25-34	3
35-49	4
50-65	5
OVER 65	6
(refused)	7

9. AND, FINALLY, IS YOUR TOTAL HOUSEHOLD INCOME UNDER OR OVER $15,000?

If under:	WOULD IT BE UNDER OR OVER $12,000	1
	1 = under 2 = over	2
If over:	WOULD IT BE UNDER OR OVER $20,000	3
	3 = under 4 = over	4
	(refused)	5

THANK YOU VERY MUCH

Interviewer: Record Sex	Male	1
	Female	2

Name ______________________

FAST FOOD SURVEY

Questionnaire Number ___2___
Phone Number Called: ________
Date/Time: ______________

HELLO, MY NAME IS ________. I'M A STUDENT AT __________ AND I'M CONDUCTING AN OPINION SURVEY ABOUT RESTAURANTS IN OUR AREA. IT WILL ONLY TAKE A FEW MINUTES OF YOUR TIME. WOULD YOU MIND IF I ASK YOU A FEW QUESTIONS?

[wait for response]

	Circle:
Yes -- Terminate and record	1
No -- Continue	2

MANY PEOPLE USE THE TERM FAST FOOD TO DESCRIBE CERTAIN RESTAURANTS.

1. FIRST OF ALL, WHAT DO THE WORDS FAST FOOD, AS IN FAST FOOD RESTAURANT, MEAN TO YOU? [probe]

____

____

2. DURING A TYPICAL MONTH ABOUT HOW OFTEN DO YOU VISIT A FAST FOOD RESTAURANT? [do not read]

never (skip to Q.7)	1
less than once a month (skip to Q.7)	2
1-2 times (continue)	3
3-4 times (continue)	4
5-9 times (continue)	5
10 or more (continue)	6

3. AT WHICH FAST FOOD RESTAURANT DO YOU EAT MOST FREQUENTLY?

____

4. CAN YOU TELL ME IF YOU RECALL SEEING OR HEARING ANY ADS FOR ANY FAST FOOD RESTAURANTS WITHIN THE PAST TWO WEEKS?

No (skip to Q.6)	1
Yes (continue)	2

5. CAN YOU TELL ME WHICH RESTAURANT YOU RECALL SEEING OR HEARING THE ADS FOR? ...... ANY OTHERS? [check if don't recall____]

first mention: ______________________

second mention: ______________________

third mention: ______________________

6. NOW, I WOULD LIKE YOU TO THINK OF ONLY FAST FOOD RESTAURANTS THAT SPECIALIZE IN HAMBURGERS. CONSIDERING ALL OF THE HAMBURGER RESTAURANTS WHICH YOU'VE RECENTLY VISITED, WOULD YOU SAY THAT THE (insert first item) AT THESE RESTAURANTS IS (ARE) EXCELLENT, GOOD, FAIR, OR POOR? [repeat items]

[rotate order of reading items]	Excellent	Good	Fair	Poor	Don't Know
a. FOOD QUALITY	1	2	3	4	5
b. SPEED OF SERVICE	1	2	3	4	5
c. CLEANLINESS OF THE RESTAURANT	1	2	3	4	5
d. VALUE FOR THE MONEY	1	2	3	4	5
e. COURTESY OF EMPLOYEES	1	2	3	4	5
f. PRICES	1	2	3	4	5

7. NOW, I'D LIKE TO ASK YOU JUST A FEW QUESTIONS ABOUT YOU AND YOUR HOUSEHOLD TO HELP US CLASSIFY YOUR ANSWERS.

ARE THERE ANY CHILDREN AGE 15 OR UNDER LIVING IN YOUR HOME?

Yes	1
No	2

8. INTO WHAT AGE GROUP DO YOU FALL? [read categories]

18 AND UNDER	1
19-24	2
25-34	3
35-49	4
50-65	5
OVER 65	6
(refused)	7

9. AND, FINALLY, IS YOUR TOTAL HOUSEHOLD INCOME UNDER OR OVER $15,000?

If under:	WOULD IT BE UNDER OR OVER $12,000	1
	1 = under 2 = over	2
If over:	WOULD IT BE UNDER OR OVER $20,000	3
	3 = under 4 = over	4
	(refused)	5

THANK YOU VERY MUCH

Interviewer:	Record Sex	Male	1
		Female	2

Name ______________________

FAST FOOD SURVEY

Questionnaire Number ___3___
Phone Number Called: __________
Date/Time: ______________

HELLO, MY NAME IS ________. I'M A STUDENT AT __________ AND I'M CONDUCTING AN OPINION SURVEY ABOUT RESTAURANTS IN OUR AREA. IT WILL ONLY TAKE A FEW MINUTES OF YOUR TIME. WOULD YOU MIND IF I ASK YOU A FEW QUESTIONS?

[wait for response]

	Circle:
Yes -- Terminate and record	1
No -- Continue	2

MANY PEOPLE USE THE TERM FAST FOOD TO DESCRIBE CERTAIN RESTAURANTS.

1. FIRST OF ALL, WHAT DO THE WORDS FAST FOOD, AS IN FAST FOOD RESTAURANT, MEAN TO YOU? [probe]

____

____

2. DURING A TYPICAL MONTH ABOUT HOW OFTEN DO YOU VISIT A FAST FOOD RESTAURANT? [do not read]

never (skip to Q.7)	1
less than once a month (skip to Q.7)	2
1-2 times (continue)	3
3-4 times (continue)	4
5-9 times (continue)	5
10 or more (continue)	6

3. AT WHICH FAST FOOD RESTAURANT DO YOU EAT MOST FREQUENTLY?

____

4. CAN YOU TELL ME IF YOU RECALL SEEING OR HEARING ANY ADS FOR ANY FAST FOOD RESTAURANTS WITHIN THE PAST TWO WEEKS?

No (skip to Q.6)	1
Yes (continue)	2

5. CAN YOU TELL ME WHICH RESTAURANT YOU RECALL SEEING OR HEARING THE ADS FOR? ...... ANY OTHERS? [check if don't recall____]

first mention: ______________________________

second mention: ______________________________

third mention: ______________________________

6. NOW, I WOULD LIKE YOU TO THINK OF ONLY FAST FOOD RESTAURANTS THAT SPECIALIZE IN HAMBURGERS. CONSIDERING ALL OF THE HAMBURGER RESTAURANTS WHICH YOU'VE RECENTLY VISITED, WOULD YOU SAY THAT THE (insert first item) AT THESE RESTAURANTS IS (ARE) EXCELLENT, GOOD, FAIR, OR POOR? [repeat items]

[rotate order of reading items]	Excellent	Good	Fair	Poor	Don't Know
a. FOOD QUALITY	1	2	3	4	5
b. SPEED OF SERVICE	1	2	3	4	5
c. CLEANLINESS OF THE RESTAURANT	1	2	3	4	5
d. VALUE FOR THE MONEY	1	2	3	4	5
e. COURTESY OF EMPLOYEES	1	2	3	4	5
f. PRICES	1	2	3	4	5

7. NOW, I'D LIKE TO ASK YOU JUST A FEW QUESTIONS ABOUT YOU AND YOUR HOUSEHOLD TO HELP US CLASSIFY YOUR ANSWERS.

ARE THERE ANY CHILDREN AGE 15 OR UNDER LIVING IN YOUR HOME?

Yes	1
No	2

8. INTO WHAT AGE GROUP DO YOU FALL? [read categories]

18 AND UNDER	1
19-24	2
25-34	3
35-49	4
50-65	5
OVER 65	6
(refused)	7

9. AND, FINALLY, IS YOUR TOTAL HOUSEHOLD INCOME UNDER OR OVER $15,000?

If under: WOULD IT BE UNDER OR OVER $12,000 1
1 = under 2 = over 2
If over: WOULD IT BE UNDER OR OVER $20,000 3
3 = under 4 = over 4
(refused) 5

THANK YOU VERY MUCH

Interviewer: Record Sex

Male	1
Female	2

Name ____________________

FAST FOOD SURVEY

Questionnaire Number ___4___
Phone Number Called: ________
Date/Time: ________________

HELLO, MY NAME IS ________. I'M A STUDENT AT ____________ AND I'M CONDUCTING AN OPINION SURVEY ABOUT RESTAURANTS IN OUR AREA. IT WILL ONLY TAKE A FEW MINUTES OF YOUR TIME. WOULD YOU MIND IF I ASK YOU A FEW QUESTIONS?

[wait for response]

	Circle:
Yes -- Terminate and record	1
No -- Continue	2

MANY PEOPLE USE THE TERM FAST FOOD TO DESCRIBE CERTAIN RESTAURANTS.

1. FIRST OF ALL, WHAT DO THE WORDS FAST FOOD, AS IN FAST FOOD RESTAURANT, MEAN TO YOU? [probe]

____

____

2. DURING A TYPICAL MONTH ABOUT HOW OFTEN DO YOU VISIT A FAST FOOD RESTAURANT? [do not read]

never (skip to Q.7)	1
less than once a month (skip to Q.7)	2
1-2 times (continue)	3
3-4 times (continue)	4
5-9 times (continue)	5
10 or more (continue)	6

3. AT WHICH FAST FOOD RESTAURANT DO YOU EAT MOST FREQUENTLY?

____

4. CAN YOU TELL ME IF YOU RECALL SEEING OR HEARING ANY ADS FOR ANY FAST FOOD RESTAURANTS WITHIN THE PAST TWO WEEKS?

No (skip to Q.6)	1
Yes (continue)	2

5. CAN YOU TELL ME WHICH RESTAURANT YOU RECALL SEEING OR HEARING THE ADS FOR? ...... ANY OTHERS? [check if don't recall____]

first mention: ______________________

second mention: ______________________

third mention: ______________________

6. NOW, I WOULD LIKE YOU TO THINK OF ONLY FAST FOOD RESTAURANTS THAT SPECIALIZE IN HAMBURGERS. CONSIDERING ALL OF THE HAMBURGER RESTAURANTS WHICH YOU'VE RECENTLY VISITED, WOULD YOU SAY THAT THE (insert first item) AT THESE RESTAURANTS IS (ARE) EXCELLENT, GOOD, FAIR, OR POOR? [repeat items]

[rotate order of reading items]	Excellent	Good	Fair	Poor	Don't Know
a. FOOD QUALITY	1	2	3	4	5
b. SPEED OF SERVICE	1	2	3	4	5
c. CLEANLINESS OF THE RESTAURANT	1	2	3	4	5
d. VALUE FOR THE MONEY	1	2	3	4	5
e. COURTESY OF EMPLOYEES	1	2	3	4	5
f. PRICES	1	2	3	4	5

7. NOW, I'D LIKE TO ASK YOU JUST A FEW QUESTIONS ABOUT YOU AND YOUR HOUSEHOLD TO HELP US CLASSIFY YOUR ANSWERS.

ARE THERE ANY CHILDREN AGE 15 OR UNDER LIVING IN YOUR HOME?

Yes	1
No	2

8. INTO WHAT AGE GROUP DO YOU FALL? [read categories]

18 AND UNDER	1
19-24	2
25-34	3
35-49	4
50-65	5
OVER 65	6
(refused)	7

9. AND, FINALLY, IS YOUR TOTAL HOUSEHOLD INCOME UNDER OR OVER $15,000?

If under:	WOULD IT BE UNDER OR OVER $12,000	1
	1 = under 2 = over	2
If over:	WOULD IT BE UNDER OR OVER $20,000	3
	3 = under 4 = over	4
	(refused)	5

THANK YOU VERY MUCH

Interviewer:	Record Sex	Male	1
		Female	2

Name ______________________

FAST FOOD SURVEY

Questionnaire Number ___5___
Phone Number Called: ________
Date/Time: ________________

HELLO, MY NAME IS ________. I'M A STUDENT AT ____________ AND I'M CONDUCTING AN OPINION SURVEY ABOUT RESTAURANTS IN OUR AREA. IT WILL ONLY TAKE A FEW MINUTES OF YOUR TIME. WOULD YOU MIND IF I ASK YOU A FEW QUESTIONS?

[wait for response]

	Circle:
Yes -- Terminate and record	1
No -- Continue	2

MANY PEOPLE USE THE TERM FAST FOOD TO DESCRIBE CERTAIN RESTAURANTS.

1. FIRST OF ALL, WHAT DO THE WORDS FAST FOOD, AS IN FAST FOOD RESTAURANT, MEAN TO YOU? [probe]

____

____

2. DURING A TYPICAL MONTH ABOUT HOW OFTEN DO YOU VISIT A FAST FOOD RESTAURANT? [do not read]

never (skip to Q.7)	1
less than once a month (skip to Q.7)	2
1-2 times (continue)	3
3-4 times (continue)	4
5-9 times (continue)	5
10 or more (continue)	6

3. AT WHICH FAST FOOD RESTAURANT DO YOU EAT MOST FREQUENTLY?

____

4. CAN YOU TELL ME IF YOU RECALL SEEING OR HEARING ANY ADS FOR ANY FAST FOOD RESTAURANTS WITHIN THE PAST TWO WEEKS?

No (skip to Q.6)	1
Yes (continue)	2

5. CAN YOU TELL ME WHICH RESTAURANT YOU RECALL SEEING OR HEARING THE ADS FOR? ...... ANY OTHERS? [check if don't recall____]

first mention: ______________________________

second mention: ______________________________

third mention: ______________________________

6. NOW, I WOULD LIKE YOU TO THINK OF ONLY FAST FOOD RESTAURANTS THAT SPECIALIZE IN HAMBURGERS. CONSIDERING ALL OF THE HAMBURGER RESTAURANTS WHICH YOU'VE RECENTLY VISITED, WOULD YOU SAY THAT THE (insert first item) AT THESE RESTAURANTS IS (ARE) EXCELLENT, GOOD, FAIR, OR POOR? [repeat items]

[rotate order of reading items]	Excellent	Good	Fair	Poor	Don't Know
a. FOOD QUALITY	1	2	3	4	5
b. SPEED OF SERVICE	1	2	3	4	5
c. CLEANLINESS OF THE RESTAURANT	1	2	3	4	5
d. VALUE FOR THE MONEY	1	2	3	4	5
e. COURTESY OF EMPLOYEES	1	2	3	4	5
f. PRICES	1	2	3	4	5

7. NOW, I'D LIKE TO ASK YOU JUST A FEW QUESTIONS ABOUT YOU AND YOUR HOUSEHOLD TO HELP US CLASSIFY YOUR ANSWERS.

ARE THERE ANY CHILDREN AGE 15 OR UNDER LIVING IN YOUR HOME?

Yes	1
No	2

8. INTO WHAT AGE GROUP DO YOU FALL? [read categories]

18 AND UNDER	1
19-24	2
25-34	3
35-49	4
50-65	5
OVER 65	6
(refused)	7

9. AND, FINALLY, IS YOUR TOTAL HOUSEHOLD INCOME UNDER OR OVER $15,000?

If under:	WOULD IT BE UNDER OR OVER $12,000	1
	1 = under 2 = over	2
If over:	WOULD IT BE UNDER OR OVER $20,000	3
	3 = under 4 = over	4
	(refused)	5

THANK YOU VERY MUCH

Interviewer:	Record Sex	Male	1
		Female	2

Name ______________________________

FAST FOOD SURVEY

Questionnaire Number ___6___
Phone Number Called: __________
Date/Time: ____________________

HELLO, MY NAME IS ________. I'M A STUDENT AT ____________ AND I'M CONDUCTING AN OPINION SURVEY ABOUT RESTAURANTS IN OUR AREA. IT WILL ONLY TAKE A FEW MINUTES OF YOUR TIME. WOULD YOU MIND IF I ASK YOU A FEW QUESTIONS?

[wait for response]

	Circle:
Yes -- Terminate and record	1
No -- Continue	2

MANY PEOPLE USE THE TERM FAST FOOD TO DESCRIBE CERTAIN RESTAURANTS.

1. FIRST OF ALL, WHAT DO THE WORDS FAST FOOD, AS IN FAST FOOD RESTAURANT, MEAN TO YOU? [probe]

____

____

2. DURING A TYPICAL MONTH ABOUT HOW OFTEN DO YOU VISIT A FAST FOOD RESTAURANT? [do not read]

never (skip to Q.7)	1
less than once a month (skip to Q.7)	2
1-2 times (continue)	3
3-4 times (continue)	4
5-9 times (continue)	5
10 or more (continue)	6

3. AT WHICH FAST FOOD RESTAURANT DO YOU EAT MOST FREQUENTLY?

____

4. CAN YOU TELL ME IF YOU RECALL SEEING OR HEARING ANY ADS FOR ANY FAST FOOD RESTAURANTS WITHIN THE PAST TWO WEEKS?

No (skip to Q.6)	1
Yes (continue)	2

5. CAN YOU TELL ME WHICH RESTAURANT YOU RECALL SEEING OR HEARING THE ADS FOR? ...... ANY OTHERS? [check if don't recall____]

first mention: ______________________________

second mention: ______________________________

third mention: ______________________________

6. NOW, I WOULD LIKE YOU TO THINK OF ONLY FAST FOOD RESTAURANTS THAT SPECIALIZE IN HAMBURGERS. CONSIDERING ALL OF THE HAMBURGER RESTAURANTS WHICH YOU'VE RECENTLY VISITED, WOULD YOU SAY THAT THE (insert first item) AT THESE RESTAURANTS IS (ARE) EXCELLENT, GOOD, FAIR, OR POOR? [repeat items]

[rotate order of reading items]	Excellent	Good	Fair	Poor	Don't Know
a. FOOD QUALITY	1	2	3	4	5
b. SPEED OF SERVICE	1	2	3	4	5
c. CLEANLINESS OF THE RESTAURANT	1	2	3	4	5
d. VALUE FOR THE MONEY	1	2	3	4	5
e. COURTESY OF EMPLOYEES	1	2	3	4	5
f. PRICES	1	2	3	4	5

7. NOW, I'D LIKE TO ASK YOU JUST A FEW QUESTIONS ABOUT YOU AND YOUR HOUSEHOLD TO HELP US CLASSIFY YOUR ANSWERS.

ARE THERE ANY CHILDREN AGE 15 OR UNDER LIVING IN YOUR HOME?

Yes	1
No	2

8. INTO WHAT AGE GROUP DO YOU FALL? [read categories]

18 AND UNDER	1
19-24	2
25-34	3
35-49	4
50-65	5
OVER 65	6
(refused)	7

9. AND, FINALLY, IS YOUR TOTAL HOUSEHOLD INCOME UNDER OR OVER $15,000?

If under:	WOULD IT BE UNDER OR OVER $12,000	1
	1 = under 2 = over	2
If over:	WOULD IT BE UNDER OR OVER $20,000	3
	3 = under 4 = over	4
	(refused)	5

THANK YOU VERY MUCH

Interviewer: Record Sex		
	Male	1
	Female	2

Name ______________________

FAST FOOD SURVEY

Questionnaire Number ___7___
Phone Number Called: __________
Date/Time: ______________________

HELLO, MY NAME IS ________. I'M A STUDENT AT ____________ AND I'M CONDUCTING AN OPINION SURVEY ABOUT RESTAURANTS IN OUR AREA. IT WILL ONLY TAKE A FEW MINUTES OF YOUR TIME. WOULD YOU MIND IF I ASK YOU A FEW QUESTIONS?

[wait for response]

	Circle:
Yes -- Terminate and record	1
No -- Continue	2

MANY PEOPLE USE THE TERM FAST FOOD TO DESCRIBE CERTAIN RESTAURANTS.

1. FIRST OF ALL, WHAT DO THE WORDS FAST FOOD, AS IN FAST FOOD RESTAURANT, MEAN TO YOU? [probe]

____

____

2. DURING A TYPICAL MONTH ABOUT HOW OFTEN DO YOU VISIT A FAST FOOD RESTAURANT? [do not read]

never (skip to Q.7)	1
less than once a month (skip to Q.7)	2
1-2 times (continue)	3
3-4 times (continue)	4
5-9 times (continue)	5
10 or more (continue)	6

3. AT WHICH FAST FOOD RESTAURANT DO YOU EAT MOST FREQUENTLY?

____

4. CAN YOU TELL ME IF YOU RECALL SEEING OR HEARING ANY ADS FOR ANY FAST FOOD RESTAURANTS WITHIN THE PAST TWO WEEKS?

No (skip to Q.6)	1
Yes (continue)	2

5. CAN YOU TELL ME WHICH RESTAURANT YOU RECALL SEEING OR HEARING THE ADS FOR? ...... ANY OTHERS? [check if don't recall____]

first mention: ______________________________

second mention: ______________________________

third mention: ______________________________

6. NOW, I WOULD LIKE YOU TO THINK OF ONLY FAST FOOD RESTAURANTS THAT SPECIALIZE IN HAMBURGERS. CONSIDERING ALL OF THE HAMBURGER RESTAURANTS WHICH YOU'VE RECENTLY VISITED, WOULD YOU SAY THAT THE (insert first item) AT THESE RESTAURANTS IS (ARE) EXCELLENT, GOOD, FAIR, OR POOR? [repeat items]

[rotate order of reading items]	Excellent	Good	Fair	Poor	Don't Know
a. FOOD QUALITY	1	2	3	4	5
b. SPEED OF SERVICE	1	2	3	4	5
c. CLEANLINESS OF THE RESTAURANT	1	2	3	4	5
d. VALUE FOR THE MONEY	1	2	3	4	5
e. COURTESY OF EMPLOYEES	1	2	3	4	5
f. PRICES	1	2	3	4	5

7. NOW, I'D LIKE TO ASK YOU JUST A FEW QUESTIONS ABOUT YOU AND YOUR HOUSEHOLD TO HELP US CLASSIFY YOUR ANSWERS.

ARE THERE ANY CHILDREN AGE 15 OR UNDER LIVING IN YOUR HOME?

Yes	1
No	2

8. INTO WHAT AGE GROUP DO YOU FALL? [read categories]

18 AND UNDER	1
19-24	2
25-34	3
35-49	4
50-65	5
OVER 65	6
(refused)	7

9. AND, FINALLY, IS YOUR TOTAL HOUSEHOLD INCOME UNDER OR OVER $15,000?

If under:	WOULD IT BE UNDER OR OVER $12,000	1
	1 = under 2 = over	2
If over:	WOULD IT BE UNDER OR OVER $20,000	3
	3 = under 4 = over	4
	(refused)	5

THANK YOU VERY MUCH

Interviewer: Record Sex		
	Male	1
	Female	2

Name ______________________

FAST FOOD SURVEY

Questionnaire Number ____8____
Phone Number Called: ________
Date/Time: ________________

HELLO, MY NAME IS ________. I'M A STUDENT AT __________ AND I'M CONDUCTING AN OPINION SURVEY ABOUT RESTAURANTS IN OUR AREA. IT WILL ONLY TAKE A FEW MINUTES OF YOUR TIME. WOULD YOU MIND IF I ASK YOU A FEW QUESTIONS?

[wait for response]

	Circle:
Yes -- Terminate and record	1
No -- Continue	2

MANY PEOPLE USE THE TERM FAST FOOD TO DESCRIBE CERTAIN RESTAURANTS.

1. FIRST OF ALL, WHAT DO THE WORDS FAST FOOD, AS IN FAST FOOD RESTAURANT, MEAN TO YOU? [probe]

____

____

2. DURING A TYPICAL MONTH ABOUT HOW OFTEN DO YOU VISIT A FAST FOOD RESTAURANT? [do not read]

never (skip to Q.7)	1
less than once a month (skip to Q.7)	2
1-2 times (continue)	3
3-4 times (continue)	4
5-9 times (continue)	5
10 or more (continue)	6

3. AT WHICH FAST FOOD RESTAURANT DO YOU EAT MOST FREQUENTLY?

____

4. CAN YOU TELL ME IF YOU RECALL SEEING OR HEARING ANY ADS FOR ANY FAST FOOD RESTAURANTS WITHIN THE PAST TWO WEEKS?

No (skip to Q.6)	1
Yes (continue)	2

5. CAN YOU TELL ME WHICH RESTAURANT YOU RECALL SEEING OR HEARING THE ADS FOR? ...... ANY OTHERS? [check if don't recall____]

first mention: ______________________________

second mention: ______________________________

third mention: ______________________________

6. NOW, I WOULD LIKE YOU TO THINK OF ONLY FAST FOOD RESTAURANTS THAT SPECIALIZE IN HAMBURGERS. CONSIDERING ALL OF THE HAMBURGER RESTAURANTS WHICH YOU'VE RECENTLY VISITED, WOULD YOU SAY THAT THE (insert first item) AT THESE RESTAURANTS IS (ARE) EXCELLENT, GOOD, FAIR, OR POOR? [repeat items]

[rotate order of reading items]	Excellent	Good	Fair	Poor	Don't Know
a. FOOD QUALITY	1	2	3	4	5
b. SPEED OF SERVICE	1	2	3	4	5
c. CLEANLINESS OF THE RESTAURANT	1	2	3	4	5
d. VALUE FOR THE MONEY	1	2	3	4	5
e. COURTESY OF EMPLOYEES	1	2	3	4	5
f. PRICES	1	2	3	4	5

7. NOW, I'D LIKE TO ASK YOU JUST A FEW QUESTIONS ABOUT YOU AND YOUR HOUSEHOLD TO HELP US CLASSIFY YOUR ANSWERS.

ARE THERE ANY CHILDREN AGE 15 OR UNDER LIVING IN YOUR HOME?

Yes	1
No	2

8. INTO WHAT AGE GROUP DO YOU FALL? [read categories]

18 AND UNDER	1
19-24	2
25-34	3
35-49	4
50-65	5
OVER 65	6
(refused)	7

9. AND, FINALLY, IS YOUR TOTAL HOUSEHOLD INCOME UNDER OR OVER $15,000?

If under:	WOULD IT BE UNDER OR OVER $12,000	1
	1 = under 2 = over	2
If over:	WOULD IT BE UNDER OR OVER $20,000	3
	3 = under 4 = over	4
	(refused)	5

THANK YOU VERY MUCH

Interviewer: Record Sex		
	Male	1
	Female	2

Name ______________________________

FAST FOOD SURVEY

Questionnaire Number ____9____
Phone Number Called: ____________
Date/Time: ______________________

HELLO, MY NAME IS __________. I'M A STUDENT AT _______________ AND I'M CONDUCTING AN OPINION SURVEY ABOUT RESTAURANTS IN OUR AREA. IT WILL ONLY TAKE A FEW MINUTES OF YOUR TIME. WOULD YOU MIND IF I ASK YOU A FEW QUESTIONS?

[wait for response]

	Circle:
Yes -- Terminate and record	1
No -- Continue	2

MANY PEOPLE USE THE TERM FAST FOOD TO DESCRIBE CERTAIN RESTAURANTS.

1. FIRST OF ALL, WHAT DO THE WORDS FAST FOOD, AS IN FAST FOOD RESTAURANT, MEAN TO YOU? [probe]

____

____

2. DURING A TYPICAL MONTH ABOUT HOW OFTEN DO YOU VISIT A FAST FOOD RESTAURANT? [do not read]

never (skip to Q.7)	1
less than once a month (skip to Q.7)	2
1-2 times (continue)	3
3-4 times (continue)	4
5-9 times (continue)	5
10 or more (continue)	6

3. AT WHICH FAST FOOD RESTAURANT DO YOU EAT MOST FREQUENTLY?

____

4. CAN YOU TELL ME IF YOU RECALL SEEING OR HEARING ANY ADS FOR ANY FAST FOOD RESTAURANTS WITHIN THE PAST TWO WEEKS?

No (skip to Q.6)	1
Yes (continue)	2

5. CAN YOU TELL ME WHICH RESTAURANT YOU RECALL SEEING OR HEARING THE ADS FOR? ...... ANY OTHERS? [check if don't recall ___]

first mention: ______________________________

second mention: ______________________________

third mention: ______________________________

6. NOW, I WOULD LIKE YOU TO THINK OF ONLY FAST FOOD RESTAURANTS THAT SPECIALIZE IN HAMBURGERS. CONSIDERING ALL OF THE HAMBURGER RESTAURANTS WHICH YOU'VE RECENTLY VISITED, WOULD YOU SAY THAT THE (insert first item) AT THESE RESTAURANTS IS (ARE) EXCELLENT, GOOD, FAIR, OR POOR? [repeat items]

[rotate order of reading items]	Excellent	Good	Fair	Poor	Don't Know
a. FOOD QUALITY	1	2	3	4	5
b. SPEED OF SERVICE	1	2	3	4	5
c. CLEANLINESS OF THE RESTAURANT	1	2	3	4	5
d. VALUE FOR THE MONEY	1	2	3	4	5
e. COURTESY OF EMPLOYEES	1	2	3	4	5
f. PRICES	1	2	3	4	5

7. NOW, I'D LIKE TO ASK YOU JUST A FEW QUESTIONS ABOUT YOU AND YOUR HOUSEHOLD TO HELP US CLASSIFY YOUR ANSWERS.

ARE THERE ANY CHILDREN AGE 15 OR UNDER LIVING IN YOUR HOME?

Yes	1
No	2

8. INTO WHAT AGE GROUP DO YOU FALL? [read categories]

18 AND UNDER	1
19-24	2
25-34	3
35-49	4
50-65	5
OVER 65	6
(refused)	7

9. AND, FINALLY, IS YOUR TOTAL HOUSEHOLD INCOME UNDER OR OVER $15,000?

If under:	WOULD IT BE UNDER OR OVER $12,000	1
	1 = under 2 = over	2
If over:	WOULD IT BE UNDER OR OVER $20,000	3
	3 = under 4 = over	4
	(refused)	5

THANK YOU VERY MUCH

Interviewer:	Record Sex	Male	1
		Female	2

Name ____________________

FAST FOOD SURVEY

Questionnaire Number ___10___
Phone Number Called: ________
Date/Time: ________________

HELLO, MY NAME IS ________. I'M A STUDENT AT __________ AND I'M CONDUCTING AN OPINION SURVEY ABOUT RESTAURANTS IN OUR AREA. IT WILL ONLY TAKE A FEW MINUTES OF YOUR TIME. WOULD YOU MIND IF I ASK YOU A FEW QUESTIONS?

[wait for response]

	Circle:
Yes -- Terminate and record	1
No -- Continue	2

MANY PEOPLE USE THE TERM FAST FOOD TO DESCRIBE CERTAIN RESTAURANTS.

1. FIRST OF ALL, WHAT DO THE WORDS FAST FOOD, AS IN FAST FOOD RESTAURANT, MEAN TO YOU? [probe]

____

____

2. DURING A TYPICAL MONTH ABOUT HOW OFTEN DO YOU VISIT A FAST FOOD RESTAURANT? [do not read]

never (skip to Q.7)	1
less than once a month (skip to Q.7)	2
1-2 times (continue)	3
3-4 times (continue)	4
5-9 times (continue)	5
10 or more (continue)	6

3. AT WHICH FAST FOOD RESTAURANT DO YOU EAT MOST FREQUENTLY?

____

4. CAN YOU TELL ME IF YOU RECALL SEEING OR HEARING ANY ADS FOR ANY FAST FOOD RESTAURANTS WITHIN THE PAST TWO WEEKS?

No (skip to Q.6)	1
Yes (continue)	2

5. CAN YOU TELL ME WHICH RESTAURANT YOU RECALL SEEING OR HEARING THE ADS FOR? ...... ANY OTHERS? [check if don't recall____]

first mention: ____________________

second mention: ____________________

third mention: ____________________

6. NOW, I WOULD LIKE YOU TO THINK OF ONLY FAST FOOD RESTAURANTS THAT SPECIALIZE IN HAMBURGERS. CONSIDERING ALL OF THE HAMBURGER RESTAURANTS WHICH YOU'VE RECENTLY VISITED, WOULD YOU SAY THAT THE (insert first item) AT THESE RESTAURANTS IS (ARE) EXCELLENT, GOOD, FAIR, OR POOR? [repeat items]

[rotate order of reading items]	Excellent	Good	Fair	Poor	Don't Know
a. FOOD QUALITY	1	2	3	4	5
b. SPEED OF SERVICE	1	2	3	4	5
c. CLEANLINESS OF THE RESTAURANT	1	2	3	4	5
d. VALUE FOR THE MONEY	1	2	3	4	5
e. COURTESY OF EMPLOYEES	1	2	3	4	5
f. PRICES	1	2	3	4	5

7. NOW, I'D LIKE TO ASK YOU JUST A FEW QUESTIONS ABOUT YOU AND YOUR HOUSEHOLD TO HELP US CLASSIFY YOUR ANSWERS.

ARE THERE ANY CHILDREN AGE 15 OR UNDER LIVING IN YOUR HOME?

Yes	1
No	2

8. INTO WHAT AGE GROUP DO YOU FALL? [read categories]

18 AND UNDER	1
19-24	2
25-34	3
35-49	4
50-65	5
OVER 65	6
(refused)	7

9. AND, FINALLY, IS YOUR TOTAL HOUSEHOLD INCOME UNDER OR OVER $15,000?

If under:	WOULD IT BE UNDER OR OVER $12,000	1
	1 = under 2 = over	2
If over:	WOULD IT BE UNDER OR OVER $20,000	3
	3 = under 4 = over	4
	(refused)	5

THANK YOU VERY MUCH

Interviewer:	Record Sex	Male	1
		Female	2

Name ______________________

FAST FOOD SURVEY

Questionnaire Number 11 (extra)
Phone Number Called: __________
Date/Time: ____________________

HELLO, MY NAME IS ________. I'M A STUDENT AT ___________ AND I'M CONDUCTING AN OPINION SURVEY ABOUT RESTAURANTS IN OUR AREA. IT WILL ONLY TAKE A FEW MINUTES OF YOUR TIME. WOULD YOU MIND IF I ASK YOU A FEW QUESTIONS?

[wait for response]

	Circle:
Yes -- Terminate and record	1
No -- Continue	2

MANY PEOPLE USE THE TERM FAST FOOD TO DESCRIBE CERTAIN RESTAURANTS.

1. FIRST OF ALL, WHAT DO THE WORDS FAST FOOD, AS IN FAST FOOD RESTAURANT, MEAN TO YOU? [probe]

____

____

2. DURING A TYPICAL MONTH ABOUT HOW OFTEN DO YOU VISIT A FAST FOOD RESTAURANT? [do not read]

never (skip to Q.7)	1
less than once a month (skip to Q.7)	2
1-2 times (continue)	3
3-4 times (continue)	4
5-9 times (continue)	5
10 or more (continue)	6

3. AT WHICH FAST FOOD RESTAURANT DO YOU EAT MOST FREQUENTLY?

____

4. CAN YOU TELL ME IF YOU RECALL SEEING OR HEARING ANY ADS FOR ANY FAST FOOD RESTAURANTS WITHIN THE PAST TWO WEEKS?

No (skip to Q.6)	1
Yes (continue)	2

5. CAN YOU TELL ME WHICH RESTAURANT YOU RECALL SEEING OR HEARING THE ADS FOR? ...... ANY OTHERS? [check if don't recall____]

first mention: ______________________________

second mention: ______________________________

third mention: ______________________________

6. NOW, I WOULD LIKE YOU TO THINK OF <u>ONLY</u> FAST FOOD RESTAURANTS THAT SPECIALIZE IN HAMBURGERS. CONSIDERING ALL OF THE HAMBURGER RESTAURANTS WHICH YOU'VE RECENTLY VISITED, WOULD YOU SAY THAT THE (insert first item) AT THESE RESTAURANTS IS (ARE) EXCELLENT, GOOD, FAIR, OR POOR? [repeat items]

[rotate order of reading items]	Excellent	Good	Fair	Poor	Don't Know
a. FOOD QUALITY	1	2	3	4	5
b. SPEED OF SERVICE	1	2	3	4	5
c. CLEANLINESS OF THE RESTAURANT	1	2	3	4	5
d. VALUE FOR THE MONEY	1	2	3	4	5
e. COURTESY OF EMPLOYEES	1	2	3	4	5
f. PRICES	1	2	3	4	5

7. NOW, I'D LIKE TO ASK YOU JUST A FEW QUESTIONS ABOUT YOU AND YOUR HOUSEHOLD TO HELP US CLASSIFY YOUR ANSWERS.

ARE THERE ANY CHILDREN AGE 15 OR UNDER LIVING IN YOUR HOME?

Yes	1
No	2

8. INTO WHAT AGE GROUP DO YOU FALL? [read categories]

18 AND UNDER	1
19-24	2
25-34	3
35-49	4
50-65	5
OVER 65	6
(refused)	7

9. AND, FINALLY, IS YOUR TOTAL HOUSEHOLD INCOME UNDER OR OVER $15,000?

If under:	WOULD IT BE UNDER OR OVER $12,000	1
	1 = under 2 = over	2
If over:	WOULD IT BE UNDER OR OVER $20,000	3
	3 = under 4 = over	4
	(refused)	5

THANK YOU VERY MUCH

Interviewer: Record Sex		
	Male	1
	Female	2

Name ____________________

FAST FOOD SURVEY

Questionnaire Number 12 (extra)
Phone Number Called: ________
Date/Time: ______________

HELLO, MY NAME IS ________. I'M A STUDENT AT __________ AND I'M CONDUCTING AN OPINION SURVEY ABOUT RESTAURANTS IN OUR AREA. IT WILL ONLY TAKE A FEW MINUTES OF YOUR TIME. WOULD YOU MIND IF I ASK YOU A FEW QUESTIONS?

[wait for response]

	Circle:
Yes -- Terminate and record	1
No -- Continue	2

MANY PEOPLE USE THE TERM FAST FOOD TO DESCRIBE CERTAIN RESTAURANTS.

1. FIRST OF ALL, WHAT DO THE WORDS FAST FOOD, AS IN FAST FOOD RESTAURANT, MEAN TO YOU? [probe]

____

____

2. DURING A TYPICAL MONTH ABOUT HOW OFTEN DO YOU VISIT A FAST FOOD RESTAURANT? [do not read]

never (skip to Q.7)	1
less than once a month (skip to Q.7)	2
1-2 times (continue)	3
3-4 times (continue)	4
5-9 times (continue)	5
10 or more (continue)	6

3. AT WHICH FAST FOOD RESTAURANT DO YOU EAT MOST FREQUENTLY?

____

4. CAN YOU TELL ME IF YOU RECALL SEEING OR HEARING ANY ADS FOR ANY FAST FOOD RESTAURANTS WITHIN THE PAST TWO WEEKS?

No (skip to Q.6)	1
Yes (continue)	2

5. CAN YOU TELL ME WHICH RESTAURANT YOU RECALL SEEING OR HEARING THE ADS FOR? ...... ANY OTHERS? [check if don't recall____]

first mention: ____________________

second mention: ____________________

third mention: ____________________

6. NOW, I WOULD LIKE YOU TO THINK OF ONLY FAST FOOD RESTAURANTS THAT SPECIALIZE IN HAMBURGERS. CONSIDERING ALL OF THE HAMBURGER RESTAURANTS WHICH YOU'VE RECENTLY VISITED, WOULD YOU SAY THAT THE (insert first item) AT THESE RESTAURANTS IS (ARE) EXCELLENT, GOOD, FAIR, OR POOR? [repeat items]

[rotate order of reading items]	Excellent	Good	Fair	Poor	Don't Know
a. FOOD QUALITY	1	2	3	4	5
b. SPEED OF SERVICE	1	2	3	4	5
c. CLEANLINESS OF THE RESTAURANT	1	2	3	4	5
d. VALUE FOR THE MONEY	1	2	3	4	5
e. COURTESY OF EMPLOYEES	1	2	3	4	5
f. PRICES	1	2	3	4	5

7. NOW, I'D LIKE TO ASK YOU JUST A FEW QUESTIONS ABOUT YOU AND YOUR HOUSEHOLD TO HELP US CLASSIFY YOUR ANSWERS.

ARE THERE ANY CHILDREN AGE 15 OR UNDER LIVING IN YOUR HOME?

Yes	1
No	2

8. INTO WHAT AGE GROUP DO YOU FALL? [read categories]

18 AND UNDER	1
19-24	2
25-34	3
35-49	4
50-65	5
OVER 65	6
(refused)	7

9. AND, FINALLY, IS YOUR TOTAL HOUSEHOLD INCOME UNDER OR OVER $15,000?

If under:	WOULD IT BE UNDER OR OVER $12,000	1
	1 = under 2 = over	2
If over:	WOULD IT BE UNDER OR OVER $20,000	3
	3 = under 4 = over	4
	(refused)	5

THANK YOU VERY MUCH

Interviewer:	Record Sex	Male	1
		Female	2

8.2 Observation Study

The purpose of this study is to determine an estimate of customer service time in fast food restaurants. More specifically, we are interested in estimating the amount of time that a customer waits before an order is taken and the amount of time needed to fill the order.

Select a fast food restaurant (such as a McDonald's). Ideally, choose a busy time of day, such as lunchtime. Randomly select customers as they enter the store. On the observation sheet, record the amount of time that it takes before each places an order and the amount of time before the order is filled. Continue until you have collected data on twenty customers. You will probably want to use a stopwatch or a watch with a second hand or elapsed timer. Be sure to get permission from the store manager before starting your observation study.

Name ______________________

OBSERVATION FORM

Restaurant: ________________

Day of Week: ________________

Time began observation: __________

Time completed: ________

Customer Number	Wait Time	Service Time
1	___ seconds	_____ seconds
2	___	_____
3	___	_____
4	___	_____
5	___	_____
6	___	_____
7	___	_____
8	___	_____
9	___	_____
10	___	_____
11	___	_____
12	___	_____
13	___	_____
14	___	_____
15	___	_____
16	___	_____
17	___	_____
18	___	_____
19	___	_____
20	___	_____

Estimate of average wait time ________________

Estimate of average service time ____________

CHAPTER 9

EDITING AND CODING

After the data collection is completed, the next task is to edit the results and prepare the information for analysis. In some instances the researcher must conduct a hand tally or analysis of the information, especially when open-ended questions have been used. Generally, the results of the research study will be coded so that the information can be entered into a computer data file for further analysis.

This section first includes an exercise in coding free responses from a survey. Next, a case study is presented with accompanying questionnaires and coding information to illustrate the coding process.

9.1 Modern Furniture Company

The owner of Modern Furniture Company was considering whether or not to add a professional interior designer to the store's staff. A mail survey of households was conducted and various questions were asked about interior decorating or design services. One such question asked if respondents had any objections to using design or decorating services offered by furniture stores. The responses of fifty of those surveyed are shown below:

Objections to using design or decorating services offered by furniture stores:

"We do our own decorating."

"prefer to do my own"

"enjoy doing it myself"

"felt the furnishings were higher priced when I could have economized on my own"

"have to buy things from that store"

"prefer to do my own decorating, rarely like decorators design"

"want personal touch"

"most are just salespersons, even in big stores"

"don't want to be told what I will like"

"looks too much like a showroom, like a personal touch"

"know how I want to decorate a room, don't feel I need professional help"

"have definite ideas about how I want my home to look"

"lost money"

"you must make all purchases at that store"

"designers have too flashy ideas."

"I shop and compare among stores, and have a background in art and trust my own decisions on decor. Some of the accessories are frivolous that decorators choose."

"It is best to have persons wanting the services to pay for them."

"I do it myself."

"Only I know what I like or would be comfortable with."

"would like to add my own touch"

"too expensive"

"They tend to decorate according to their views and professional tastes need to communicate more with customers."

"They have set ideas of design concepts."

"The only problem I've had is I'm usually not buying many pieces of furniture at one time, therefore each time I could be talking to a different designer and not getting the same advice, in order to carry through a coordinated look."

"prefer my own choices"

"felt the furnishings were higher priced when I could have economized on my own"

"I don't like the snobbish attitude of decorators in thinking their taste is superior to mine. I do like the aid of someone who knows what is available."

"use my own judgment; decorators get carried away"

"They are not likely to stay within the price and style guidelines I require as a matter of economy."

"I use old furniture as long as possible and replace only one piece at a time."

"I might use decorator service if I needed it."

"prefer doing own decorating"

"I want my house to reflect my ideas and designs, not someone else's."

"want to decorate on my own"

"prefer my own ideas"

"I know what I like and want, I can decide for myself."

"This service would be unnecessary in my income bracket."

"cost"

"You're limited to use of merchandise sold at that store."

"Stores do not offer much selection, and decorators often push design not suitable to our lifestyle."

"I like to use my own taste and imagination, not someone else's."

"My time is very limited and I prefer to trust my own tastes and judgment."

"I know my own taste."

"rather do it myself"

"Using someone else's ideas does not reflect one's own personality and tastes."

"I know what I like and would like to design my own house."

"like designing my own home with personal touch"

"prefer to do my own"

"trust my own design sense, know my own needs better"

Name ____________________

CODING ASSIGNMENT -- MODERN FURNITURE COMPANY

Read through the survey responses and formulate a set of coding categories which describes the results. Tabulate the results using your coding procedure. [Hint: including an "other" category, you will probably want about five separate categories.]

	Category Description	Number Responding	Percent Responding
1.			
2.			
3.			
4.			
5.			
6.*			
7.*			
8.*			
TOTAL		50	100%

*if needed

San Diego Convention And Visitors Bureau (A)

One of the major industries of the city of San Diego, California is tourism. To promote San Diego as a visitor destination, a separate information and marketing agency was formed a number of years ago. The San Diego Convention and Visitors Bureau (CONVIS) is responsible for an annual budget of approximately $2.5 million which is devoted to promoting the location as a travel destination or convention site. This is in addition to roughly $25 million which is spent by the city's travel and tourism industry, including such attractions as Sea World, San Diego Zoo and San Diego Wild Animal Park.

The marketing effort of CONVIS is divided into three major areas: 1) conventions; 2) international tours and visitors; and 3) visitor marketing. The latter area is responsible for promoting San Diego as a destination for domestic travelers.

Visitor marketing is, in turn, divided into three major areas of responsibility. These include: 1) working with travel agents who plan or book tours and itineraries; 2) cooperative marketing with the airlines which serve the San Diego market; and 3) direct advertising to prospective visitors. The advertising program has accounted for the bulk of the visitor marketing budget, with nearly $500,000 devoted to magazine, radio and newspaper advertising.

Ronni Hawthorne, the new director of visitor marketing, was interested in devising a method to help evaluate the effectiveness of the advertising program. Consequently, she developed an advertising campaign which was based on a clip-out coupon response program.

Ads appearing in print media were accompanied by a coupon with which prospective visitors could request information about San Diego. Respondents were sent a check-card listing specific brochures which also asked for the date of any planned visit. After the date of the planned visit, a survey questionnaire (Exhibit 8) was sent to those returning the response card. The codebook (coding details) for this survey is shown in Exhibit 9.

Exhibit 8

SURVEY QUESTIONNAIRE

VISITOR SURVEY

I. ABOUT YOUR TRIP

1. How many nights in total were you away from home? ______

2. How many nights were you in San Diego? ______
Did not stay overnight ☐

3. Was San Diego your *primary* destination?
☐ Yes ☐ No → what was? ______

4. What other areas did you visit on your trip?
   - ☐ Areas in San Diego County
   - ☐ Tijuana/Baja California
   - ☐ Anaheim/Disneyland
   - ☐ Los Angeles
   - ☐ Other California City
   - ☐ Arizona
   - ☐ Nevada
   - ☐ Other Western State

5. Mode of transportation you used to arrive in San Diego?
   - ☐ private auto ☐ motor home/RV
   - ☐ rental auto ☐ train
   - ☐ airplane ☐ bus
   - ☐ Other

6. Mode of transportation used in San Diego?
   - ☐ private auto ☐ public bus
   - ☐ rental auto ☐ taxi
   - ☐ RV/van ☐ other

7. What type of lodging did you stay in?
   - ☐ did not stay overnight ☐ RV/camper park
   - ☐ hotel/motel ☐ rental/condo/apt.
   - ☐ private home ☐ other

8. About how much money would you estimate you spent in a typical day in San Diego?
$ ______
How much do you estimate you spent during your total visit in San Diego?
$ ______

9. What attractions did you visit while in San Diego? (Check all that apply)
   - ☐ Zoo ☐ Balboa Park Museums
   - ☐ Sea World ☐ Missions
   - ☐ Wild Animal Park ☐ Beaches
   - ☐ Cabrillo Monument ☐ Harbor Area
   - ☐ Coronado ☐ Mission Bay
   - ☐ La Jolla ☐ Old Town
   - ☐ East County/Mountains ☐ Downtown San Diego
   - ☐ Others ______

II. PLANNING FOR YOUR TRIP

10. Did you use a ☐ travel agent ☐ auto club
to help you: ☐ book airlines ☐ hotel/motel ☐ attractions ☐ tour package
☐ Did not use

11. How far in advance did you plan this trip?
No. of weeks ☐ No. of months ☐

12. On what date(s) were you in San Diego?
______ to ______

13. Have you been to San Diego before?
☐ No ☐ Yes → No. of times ______

14. How important were the following in your decision to visit San Diego (Check one for each item)

	VERY IMPORTANT	SOMEWHAT IMPORTANT	NOT TOO IMPORTANT
Climate	☐	☐	☐
Cost of travel	☐	☐	☐
Family oriented	☐	☐	☐
Educational/historical aspects	☐	☐	☐
Familiarity w/area	☐	☐	☐
Advertising	☐	☐	☐

Where ad seen ______

Please tape or staple closed

III. ABOUT YOU

15 ⓐ How many people including yourself came to San Diego in your group? ____________

ⓑ traveled with
☐ friends ☐ relatives ☐ alone

16 How many are (No.) ____________ under 18
____________ over 18

17 Which one of the following best describes your total annual household income?

☐ less than $5,000
☐ $5,000-$9,999
☐ $10,000-$14,999
☐ $15,000-$19,999
☐ $20,000-$24,999
☐ $25,000 and over

18 Which one of the following best describes your household?

☐ head of household under 45, not married
☐ head under 45, married, no children
☐ head married, youngest child under 6
☐ head married, youngest child over 6
☐ head over 45, married, older children, none at home
☐ head over 45, not married
☐ single parent, other household type.

19 What are your favorite magazines? (Please list)

Ⓐ____________ Ⓒ____________
Ⓑ____________ Ⓓ____________

Please tape or staple closed

NO POSTAGE
NECESSARY
IF MAILED
IN THE
UNITED STATES

BUSINESS REPLY MAIL

FIRST CLASS PERMIT NO. SAN DIEGO, CA 92101

POSTAGE WILL BE PAID BY ADDRESSEE

Attention: Visitor Marketing Dept.

Exhibit 9

CODEBOOK: VISITOR SURVEY

Question Number	Card Column	Variable Number	Variable Name	Code	Value Label
	1-4			Respondent number	
	5			(blank)	
1	6	V1	Nights away from home total	1	daytrip
				2	1 night
				3	2-3 nights
				4	4-7 nights
				5	8-14 nights (1-2 weeks)
				6	15-28 nights (2-4 weeks)
				7	1-2 months
				8	2-4 months
				9	4+ months
2	7	V2	Nights in San Diego	1	daytrip
				2	1 night
				3	2-3 nights
				4	4-7 nights
				5	8-14 nights (1-2 weeks)
				6	15-28 nights (2-4 weeks)
				7	1-2 months
				8	2-4 months
				9	4+ months
3	8	V3	Primary destination	1	San Diego
				2	L.A.-Anaheim
				3	other Southern California
				4	other California city
				5	California in general
				6	Mexico
				7	other western state
				8	western U.S.
				9	other destination
4	9	V4	Visited S.D. County	1	yes (otherwise blank)
	10	V5	Visited Tijuana-Baja California	1	yes
	11	V6	Visited Anaheim-Disneyland	1	yes
	12	V7	Visited Los Angeles	1	yes
	13	V8	Visited other California city	1	yes
	14	V9	Visited Arizona	1	yes

	15	V10	Visited Nevada	1	yes
	16	V11	Visited other western states	1	yes
5	17	V12	Arrival transportation	1 2 3 4 5 6 7	private auto rental auto air motor home/RV train bus other
6	18	V13	Used private auto in San Diego	1	yes
	19	V14	Used rental auto in San Diego	1	yes
	20	V15	Used RV-van in SD	1	yes
	21	V16	Used public bus	1	yes
	22	V17	Used taxi in SD	1	yes
	23	V18	Used other transportation in SD	1	yes
7	24	V19	Type of lodging used	1 2 3 4 5 6	daytrip hotel/motel private home RV-camper park rental-condo-apt other
8	25,26,27	V20	Daily expenditure in San Diego		[right justify]
	28,29,30,31	V21	Total expenditure in San Diego		[right justify]
9	32	V22	Visited zoo-museums	1	yes
	33	V23	Visited Sea World	1	yes
	34	V24	Visited Wild Animal Park	1	yes
	35	V25	Visited Cabrillo Monument	1	yes
	36	V26	Visited Coronado	1	yes

	37	V27	Visited La Jolla	1	yes
	38	V28	Visited East County	1	yes
	39	V29	Visited Balboa Park	1	yes
	40	V30	Visited missions	1	yes
	41	V31	Visited beaches	1	yes
	42	V32	Visited harbor area	1	yes
	43	V33	Visited Mission Bay	1	yes
	44	V34	Visited Old Town	1	yes
	45	V35	Visited downtown	1	yes
	46	V36	Visited other areas	1	yes
10	47	V37	Use of travel agent	1 2 3	used travel agent used auto club used neither
	48	V38	Agent booked airlines	1	yes
	49	V39	Agent booked hotel-motel	1	yes
	50	V40	Agent booked attractions	1	yes
	51	V41	Agent booked tour package	1	yes
11	52	V42	When trip planned?	1 2 3 4 5 6 7	1-3 weeks prior 4-7 weeks prior 2-3 months prior 4-6 months prior 7-9 months prior 10-12 months prior 12+ months prior
				(choose closest time period)	
12	53	V43	When in San Diego?	1 2 3 4 5 6	Jan-Feb Mar-Apr May-Jun Jul-Aug Sep-Oct Nov-Dec

13	54	V44	Visited San Diego before?	1	once
				2	2 times
				3	3
				4	4
				5	5
				6	6
				7	7
				8	8 or more
				9	no (first time visitor)
14	55	V45	Importance of climate	1	not too important
				2	somewhat important
				3	very important
	56	V46	Importance of cost of travel	1	not too important
				2	somewhat important
				3	very important
	57	V47	Importance of family orientation	1	not too important
				2	somewhat important
				3	very important
	58	V48	Importance of educational/historical aspects	1	not too important
				2	somewhat important
				3	very important
	59	V49	Importance of familiarity with area	1	not too important
				2	somewhat important
				3	very important
	60	V50	Importance of advertising	1	not too important
				2	somewhat important
				3	very important
	61	V51	Where ad seen?	1	Sunset Magazine
				2	Readers Digest
				3	Good Housekeeping
				4	travel magazines
				5	golf magazines
				6	magazines (other or general)
				7	local newspaper
				8	brochure, pamphlet
				9	other
15a	62	V52	Total visitors	1	alone
				2	2
				3	3
				4	4
				5	5
				6	6
				7	7
				8	8
				9	9 or more

15b	63	V53	Traveled with	1	friends
				2	relatives
				3	alone
16	64	V54	Number under 18	1	1 or alone
				2	2
				3	3
				4	4
				5	5
				6	6
				7	7
				8	8
				9	9 or more
	65	V55	Number over 18	1	1 or alone
				2	2
				3	3
				4	4
				5	5
				6	6
				7	7
				8	8
				9	9 or more
17	66	V56	Annual household income	1	less than $5,000
				2	$5,000-$9,999
				3	$10,000-$14,999
				4	$15,000-$19,999
				5	$20,000-$24,999
				6	$25,000 or more
18	67	V57	Family status	1	head of household under 45 not married
				2	head under 45, married no children
				3	head married, youngest child under 6
				4	head married, youngest child over 6
				5	head over 45, married older children, none at home
				6	head over 45, not married
				7	single parent, other household type
19	68-69	V58	Favorite magazine A	(see list)	
	70-71	V59	Favorite magazine B	(see list)	
	72-73	V60	Favorite magazine C	(see list)	
	74-75	V61	Favorite magazine D	(see list)	
	76	V62	Sex of respondent	1	female
				2	male
				0	not known

Magazine Codes

Code	Magazine
01	Sunset
02	Time
03	Newsweek
04	Readers Digest
05	New Yorker
06	Good Housekeeping
07	Better Homes & Gardens
08	Ladies Home Journal
09	Family Circle
10	Smithsonian
11	National Geographic
12	Forbes
13	Fortune
14	Life
15	Playboy
16	MacCleans
17	Prevention
18	Sports Illustrated
19	Popular Mechanics
20	People
21	US News and World Report
22	Travel magazines (misc.)
23	Golf magazines (misc.)
24	other magazines

Name ______________________________

9.2 Measurement Scales Exercise (B)

Review the CONVIS questionnaire and codebook carefully to determine the scale of measurement used for each question. How is each of the following "variables" measured?

	Variable	Variable Number	Question Number	Scale of Measurement
1.	Nights away from home total	V1	1	ordinal
2.	Visited San Diego County	V4	4	nominal
3.	Primary destination	V3	2	______
4.	Arrival transportation	V12	5	______
5.	Daily expenditure in San Diego	V20	8	______
6.	Visited San Diego before?	V44	13	______
7.	Importance of climate	V45	14	______
8.	Total visitors	V52	15	______
9.	Annual household income	V56	17	______
10.	Favorite magazine (A)	V58	19	______

9.3 Questionnaire Coding

The next step in data processing is to transform the answers on the questionnaire to numbers which can be read by the computer. Using the CONVIS codebook presented in the last section, you are ready to edit and code the returned survey forms.

Enclosed are copies of ten actual returns from the CONVIS visitor survey. The first one (#624) has already been coded on the coding form provided.

1. Review the codes assigned to Case 624. Notice in particular, the answers to questions 7 and 16. The response to question 7 did not "fit" the code. The response to question 16 was inconsistent with question 15. Both responses have been left blank in the data file and have been treated as "missing data."

2. Code the following nine survey forms on the coding form (Exhibit 10) provided. Be prepared for responses which do not conform to the codebook; make note of how you handle these instances. Record any specific problems encountered on the summary form.

3. How could the survey questionnaire be improved? Comment on any specific questions or codes which need improvement.

Exhibit 10

Questionnaire Coding

1	2	3	4	5	6	7	8	9	10	11	12	13	14	15	16	17	18	19	20	21	22	23	24	25	26	27	28	29	30	31	32	33	34	35	36	37	38	39	40	41	42	43	44	45	46	47	48	49	50	51	52	53	54	55	56	57	58	59	60	61	62	63	64	65	66	67	68	69	70	71	72	73	74	75	76	77	78	79	80
	6	2	4		4	4	1	1								1	1								6	5		2	5	ø					1								1			3					5	3	2	1	1	2	1	2	1		2	2			5	5	ø	1	1	1	ø	2			ø				

VISITOR SURVEY No. 624

I. ABOUT YOUR TRIP

1. How many nights in total were you away from home? 7

2. How many nights were you in San Diego? 4
Did not stay overnight ☐

3. Was San Diego your *primary* destination?
☑ Yes ☐ No → what was? ______

4. What other areas did you visit on your trip?
☑ Areas in San Diego County
☐ Tijuana/Baja California
☐ Anaheim/Disneyland
☐ Los Angeles
☐ Other California City
☐ Arizona
☐ Nevada
☐ Other Western State

5. Mode of transportation you used to arrive in San Diego?
☑ private auto ☐ motor home/RV
☐ rental auto ☐ train
☐ airplane ☐ bus
☐ Other

6. Mode of transportation used in San Diego?
☑ private auto ☐ public bus
☐ rental auto ☐ taxi
☐ RV/van ☐ other

7. What type of lodging did you stay in?
☐ did not stay overnight ☐ RV/camper park
☑ hotel/motel ☐ rental/condo/apt.
☑ private home ☐ other

8. About how much money would you estimate you spent in a typical day in San Diego?
$ 65
How much do you estimate you spent during your total visit in San Diego?
$ 250

9. What attractions did you visit while in San Diego? (Check all that apply)
☐ Zoo ☐ Balboa Park Museums
☐ Sea World ☐ Missions
☐ Wild Animal Park ☐ Beaches
☐ Cabrillo Monument ☐ Harbor Area
☑ Coronado ☐ Mission Bay
☐ La Jolla ☑ Old Town
☐ East County/Mountains ☐ Downtown San Diego
☐ Others ______

II. PLANNING FOR YOUR TRIP

10. Did you use a ☐ travel agent ☐ auto club
to help you: ☐ book airlines
☐ hotel/motel
☐ attractions
☐ tour package
☑ Did not use

11. How far in advance did you plan this trip?
No. of weeks ☐ No. of months 7

12. On what date(s) were you in San Diego?
27 Jun 79 to 1 Jul 79

13. Have you been to San Diego before?
☐ No ☑ Yes → No. of times 2

14. How important were the following in your decision to visit San Diego (Check one for each item)

	VERY IMPORTANT	SOMEWHAT IMPORTANT	NOT TOO IMPORTANT
Climate	☐	☐	☑
Cost of travel	☐	☐	☑
Family oriented	☐	☑	☐
Educational/historical aspects	☐	☐	☑
Familiarity w/area	☐	☑	☐
Advertising	☐	☐	☑

Where ad seen ______

Please tape or staple closed

III. ABOUT YOU

15 ⓐ How many people including yourself came to San Diego in your group? 2

ⓑ traveled with
☐ friends ☑ relatives ☐ alone

16 How many are (No.) 0 under 18
1 over 18

17 Which one of the following best describes your total annual household income?

☐ less than $5,000 ☐ $15,000-$19,999
☐ $5,000-$9,999 ☑ $20,000-$24,999
☐ $10,000-$14,999 ☐ $25,000 and over

18 Which one of the following best describes your household?

☐ head of household under 45, not married
☐ head under 45, married, no children
☐ head married, youngest child under 6
☐ head married, youngest child over 6
☑ head over 45, married, older children, at home
☐ head over 45, not married
☐ single parent, other household type.

19 What are your favorite magazines? (Please list)

Ⓐ Sunset Ⓒ Time
Ⓑ Nat. Geographic Ⓓ

Please tape or staple closed

NO POSTAGE
NECESSARY
IF MAILED
IN THE
UNITED STATES

BUSINESS REPLY MAIL

FIRST CLASS PERMIT NO. SAN DIEGO, CA 92101

POSTAGE WILL BE PAID BY ADDRESSEE

Attention: Visitor Marketing Dept.

(ZIP)

VISITOR SURVEY No. 629

I. ABOUT YOUR TRIP

1. How many nights in total were you away from home? 12

2. How many nights were you in San Diego? 4
Did not stay overnight ☐

3. Was San Diego your *primary* destination?
☒ Yes ☐ No → what was? ____

4. What other areas did you visit on your trip?
☒ Areas in San Diego County
☒ Tijuana/Baja California
☒ Anaheim/Disneyland
☒ Los Angeles
☐ Other California City
☐ Arizona
☒ Nevada
☐ Other Western State

5. Mode of transportation you used to arrive in San Diego?
☒ private auto ☐ motor home/RV
☐ rental auto ☐ train
☐ airplane ☐ bus
☐ Other

6. Mode of transportation used in San Diego?
☒ private auto ☐ public bus
☐ rental auto ☐ taxi
☐ RV/van ☐ other

7. What type of lodging did you stay in?
☐ did not stay overnight ☐ RV/camper park
☒ hotel/motel ☐ rental/condo/apt.
☐ private home ☐ other

8. About how much money would you estimate you spent in a typical day in San Diego?
$ 50.00
How much do you estimate you spent during your total visit in San Diego?
$ 200.00

9. What attractions did you visit while in San Diego? (Check all that apply)
☒ Zoo ☒ Balboa Park
Museums
☒ Sea World ☐ Missions
☒ Wild Animal Park ☐ Beaches
☐ Cabrillo Monument ☒ Harbor Area
☐ Coronado ☐ Mission Bay
☐ La Jolla ☐ Old Town
☐ East County/Mountains ☐ Downtown San Diego
☐ Others ____

II. PLANNING FOR YOUR TRIP

10. Did you use a ☐ travel agent ☐ auto club
to help you: ☐ book airlines
☐ hotel/motel
☐ attractions
☐ tour package
☐ Did not use

11. How far in advance did you plan this trip?
No. of weeks ☐ No. of months 6

12. On what date(s) were you in San Diego?
7-9-79 to 7-12-79

13. Have you been to San Diego before?
☐ No ☒ Yes → No. of times 1

14. How important were the following in your decision to visit San Diego (Check one for each item)

	VERY IMPORTANT	SOMEWHAT IMPORTANT	NOT TOO IMPORTANT
Climate	☐	☒	☐
Cost of travel	☐	☒	☐
Family oriented	☒	☐	☐
Educational/historical aspects	☒	☐	☐
Familiarity w/area	☐	☐	☒
Advertising	☐	☐	☒

Where ad seen ____

Please tape or staple closed

III. ABOUT YOU

15 ⓐ How many people including yourself came to San Diego in your group? 3

ⓑ traveled with
☐ friends ☒ relatives ☐ alone

16 How many are (No.) 1 under 18
2 over 18

17 Which one of the following best describes your total annual household income?

☐ less than $5,000 ☒ $15,000-$19,999
☐ $5,000-$9,999 ☐ $20,000-$24,999
☐ $10,000-$14,999 ☐ $25,000 and over

18 Which one of the following best describes your household?

☐ head of household under 45, not married
☐ head under 45, married, no children
☐ head married, youngest child under 6
☒ head married, youngest child over 6
☐ head over 45, married, older children, none at home
☐ head over 45, not married
☐ single parent, other household type.

19 What are your favorite magazines? (Please list)

Ⓐ Sunset Ⓒ Better Homes
Ⓑ Time Ⓓ ~~[illegible]~~ Reader's D

Please tape or staple closed

NO POSTAGE NECESSARY IF MAILED IN THE UNITED STATES

BUSINESS REPLY MAIL

FIRST CLASS PERMIT NO. SAN DIEGO, CA 92101

POSTAGE WILL BE PAID BY ADDRESSEE

Attention: Visitor Marketing Dept.

VISITOR SURVEY No. 633

I. ABOUT YOUR TRIP

1 How many nights in total were you away from home? 8

2 How many nights were you in San Diego? 4
Did not stay overnight ☐

3 Was San Diego your *primary* destination?
☐ Yes ☒ No →what was? Las Vegas, NV

4 What other areas did you visit on your trip?
- ☑ Areas in San Diego County
- ☐ Tijuana/Baja California
- ☐ Anaheim/Disneyland
- ☐ Los Angeles
- ☐ Other California City
- ☐ Arizona
- ☑ Nevada
- ☐ Other Western State

5 Mode of transportation you used to arrive in San Diego?
- ☐ private auto
- ☐ motor home/RV
- ☐ rental auto
- ☐ train
- ☑ airplane
- ☐ bus
- ☐ Other

6 Mode of transportation used in San Diego?
- ☐ private auto
- ☐ public bus
- ☑ rental auto
- ☐ taxi
- ☐ RV/van
- ☐ other

7 What type of lodging did you stay in?
- ☐ did not stay overnight
- ☐ RV/camper park
- ☑ hotel/motel
- ☐ rental/condo/apt.
- ☐ private home
- ☐ other

8 About how much money would you estimate you spent in a typical day in San Diego?
$ 60.00

How much do you estimate you spent during your total visit in San Diego?
$ $340.00

9 What attractions did you visit while in San Diego? (Check all that apply)
- ☐ Zoo
- ☐ Balboa Park Museums
- ☑ Sea World
- ☐ Missions
- ☑ Wild Animal Park
- ☑ Beaches
- ☐ Cabrillo Monument
- ☐ Harbor Area
- ☐ Coronado
- ☑ Mission Bay
- ☑ La Jolla
- ☑ Old Town
- ☐ East County/Mountains
- ☐ Downtown San Diego
- ☐ Others ______

II. PLANNING FOR YOUR TRIP

10 Did you use a ☐ travel agent ☑ auto club to help you:
- ☑ book airlines
- ☐ hotel/motel
- ☐ attractions
- ☐ tour package
- ☐ Did not use

11 How far in advance did you plan this trip?
No. of weeks ☐ No. of months 4

12 On what date(s) were you in San Diego?
June 22 to June 25

13 Have you been to San Diego before?
☐ No ☑ Yes → No. of times 2

14 How important were the following in your decision to visit San Diego (Check one for each item)

	VERY IMPORTANT	SOMEWHAT IMPORTANT	NOT TOO IMPORTANT
Climate	☑	☐	☐
Cost of travel	☐	☑	☐
Family oriented	☐	☐	☑
Educational/historical aspects	☐	☑	☐
Familiarity w/area	☐	☐	☑
Advertising	☐	☐	☑

Where ad seen ______

Please tape or staple closed

III. ABOUT YOU

15 (a) How many people including yourself came to San Diego in your group? 2

(b) traveled with

☑ friends ☐ relatives ☐ alone

16 How many are (No.) ______ under 18

2 over 18

17 Which one of the following best describes your total annual household income?

☐ less than $5,000 ☐ $15,000-$19,999
☐ $5,000-$9,999 ☐ $20,000-$24,999
☑ $10,000-$14,999 ☐ $25,000 and over

18 Which one of the following best describes your household?

☑ head of household under 45, not married
☐ head under 45, married, no children
☐ head married, youngest child under 6
☐ head married, youngest child over 6
☐ head over 45, married, older children, none at home
☐ head over 45, not married
☐ single parent, other household type.

19 What are your favorite magazines? (Please list)

(A) National Geographic (C) Time
(B) Glamour (D) Newsweek

Please tape or staple closed

NO POSTAGE NECESSARY IF MAILED IN THE UNITED STATES

BUSINESS REPLY MAIL

FIRST CLASS PERMIT NO. SAN DIEGO, CA 92101

POSTAGE WILL BE PAID BY ADDRESSEE

Attention: Visitor Marketing Dept.

(ZIP)

Dickmann

VISITOR SURVEY No. 634

I. ABOUT YOUR TRIP

1. How many nights in total were you away from home? 8

2. How many nights were you in San Diego? 6
Did not stay overnight ☐

3. Was San Diego your *primary* destination?
☒ Yes ☐ No → what was? ____

4. What other areas did you visit on your trip?
☒ Areas in San Diego County
☒ Tijuana/Baja California
☐ Anaheim/Disneyland
☐ Los Angeles
☒ Other California City
☐ Arizona
☐ Nevada
☐ Other Western State

5. Mode of transportation you used to arrive in San Diego?
☒ private auto ☐ motor home/RV
☐ rental auto ☐ train
☐ airplane ☐ bus
☐ Other

6. Mode of transportation used in San Diego?
☒ private auto ☐ public bus
☐ rental auto ☐ taxi
☐ RV/van ☐ other

7. What type of lodging did you stay in?
☐ did not stay overnight ☐ RV/camper park
☒ hotel/motel ☐ rental/condo/apt.
☐ private home ☐ other

8. About how much money would you estimate you spent in a typical day in San Diego?
$ 70-75
How much do you estimate you spent during your total visit in San Diego?
$ $420

9. What attractions did you visit while in San Diego? (Check all that apply)
☒ Zoo ☒ Balboa Park
Museums
☐ Sea World ☒ Missions
☐ Wild Animal Park ☒ Beaches
☒ Cabrillo Monument ☒ Harbor Area
☒ Coronado ☒ Mission Bay
☒ La Jolla ☒ Old Town
☐ East County/Mountains ☒ Downtown San Diego
☐ Others ____

II. PLANNING FOR YOUR TRIP

10. Did you use a ☐ travel agent ☐ auto club
to help you: ☐ book airlines
☐ hotel/motel
☐ attractions
☐ tour package
☒ Did not use

11. How far in advance did you plan this trip?
No. of weeks [3] No. of months [ ]

12. On what date(s) were you in San Diego?
July 8 to July 13

13. Have you been to San Diego before?
☐ No ☒ Yes → No. of times 10-12

14. How important were the following in your decision to visit San Diego (Check one for each item)

	VERY IMPORTANT	SOMEWHAT IMPORTANT	NOT TOO IMPORTANT
Climate	☒	☐	☐
Cost of travel	☐	☐	☒
Family oriented	☐	☒	☐
Educational/historical aspects	☐	☒	☐
Familiarity w/area	☒	☐	☐
Advertising	☐	☒	☐

Where ad seen ____

Please tape or staple closed

III. ABOUT YOU

15 ⓐ How many people including yourself came to San Diego in your group? 2

ⓑ traveled with

☐ friends ☐ relatives ☐ alone

16 How many are (No.) ______ under 18

2 over 18

17 Which one of the following best describes your total annual household income?

☐ less than $5,000 ☐ $15,000-$19,999
☐ $5,000-$9,999 ☐ $20,000-$24,999
☐ $10,000-$14,999 ☒ $25,000 and over

18 Which one of the following best describes your household?

☐ head of household under 45, not married
☐ head under 45, married, no children
☐ head married, youngest child under 6
☒ head married, youngest child over 6
☐ head over 45, married, older children, none at home
☐ head over 45, not married
☐ single parent, other household type.

19 What are your favorite magazines? (Please list

Ⓐ Sunset Ⓒ Arch. Rec
Ⓑ Ariz Highways Ⓓ ______

Please tape or staple closed

NO POSTAGE NECESSARY IF MAILED IN THE UNITED STATES

BUSINESS REPLY MAIL

FIRST CLASS PERMIT NO. SAN DIEGO, CA 92101

POSTAGE WILL BE PAID BY ADDRESSEE

Attention: Visitor Marketing Dept.

(zip)

ORDEN

VISITOR SURVEY No. 638

I. ABOUT YOUR TRIP

1. How many nights in total were you away from home? *16*

2. How many nights were you in San Diego? *14*
   Did not stay overnight ☐

3. Was San Diego your *primary* destination?
   ☑ Yes ☐ No → what was? ______

4. What other areas did you visit on your trip?
   - ☑ Areas in San Diego County
   - ☑ Tijuana/Baja California
   - ☑ Anaheim/Disneyland
   - ☑ Los Angeles
   - ☐ Other California City
   - ☐ Arizona
   - ☑ Nevada
   - ☐ Other Western State

5. Mode of transportation you used to arrive in San Diego?
   - ☐ private auto
   - ☐ rental auto
   - ☑ airplane
   - ☐ motor home/RV
   - ☐ train
   - ☐ bus
   - ☐ Other

6. Mode of transportation used in San Diego?
   - ☐ private auto
   - ☐ rental auto
   - ☑ RV/van
   - ☐ public bus
   - ☐ taxi
   - ☐ other

7. What type of lodging did you stay in?
   - ☐ did not stay overnight
   - ☐ hotel/motel
   - ☑ private home
   - ☐ RV/camper park
   - ☐ rental/condo/apt.
   - ☐ other

8. About how much money would you estimate you spent in a typical day in San Diego?
   $ *65.00*

   How much do you estimate you spent during your total visit in San Diego?
   $ *900.00*

9. What attractions did you visit while in San Diego? (Check all that apply)
   - ☑ Zoo
   - Museums
   - ☐ Sea World
   - ☑ Wild Animal Park
   - ☑ Cabrillo Monument
   - ☐ Coronado
   - ☑ La Jolla
   - ☐ East County/Mountains
   - ☑ Balboa Park
   - ☐ Missions
   - ☐ Beaches
   - ☑ Harbor Area
   - ☐ Mission Bay
   - ☑ Old Town
   - ☑ Downtown San Diego
   - ☑ Others *Harbor Cruise*

II. PLANNING FOR YOUR TRIP

10. Did you use a ☑ travel agent ☐ auto club

    to help you:
    - ☑ book airlines
    - ☐ hotel/motel
    - ☐ attractions
    - ☐ tour package
    - ☐ Did not use

11. How far in advance did you plan this trip?
    No. of weeks ☐ No. of months *6*

12. On what date(s) were you in San Diego?
    June 27 to *July 13*

13. Have you been to San Diego before?
    ☑ No ☐ Yes → No. of times ______

14. How important were the following in your decision to visit San Diego (Check one for each item)

	VERY IMPORTANT	SOMEWHAT IMPORTANT	NOT TOO IMPORTANT
Climate	☐	☑	☐
Cost of travel	☑	☐	☐
Family oriented	☑	☐	☐
Educational/historical aspects	☐	☑	☐
Familiarity w/area	☐	☐	☑
Advertising	☐	☐	☑

Where ad seen ______

Please tape or staple closed

III. ABOUT YOU

15 ⓐ How many people including yourself came to San Diego in your group? 3

ⓑ traveled with
☐ friends ☑ relatives ☐ alone

16 How many are (No.) ______ under 18
3 over 18

17 Which one of the following best describes your total annual household income?

☐ less than $5,000 ☐ $15,000-$19,999
☐ $5,000-$9,999 ☐ $20,000-$24,999
☐ $10,000-$14,999 ☑ $25,000 and over

18 Which one of the following best describes your household?

☐ head of household under 45, not married
☐ head under 45, married, no children
☐ head married, youngest child under 6
☐ head married, youngest child over 6
☑ head over 45, married, older children, none at home
☐ head over 45, not married
☐ single parent, other household type.

19 What are your favorite magazines? (Please list)

Ⓐ ______ Ⓒ ______
Ⓑ ______ Ⓓ ______

Please tape or staple closed

Attention: Visitor Marketing Dept.

POSTAGE WILL BE PAID BY ADDRESSEE

FIRST CLASS PERMIT NO. SAN DIEGO, CA 92101

BUSINESS REPLY MAIL

(ZIP)

NO POSTAGE NECESSARY IF MAILED IN THE UNITED STATES

VISITOR SURVEY No. 645

I. ABOUT YOUR TRIP

1 How many nights in total were you away from home? 5

2 How many nights were you in San Diego? 2
Did not stay overnight ☒

3 Was San Diego your *primary* destination?
☒ Yes ☐ No → what was? ______

4 What other areas did you visit on your trip?
- ☒ Areas in San Diego County
- ☒ Tijuana/Baja California
- ☐ Anaheim/Disneyland
- ☐ Los Angeles
- ☐ Other California City
- ☐ Arizona
- ☐ Nevada
- ☐ Other Western State

5 Mode of transportation you used to arrive in San Diego?
- ☐ private auto
- ☐ rental auto
- ☒ airplane
- ☐ motor home/RV
- ☐ train
- ☐ bus
- ☐ Other

6 Mode of transportation used in San Diego?
- ☐ private auto
- ☐ rental auto
- ☐ RV/van
- ☒ public bus
- ☐ taxi
- ☒ other

7 What type of lodging did you stay in?
- ☐ did not stay overnight
- ☒ hotel/motel
- ☐ private home
- ☐ RV/camper park
- ☐ rental/condo/apt.
- ☐ other

8 About how much money would you estimate you spent in a typical day in San Diego?
$ ~60

How much do you estimate you spent during your total visit in San Diego?
$ ~200

9 What attractions did you visit while in San Diego? (Check all that apply)
- ☒ Zoo
- Museums
- ☐ Sea World
- ☐ Wild Animal Park
- ☐ Cabrillo Monument
- ☒ Coronado
- ☐ La Jolla
- ☐ East County/ Mountains
- ☒ Balboa Park
- ☐ Missions
- ☒ Beaches
- ☒ Harbor Area
- ☒ Mission Bay
- ☒ Old Town
- ☒ Downtown San Diego
- ☐ Others ______

II. PLANNING FOR YOUR TRIP

10 Did you use a ☐ travel agent ☐ auto club
to help you:
- ☐ book airlines
- ☐ hotel/motel
- ☐ attractions
- ☐ tour package
- ☐ Did not use

11 How far in advance did you plan this trip?
No. of weeks [—] No. of months [3]

12 On what date(s) were you in San Diego?
5/17 to 5/19

13 Have you been to San Diego before?
☒ No ☐ Yes → No. of times ______

14 How important were the following in your decision to visit San Diego (Check one for each item)

	VERY IMPORTANT	SOMEWHAT IMPORTANT	NOT TOO IMPORTANT
Climate	☐	☒	☐
Cost of travel	☐	☒	☐
Family oriented	☒	☐	☐
Educational/ historical aspects	☐	☒	☐
Familiarity w/area	☐	☐	☒
Advertising	☐	☒	☐

Where ad seen ______

Please tape or staple closed

III. ABOUT YOU

15 ⓐ How many people including yourself came to San Diego in your group? one

ⓑ traveled with

☐ friends ☐ relatives ☒ alone

16 How many are (No.) — under 18

1 over 18

17 Which one of the following best describes your total annual household income?

☐ less than $5,000 ☐ $15,000-$19,999

☐ $5,000-$9,999 ☐ $20,000-$24,999

☒ $10,000-$14,999 ☐ $25,000 and over

18 Which one of the following best describes your household?

☒ head of household under 45, not married

☐ head under 45, married, no children

☐ head married, youngest child under 6

☐ head married, youngest child over 6

☐ head over 45, married, older children, none at home

☐ head over 45, not married

☐ single parent, other household type.

19 What are your favorite magazines? (Please list)

Ⓐ SUNSET Ⓒ NAT'L GEO

Ⓑ TIME Ⓓ SCIENTIFIC AMERICAN

Please tape or staple closed

Attention: Visitor Marketing Dept.

POSTAGE WILL BE PAID BY ADDRESSEE

FIRST CLASS PERMIT SAN DIEGO, CA 92101

BUSINESS REPLY MAIL

NO POSTAGE NECESSARY IF MAILED IN THE UNITED STATES

VISITOR SURVEY No. 848

I. ABOUT YOUR TRIP

1. How many nights in total were you away from home? 8
2. How many nights were you in San Diego? 4
   Did not stay overnight ☐
3. Was San Diego your *primary* destination?
   ☐ Yes ☒ No → what was? L.A.
4. What other areas did you visit on your trip?
   - ☐ Areas in San Diego County
   - ☒ Tijuana/Baja California
   - ☒ Anaheim/Disneyland
   - ☒ Los Angeles
   - ☐ Other California City
   - ☐ Arizona
   - ☐ Nevada
   - ☐ Other Western State
5. Mode of transportation you used to arrive in San Diego?
   - ☐ private auto
   - ☐ motor home/RV
   - ☐ rental auto
   - ☐ train
   - ☒ airplane
   - ☐ bus
   - ☐ Other
6. Mode of transportation used in San Diego?
   - ☐ private auto
   - ☐ public bus
   - ☒ rental auto
   - ☐ taxi
   - ☐ RV/van
   - ☐ other
7. What type of lodging did you stay in?
   - ☐ did not stay overnight
   - ☐ RV/camper park
   - ☒ hotel/motel
   - ☐ rental/condo/apt.
   - ☐ private home
   - ☐ other
8. About how much money would you estimate you spent in a typical day in San Diego?
   $ 45.
   How much do you estimate you spent during your total visit in San Diego?
   $ 225.
9. What attractions did you visit while in San Diego? (Check all that apply)
   - ☒ Zoo
   - ☐ Balboa Park Museums
   - ☒ Sea World
   - ☒ Missions
   - ☐ Wild Animal Park
   - ☐ Beaches
   - ☐ Cabrillo Monument
   - ☐ Harbor Area
   - ☐ Coronado
   - ☐ Mission Bay
   - ☐ La Jolla
   - ☒ Old Town
   - ☐ East County/Mountains
   - ☐ Downtown San Diego
   - ☐ Others ______

II. PLANNING FOR YOUR TRIP

10. Did you use a ☐ travel agent ☐ auto club
    to help you: ☐ book airlines ☐ hotel/motel ☐ attractions ☐ tour package
    ☒ Did not use
11. How far in advance did you plan this trip?
    No. of weeks ☐ No. of months 3
12. On what date(s) were you in San Diego?
    June 23 to June 27
13. Have you been to San Diego before?
    ☒ No ☐ Yes → No. of times ______
14. How important were the following in your decision to visit San Diego (Check one for each item)

	VERY IMPORTANT	SOMEWHAT IMPORTANT	NOT TOO IMPORTANT
Climate	☒	☐	☐
Cost of travel	☐	☐	☒
Family oriented	☐	☐	☒
Educational/historical aspects	☒	☐	☐
Familiarity w/area	☐	☐	☒
Advertising	☐	☒	☐

Where ad seen local newspaper — Sunday Democrat and Chronicle

Please tape or staple closed

III. ABOUT YOU

15 ⓐ How many people including yourself came to San Diego in your group? 1

ⓑ traveled with
☒ friends ☐ relatives ☐ alone

16 How many are (No.) ______ under 18
2 over 18

17 Which one of the following best describes your total annual household income?

☐ less than $5,000 ☐ $15,000-$19,999
☐ $5,000-$9,999 ☐ $20,000-$24,999
☒ $10,000-$14,999 ☐ $25,000 and over

18 Which one of the following best describes your household?

☒ head of household under 45, not married
☐ head under 45, married, no children
☐ head married, youngest child under 6
☐ head married, youngest child over 6
☐ head over 45, married, older children, none at home
☐ head over 45, not married
☐ single parent, other household type.

19 What are your favorite magazines? (Please list)

Ⓐ Mother Earth News Ⓒ Rona Barrett's
Ⓑ National Geographic Ⓓ New Mexico World magazine

Please tape or staple closed

Attention: Visitor Marketing Dept.

POSTAGE WILL BE PAID BY ADDRESSEE

FIRST CLASS PERMIT NO. SAN DIEGO, CA 92101

BUSINESS REPLY MAIL

NO POSTAGE NECESSARY IF MAILED IN THE UNITED STATES

(ZIP)

SALMINEN

VISITOR SURVEY No. 857

I. ABOUT YOUR TRIP

1. How many nights in total were you away from home? 50

2. How many nights were you in San Diego? 3
Did not stay overnight ☐

3. Was San Diego your *primary* destination?
☐ Yes ☒ No → what was? Around the world

4. What other areas did you visit on your trip?
- ☐ Areas in San Diego County
- ☐ Tijuana/Baja California
- ☐ Anaheim/Disneyland
- ☒ Los Angeles
- ☒ Other California City
- ☐ Arizona
- ☐ Nevada
- ☐ Other Western State

5. Mode of transportation you used to arrive in San Diego?
- ☐ private auto
- ☒ rental auto
- ☐ airplane
- ☐ motor home/RV
- ☐ train
- ☐ bus
- ☐ Other

6. Mode of transportation used in San Diego?
- ☐ private auto
- ☒ rental auto
- ☐ RV/van
- ☐ public bus
- ☐ taxi
- ☐ other

7. What type of lodging did you stay in?
- ☐ did not stay overnight
- ☒ hotel/motel
- ☐ private home
- ☐ RV/camper park
- ☐ rental/condo/apt.
- ☐ other

8. About how much money would you estimate you spent in a typical day in San Diego?
$ 100.00
How much do you estimate you spent during your total visit in San Diego?
$ 300.00

9. What attractions did you visit while in San Diego? (Check all that apply)
- ☐ Zoo
- ☐ Balboa Park Museums
- ☐ Sea World
- ☐ Wild Animal Park
- ☐ Cabrillo Monument
- ☐ Coronado
- ☐ La Jolla
- ☐ East County/Mountains
- ☐ Missions
- ☒ Beaches
- ☐ Harbor Area
- ☐ Mission Bay
- ☐ Old Town
- ☐ Downtown San Diego
- ☐ Others ______

II. PLANNING FOR YOUR TRIP

10. Did you use a ☐ travel agent ☐ auto club
to help you:
- ☐ book airlines
- ☐ hotel/motel
- ☐ attractions
- ☐ tour package
- ☒ Did not use

11. How far in advance did you plan this trip?
No. of weeks ☐ No. of months 6

12. On what date(s) were you in San Diego?
June 28 to June 30

13. Have you been to San Diego before?
☐ No ☒ Yes → No. of times Former res[illegible]

14. How important were the following in your decision to visit San Diego (Check one for each item)

	VERY IMPORTANT	SOMEWHAT IMPORTANT	NOT TOO IMPORTANT
Climate	☒	☐	☐
Cost of travel	☐	☐	☒
Family oriented	☒	☐	☐
Educational/historical aspects	☒	☐	☐
Familiarity w/area	☒	☐	☐
Advertising	☐	☐	☒

Where ad seen ______

Please tape or staple closed

III. ABOUT YOU

15 ⓐ How many people including yourself came to San Diego in your group? 2

ⓑ traveled with
☐ friends ☒ relatives ☐ alone

16 How many are (No.) ______ under 18
2 over 18

17 Which one of the following best describes your total annual household income?

☐ less than $5,000 ☐ $15,000-$19,999
☐ $5,000-$9,999 ☐ $20,000-$24,999
☐ $10,000-$14,999 ☒ $25,000 and over

18 Which one of the following best describes you household?

☐ head of household under 45, not married
☐ head under 45, married, no children
☐ head married, youngest child under 6
☐ head married, youngest child over 6
☒ head over 45, married, older children, none at home
☐ head over 45, not married
☐ single parent, other household type.

19 What are your favorite magazines? (Please lis

Ⓐ Orientations Ⓒ Arts of Asia
Ⓑ Sunset Ⓓ Time

Please tape or staple closed

Attention: Visitor Marketing Dept.

POSTAGE WILL BE PAID BY ADDRESSEE

FIRST CLASS PERMIT NO. SAN DIEGO, CA 92101

BUSINESS REPLY MAIL

NO POSTAGE NECESSARY IF MAILED IN THE UNITED STATES

(ZIP)

GE R. BROSIUS

VISITOR SURVEY No. 858

I. ABOUT YOUR TRIP

1. How many nights in total were you away from home? 9

2. How many nights were you in San Diego? 9
Did not stay overnight ☐

3. Was San Diego your *primary* destination?
☒ Yes ☐ No →what was? ____

4. What other areas did you visit on your trip?
☒ Areas in San Diego County
☐ Tijuana/Baja California
☐ Anaheim/Disneyland
☐ Los Angeles
☐ Other California City
☐ Arizona
☐ Nevada
☐ Other Western State

5. Mode of transportation you used to arrive in San Diego?
☐ private auto ☐ motor home/RV
☐ rental auto ☐ train
☒ airplane ☐ bus
☐ Other

6. Mode of transportation used in San Diego?
☒ private auto ☐ public bus
☐ rental auto ☐ taxi
☐ RV/van ☐ other

7. What type of lodging did you stay in?
☐ did not stay overnight ☐ RV/camper park
☐ hotel/motel ☐ rental/condo/apt.
☒ private home ☐ other

8. About how much money would you estimate you spent in a typical day in San Diego?
$ 30→50
How much do you estimate you spent during your total visit in San Diego?
$ 400→500

9. What attractions did you visit while in San Diego? (Check all that apply)
☒ Zoo ☒ Balboa Park
Museums
*☒ Sea World ☐ Missions
☐ Wild Animal Park ☒ Beaches
☒ Cabrillo Monument ☒ Harbor Area
☐ Coronado ☒ Mission Bay
☒ La Jolla ☐ Old Town
☒ East County/Mountains ☐ Downtown San Diego
☐ Others
Sea world

II. PLANNING FOR YOUR TRIP

10. Did you use a ☒ travel agent ☐ auto club
to help you: ☒ book airlines
☐ hotel/motel
☐ attractions
☐ tour package
☐ Did not use

11. How far in advance did you plan this trip?
No. of weeks ☐ No. of months 1½

12. On what date(s) were you in San Diego?
June 20 to June 29

13. Have you been to San Diego before?
☐ No ☒ Yes → No. of times one

14. How important were the following in your decision to visit San Diego (Check one for each item)

	VERY IMPORTANT	SOMEWHAT IMPORTANT	NOT TOO IMPORTANT
Climate	☒	☐	☐
Cost of travel	☒	☐	☐
Family oriented	☐	☒	☐
Educational/historical aspects	☐	☐	☒
Familiarity w/area	☐	☒	☐
Advertising	☐	☐	☒

Where ad seen ____

Please tape or staple closed

III. ABOUT YOU

15 ⓐ How many people including yourself came to San Diego in your group? 2

ⓑ traveled with
☐ friends ☒ relatives ☐ alone

16 How many are (No.) — under 18
2 over 18

17 Which one of the following best describes your total annual household income?

☐ less than $5,000 ☐ $15,000-$19,999
☐ $5,000-$9,999 ☒ $20,000-$24,999
☐ $10,000-$14,999 ☐ $25,000 and over

18 Which one of the following best describes you household?

☐ head of household under 45, not married
☒ head under 45, married, no children
☐ head married, youngest child under 6
☐ head married, youngest child over 6
☐ head over 45, married, older children, none at home
☐ head over 45, not married
☐ single parent, other household type.

19 What are your favorite magazines? (Please lis

Ⓐ Time Ⓒ Good House

Ⓑ National Geog. Ⓓ Cosmopoli

Please tape or staple closed

NO POSTAGE
NECESSARY
IF MAILED
IN THE
UNITED STATES

BUSINESS REPLY MAIL

FIRST CLASS PERMIT NO. SAN DIEGO, CA 92101

POSTAGE WILL BE PAID BY ADDRESSEE

Attention: Visitor Marketing Dept.

(ZIP)

VISITOR SURVEY No. 919

I. ABOUT YOUR TRIP

1. How many nights in total were you away from home? 9

2. How many nights were you in San Diego? 9
Did not stay overnight ☐

3. Was San Diego your *primary* destination?
☒ Yes ☐ No → what was? ______

4. What other areas did you visit on your trip?
☒ Areas in San Diego County
☒ Tijuana/Baja California
☐ Anaheim/Disneyland
☒ Los Angeles
☒ Other California City
☐ Arizona
☐ Nevada
☐ Other Western State

5. Mode of transportation you used to arrive in San Diego?
☐ private auto ☐ motor home/RV
☐ rental auto ☐ train
☒ airplane ☐ bus
☐ Other

6. Mode of transportation used in San Diego?
☐ private auto ☐ public bus
☒ rental auto ☐ taxi
☐ RV/van ☐ other

7. What type of lodging did you stay in?
☐ did not stay overnight ☐ RV/camper park
☒ hotel/motel ☐ rental/condo/apt.
☐ private home ☐ other

8. About how much money would you estimate you spent in a typical day in San Diego?
$ $ 50.00
How much do you estimate you spent during your total visit in San Diego?
$ $ 900.00

9. What attractions did you visit while in San Diego? (Check all that apply)
☒ Zoo ☐ Balboa Park Museums
☒ Sea World ☒ Missions
☐ Wild Animal Park ☒ Beaches
☐ Cabrillo Monument ☐ Harbor Area
☐ Coronado ☒ Mission Bay
☒ La Jolla ☐ Old Town
☒ East County/Mountains ☒ Downtown San Diego
☒ Others Comedy Store
Disney world

II. PLANNING FOR YOUR TRIP

10. Did you use a ☒ travel agent ☐ auto club
to help you: ☒ book airlines
☐ hotel/motel
☐ attractions
☐ tour package
☐ Did not use

11. How far in advance did you plan this trip?
No. of weeks [4] No. of months [ ]

12. On what date(s) were you in San Diego?
July 13 to July 22

13. Have you been to San Diego before?
☐ No ☒ Yes → No. of times 1

14. How important were the following in your decision to visit San Diego (Check one for each item)

	VERY IMPORTANT	SOMEWHAT IMPORTANT	NOT TOO IMPORTANT
Climate	☐	☒	☐
Cost of travel	☐	☒	☐
Family oriented	☐	☐	☒
Educational/historical aspects	☐	☐	☒
Familiarity w/area	☐	☒	☐
Advertising	☐	☒	☐

Where ad seen Toronto Newspaper

Please tape or staple closed

III. ABOUT YOU

15 ⓐ How many people including yourself came to San Diego in your group? 4

ⓑ traveled with
☒ friends ☐ relatives ☐ alone

16 How many are (No.) ______ under 18
4 over 18

17 Which one of the following best describes your total annual household income?

☐ less than $5,000 ☐ $15,000-$19,999
☐ $5,000-$9,999 ☒ $20,000-$24,999
☐ $10,000-$14,999 ☐ $25,000 and over

18 Which one of the following best describes your household?

☒ head of household under 45, not married
☐ head under 45, married, no children
☐ head married, youngest child under 6
☐ head married, youngest child over 6
☐ head over 45, married, older children, none at home
☐ head over 45, not married
☐ single parent, other household type.

19 What are your favorite magazines? (Please lis

Ⓐ Starlog Ⓒ National Lamp
Ⓑ Audio Scene Canada Ⓓ Toronto Life

Please tape or staple closed

NO POSTAGE NECESSARY IF MAILED IN THE UNITED STATES

BUSINESS REPLY MAIL

FIRST CLASS PERMIT NO. SAN DIEGO, CA 92101

POSTAGE WILL BE PAID BY ADDRESSEE

Attention: Visitor Marketing Dept.

Name ______________________

QUESTIONNAIRE CODING

Record special coding problems encountered for each questionnaire:

Questionnaire	Problem
624	______________________
	______________________
629	______________________
	______________________
633	______________________
	______________________
634	______________________
	______________________
638	______________________
	______________________
645	______________________
	______________________
848	______________________
	______________________
857	______________________
	______________________
858	______________________
	______________________
919	______________________
	______________________

CHAPTER 10

DATA ANALYSIS

Data analysis procedures may range from a simple count of the frequency of occurrence of a certain survey result to the use of fairly sophisticated statistical tools. The most straight forward form of analysis is to tally the number of times a particular result is observed in the sample. Measures used to describe the central tendency of results are the mode, median and mean. Commonly used measures of dispersion are the variance and standard deviation.

Cross tabulation is a very commonly used method to compare the results of two variables in a sample. The Chi-square statistic can be used to analyze the cross tabulation table to determine if the variables are statistically interrelated. Correlation analysis can be used to determine the degree of association between variables. A scatter diagram can be used to plot results for two variables. A t-test can be utilized to determine if two sample means are statistically different.

This chapter provides a number of exercises to provide experience with these commonly used techniques. Although not covered here, marketing researchers have numerous other statistical methods available to them, such as regression, factor and discriminant analysis.

10.1 Design Showroom - Descriptive Statistics

Design Showroom is a chain of wholesale furniture showrooms which sells to interior designers and decorators. Products sold include furniture, lamps, accessories, wallpaper, fabric, carpeting and floor covering.

The management of Design Showroom recently conducted a sales audit of the accounts of the Denver showroom. A sample of 50 active accounts was drawn from the files. The total number of items purchased within the past six month period and the total dollar sales amount for each account were recorded.

The results for the 50 accounts are shown on the following page.

DESIGN SHOWROOM

Account	Total Items Purchased Last Six Months	Total Sales Last Six Months	Sales Territory
1	2	$224	East
2	1	2,795	North
3	16	6,380	East
4	1	286	North
5	5	1,963	West
6	2	85	South
7	1	1,319	South
8	4	149	East
9	8	1,292	West
10	1	195	North
11	1	216	North
12	5	511	East
13	1	78	South
14	33	5,160	West
15	67	7,738	North
16	1	297	West
17	1	108	South
18	3	225	East
19	6	1,660	East
20	8	4,395	North
21	3	1,099	West
22	3	900	South
23	1	1,784	East
24	11	1,822	North
25	15	2,315	West
26	5	453	South
27	13	1,532	South
28	1	79	East
29	10	3,788	North
30	8	4,796	South
31	1	472	West
32	3	313	East
33	6	744	North
34	17	4,587	West
35	1	178	North
36	4	510	East
37	3	3,014	West
38	1	649	South
39	5	936	South
40	43	4,250	East
41	1	398	South
42	1	132	West
43	3	2,077	East
44	1	9	West
45	9	2,197	North
46	9	5,898	West
47	1	17	North
48	10	2,361	South
49	5	769	South
50	4	788	East

Name ______________________

DESIGN SHOWROOM

1. Compute the following descriptive statistics:

	Total Items	Total Sales ($)
Mean	________	________
Median	________	________
Range	________	________
Variance	________	________
Standard deviation	________	________
Standard error	________	________

2. For the question above, which would be a better measure of central tendency for total items and total sales. The mean or the median? Explain.

Total Items:

Total Sales:

3. Complete the following table of absolute and relative frequencies for total items sold by category.

Category	Absolute Frequency	Relative Frequency
5 or less	(33)	(66%)
6 to 10	( )	( )
11 to 15	( )	( )
16 to 20	( )	( )
21 to 25	( )	( )
26 or more	( )	( )
Total	(50)	(100%)

4. Complete the following table of absolute and relative frequency for number of accounts per territory.

Territory	Absolute Frequency	Relative Frequency
North	( )	( )
South	( )	( )
East	( )	( )
West	( )	( )
Total	(50)	(100%)

5. Determine the distribution of total sales in each account category by territory.

	Number of Accounts in Each Sales Category		
Territory	Under $1,000	$1,000-$3,000	Over $3,000
North	( )	( )	( )
South	( )	( )	( )
East	( )	( )	( )
West	( )	( )	( )

	Percent of Accounts in Each Category		
Territory	Under $1,000	$1,000-$3,000	Over $3,000
North	( )	( )	( )
South	( )	( )	( )
East	( )	( )	( )
West	( )	( )	( )

6. Write a short paragraph to describe the "typical" Design Showroom account.

10.2 New Car Buyer Survey (A) - Descriptive Statistics

A recent survey of buyers of new automobiles asked, among other questions, the following:

1. Class of automobile purchased
2. Number of dealerships visted before final purchase
3. Buyer's household income

The research analyst asked for a computer run on these questions. The computer program produced a frequency analysis for each question and calculated the following descriptive statistics:

1. Mean
2. Mode
3. Median
4. Standard deviation
5. Variance
6. Range
7. Standard error

The results for each question are shown on the following pages.

CLASS OF AUTOMOBILE PURCHASED

Category	Code*	Absolute Frequency	Relative Frequency (percent)	Adjusted Frequency (percent)	Cumulative Frequency (percent)
Domestic Subcompact	1	138	18.3	18.3	18.3
Foreign Subcompact	2	82	10.9	10.9	29.1
Domestic Compact	3	112	14.8	14.8	44.0
Foreign Compact	4	110	14.6	14.6	58.5
Domestic Large	5	144	19.1	19.1	77.6
Foreign Large	6	169	22.4	22.4	100.0
TOTAL		755	100.0	100.0	

Mean	3.725
Mode	6.000
Median	3.914
Range	5.000
Variance	3.242
Std. Dev.	1.801
Std. Err.	0.066

*Computer code for each category

NUMBER OF DEALERSHIPS VISITED BEFORE FINAL PURCHASE

Code*	Absolute Frequency	Relative Frequency (percent)	Adjusted Frequency (percent)	Cumulative Frequency (percent)
1	113	15.0	15.7	15.7
2	118	15.6	16.4	32.1
3	140	18.5	19.4	51.5
4	102	13.5	14.2	65.7
5	82	10.9	11.4	77.1
6	50	6.6	6.9	84.0
7	23	3.0	3.2	87.2
8	20	2.6	2.8	90.0
9	10	1.3	1.4	91.4
10	31	4.1	4.3	95.7
11	6	0.8	0.8	96.5
12	8	1.1	1.1	97.6
13	2	0.3	0.3	97.9
14	2	0.3	0.3	98.2
15	3	0.4	0.4	98.6
16	1	0.1	0.1	98.8
18	1	0.1	0.1	98.9
20	7	0.9	1.0	99.9
38	1	0.1	0.1	100.0
	35	4.6	MISSING	
TOTAL	755	100.0	100.0	

mean	4.279
mode	3.000
median	3.421
range	37.000
variance	11.915
std. dev.	3.452
std. err.	0.129

*actual number visited

BUYER'S FAMILY INCOME

Category	Code	Absolute Frequency	Relative Frequency (percent)	Adjusted Frequency (percent)	Cumulative Frequency (percent)
<$5,000	1	17	2.3	2.3	2.3
$5,000-$9,999	2	65	8.6	8.9	11.3
$10,000-$14,999	3	112	14.8	15.4	26.7
$15,000-$19,999	4	120	15.9	16.5	43.2
$20,000-$24,999	5	129	17.1	17.7	60.9
$25,000-$29,999	6	85	11.3	11.7	72.6
$30,000-$34,999	7	57	7.5	7.8	80.5
>$35,000	8	142	18.8	19.5	100.0
		28	3.7	MISSING	100.0
Total		755	100.0	100.0	

mean	5.025
mode	8.000
median	4.884
range	7.000
variance	4.154
std. dev.	2.038
std. err.	0.076

Name ______________________________

NEW CAR BUYER SURVEY (A)

1. Which statistical measures could the analyst utilize for each variable in the study? Check each measure which could be used.

	Class of Automobile	Dealerships Visited	Income Category
percent	( )	( )	( )
mean	( )	( )	( )
mode	( )	( )	( )
median	( )	( )	( )
range	( )	( )	( )
variance	( )	( )	( )
std. dev.	( )	( )	( )
std. error	( )	( )	( )

2. Write a short paragraph which describes the "typical" buyer in terms of these three variables.

Class of automobile purchased

Dealerships visited

Income

10.3 San Diego Convention and Visitors Bureau (B) - Descriptive Statistics

Chapter 8 presented a case involving the San Diego Convention and Visitors Bureau (CONVIS) and a mail survey involving print advertising effectiveness. In that chapter, 10 completed questionnaires were shown as they might look prior to editing and coding. Appendix A contains a complete data file generated from 200 respondents to that survey. These are in much the same form as they might be read into a computer file.

From that Appendix, draw a sample of 25 cases. You might select them randomly (with a random number table) systematically (by selecting every 8th case) or as a cluster sample (by selecting one page). As illustrated by the following page, determine for each case in your sample, daily expenditure and total expenditure in San Diego, whether or not the visitor visited Sea World, previous visits to San Diego and the visitor's household income. Record the information on the accompanying worksheet.

Exhibit 11

Example of CONVIS Data File

Respondent No. 730 — Daily Expenditure in San Diego — Total Expenditure in San Diego — Visited Seaworld? — Previous Visits to San Diego — Income Level

Column No.

```
         1111111111222222222233333333334444444444555555555566666666667777777778
12345678901234567890123456789012345678901234567890123456789012345678901234567890
 720 5311  11   2 2      60 200 1 1 11   11  1111  331211223 41 46611241 5  2
 721 64111   1  11     2 75 32511  11  1   13      343321221721 2661124242422
 723 6421 111   2 1    2100 50011 1 1   1  9  3    44 3113 3 21 26211222    2
 724 635   1    13 1    2120 240   111  111 1 1111  3424     741   51122 2142
 725 4411  1    3 1    6    720111 11 1 11111 3    333211111 2  2632424 622
 726 551  11    3 1    3100100011   1 1 1 1 1 3    3492231  65 3234202 13242
 727 531     1  3 1    2125 350    1   111 11 3    44913  2  2  265242411151
 728 5411  1  1 3 1    2  40 15011111 1 11111111 111  349311122 2  25 2424 7  1
 729 4141   1   2 1    2  75  75      1     11 3    429321211 21 221242411241
 730 44111      11     2100 500    11   11   13    228311111631126124 24 2152
 731 618     1113 41   1       11    11  1 11 2   14 91213128 21 231242224241
 732 64411 11   3 1    2  5010001   1111 11 1  11   42932   2521 2 1232323242
 733 542 1 11 1 2 1    2  60 700    11 1  11   11   321322222 21 2251242424
 734 5511111    1      3  50 6751     1  11 11 11 1 329322212 21 16 242424242
 735 6381111111111     2  30  63111    1   11  3    439121212631 3212424 6 71
 736 541   1    3 1    2  75 800        111 11 11   339311222 2112662224 2132
 737 7411 11111111     21001000   111111111111 2 1  338322332631 366222412242
 738 6311111111114  1   4  40 200 1         111  12     31223333491365422222    1
 740 5411   1 1 31      100 5001    11   1 111 5493       21 231242424241
 741 514   11   6     11 50  50 11      1   1 1   3493322    21 23 242424241
 742 3311       11     2  45 15011  1   1111 1 3    148331111 21 23124212424
 743 3311       31    12100 300 1   1   11  1 21   441311111 91  662224 7 22
 744 55111 11   3 1    2  50 90011   11 11 1 11111  241221122741 45124242424
 870 7111 1  1 111     6  40120011 1 1 1 11    3    443222321 422253 21124 1
 269 6411  1    3 1    2  75 300               3    22131112  22 256211224 8
```

Name ______________________________

CONVIS WORKSHEET

Questionnaire Number	Daily Expenditure	Total Expenditure	Visited Sea World?	Previous Visits to San Diego	Household Income
1.	____	____	____	____	____
2.	____	____	____	____	____
3.	____	____	____	____	____
4.	____	____	____	____	____
5.	____	____	____	____	____
6.	____	____	____	____	____
7.	____	____	____	____	____
8.	____	____	____	____	____
9.	____	____	____	____	____
10.	____	____	____	____	____
11.	____	____	____	____	____
12.	____	____	____	____	____
13.	____	____	____	____	____
14.	____	____	____	____	____
15.	____	____	____	____	____
16.	____	____	____	____	____
17.	____	____	____	____	____
18.	____	____	____	____	____
19.	____	____	____	____	____
20.	____	____	____	____	____
21.	____	____	____	____	____
22.	____	____	____	____	____
23.	____	____	____	____	____
24.	____	____	____	____	____
25.	____	____	____	____	____

Name ______________________________

From your sample, describe the typical visitor in terms of

1. daily expenditure in San Diego.

2. total expenditure in San Diego.

3. visit(s) to Sea World.

4. previous visits to San Diego.

5. household income.

Name ______________________________

10.4 Public Attitudes Toward Gun Control - Cross Tabulation

A national probability opinion survey asked the following two questions concerning gun control:

Q1: Should citizens retain the right to keep a firearm for personal protection?

Q2: Should citizens be made to register personal firearms?

The results of the survey by sex of the respondent are shown below:

Q1. Personal Protection

	Female	Male	Total
Yes	541	682	1,223
No	106	128	234
	647	810	1,457

Q2. Registration

	Female	Male	Total
Yes	322	346	668
No	329	450	779
	651	796	1,447

Name ____________________

1. Complete the following cross classification tables:

PERCENT OF SAMPLE AGREEING OR DISAGREEING

Q1. Personal Protection

	Female	Male	Total
Yes	( )	( )	( )
No	( )	( )	( )
	100.0%	100.0%	100.0%

Q2. Registration

	Female	Male	Total
Yes	( )	( )	( )
No	( )	( )	( )
	100.0%	100.0%	100.0%

2. Without any further computation, does it appear as if men and women differ on either of these two questions? Explain.

3. Using the format below, compute the chi-square statistic and test for the difference in opinion by sex of the respondent. Test at the 95 percent level of confidence.

Q1. Personal Protection

Research Question: Do attitudes on the right to keep a firearm for personal protection differ by sex?

Null hypothesis: ____________________
Alternative hypothesis ____________________
Degrees of freedom: ____________________
Critical value of chi-square: ____________________
Calculated value of chi-square: ____________________

O_i	E_i	(O_i-E_i)	$(O_i-E_i)^2$	$\frac{(O_i-E_i)^2}{E_i}$*
( )	( )	( )	( )	( )
( )	( )	( )	( )	( )
( )	( )	( )	( )	( )
( )	( )	( )	( )	( )
			SUM =	( )

Your analysis: ____________________
____

Q2. Registration

Research Question: ____________________
____

Null hypothesis: ____________________
Alternative hypothesis: ____________________
Degrees of freedom: ____________________
Critical value of chi-square: ____________________
Calculated value of chi-square: ____________________

O_i	E_i	(O_i-E_i)	$(O_i-E_i)^2$	$\frac{(O_i-E_i)^2}{E_i}$
( )	( )	( )	( )	( )
( )	( )	( )	( )	( )
( )	( )	( )	( )	( )
( )	( )	( )	( )	( )
			SUM =	( )

Your analysis: ____________________
____

* Chi Square $=\sum\frac{(O_1 - E_1)^2}{E_1}$ O_1 = observed number

E_1 = expected number

Name ______________________________

10.5 San Diego Convention and Visitors Bureau (C) - Cross Tabulation

Analyze the results of a sample of 25 visitors (exercise 10.3) by comparing first time visitors to previous visitors to San Diego in terms of whether or not they visited Sea World. Treat all previous visitors to San Diego (regardless of number of visits) as belonging to one category.

1. Total Sample

	First time visitor		
Visted Sea World	Yes*	No**	Total
Yes	( )	( )	( )
No	( )	( )	( )
	( )	( )	(25)

*Code = 9
**Code = 1 through 8

2. Percent of Sample

	First time visitor		
Visited Sea World	Yes	No	Total
Yes	( )	( )	( )
No	( )	( )	( )
	( )	( )	(100.0)

3. Without any further computation, does it appear as if first time visitors are more likely to have visited Sea World? Explain.

4. Using the format below, compute the chi-square statistic and test for the difference in visit behavior by previous visits to San Diego. Test at the 95 percent level of confidence.

Research Question: ______________________________

____

____

Null hypothesis: ______________________________

Alternative hypothesis: ______________________________

Degrees of freedom: ______________________________

Critical value of chi-square: ______________________________

Calculated value of chi-square: __________

O_i	E_i	$(O_i - E_i)$	$(O_i - E_i)^2$	$\frac{(O_i - E_i)^2}{E_i}$
( )	( )	( )	( )	( )
( )	( )	( )	( )	( )
( )	( )	( )	( )	( )
( )	( )	( )	( )	( )
			SUM =	( )

Your analysis: ______________________________

____

____

Name ______________________________

10.6 San Diego Convention and Visitors Bureau (D) - Correlation Analysis

Analyze the results of a sample of 25 visitors (exercise 10.3) by comparing daily expenditure to total expenditure in San Diego.

1. Plot the data on a scatter diagram.

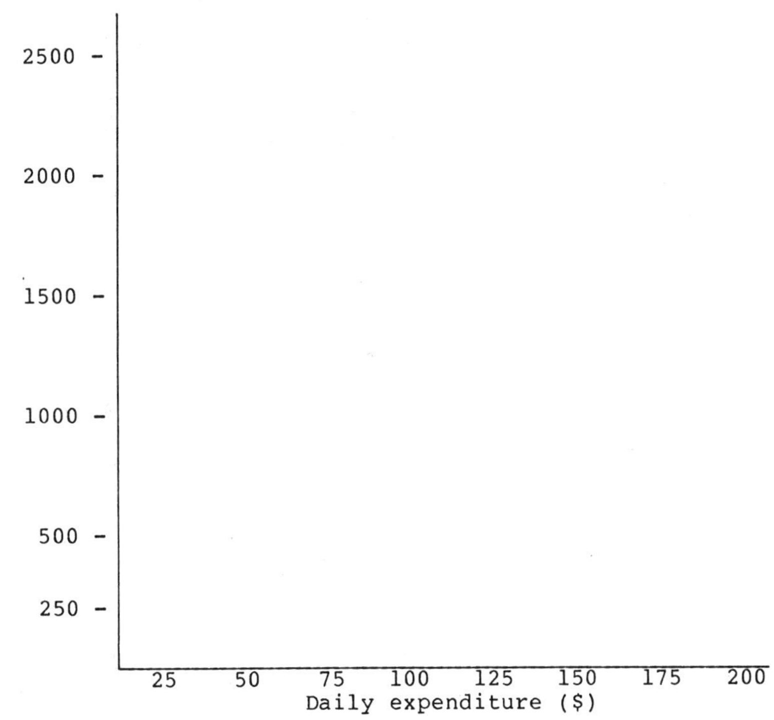

2. Compute the correlation between these two sets of data using the format below:

X = daily expenditure
Y = total expenditure

No.	X	Y	$x=(X-\bar{X})$	$y=(Y-\bar{Y})$	xy	x^2	y^2
1.	___	___	___	___	___	___	___
2.	___	___	___	___	___	___	___
3.	___	___	___	___	___	___	___
4.	___	___	___	___	___	___	___
5.	___	___	___	___	___	___	___
6.	___	___	___	___	___	___	___
7.	___	___	___	___	___	___	___
8.	___	___	___	___	___	___	___
9.	___	___	___	___	___	___	___
10.	___	___	___	___	___	___	___
11.	___	___	___	___	___	___	___
12.	___	___	___	___	___	___	___
13.	___	___	___	___	___	___	___
14.	___	___	___	___	___	___	___
15.	___	___	___	___	___	___	___
16.	___	___	___	___	___	___	___
17.	___	___	___	___	___	___	___
18.	___	___	___	___	___	___	___
19.	___	___	___	___	___	___	___
20.	___	___	___	___	___	___	___
21.	___	___	___	___	___	___	___
22.	___	___	___	___	___	___	___
23.	___	___	___	___	___	___	___
24.	___	___	___	___	___	___	___
25.	___	___	___	___	___	___	___

ΣX = ____ $\bar{X}$ = ____ ΣY = ____ $\bar{Y}$ = ____

Σxy = ____ Σx^2 = ____ Σy^2 = ____

$$r_{xy} = \frac{\Sigma xy}{\sqrt{(\Sigma x^2)(\Sigma y^2)}} = \_\_\_\_\_\_\_\_$$

Name ______________________

10.7 San Diego Convention and Visitors Bureau (E) - Comparison of Mean Differences

Using the formula below, compare the daily average expenditure between first time and repeat visitors from a sample of 25 visitors (exercise 10.3). Compare the differences at the 95 percent level of confidence.

1. Research question: ______________________

____

2. Null hypothesis: ______________________

3. Alternative hypothesis: ______________________

4. Critical value of t: ______________________

5. Calculated value of t: ______________________

$\bar{x}_1$ = average expenditure for first time visitors

$\bar{x}_2$ = average expenditure for repeat visitors

s_1^2 = sample variance of expenditures for first time visitors

s_2^2 = sample variance of expenditures for repeat visitors

n_1 = number of first time visitors in sample

n_2 = number of repeat visitors in sample

$\bar{x}_1$ = (   ) $\bar{x}_2$ = (   )

s_2^2 = (   ) s_2^2 = (   )

n_1 = (   ) n_2 = (   )

$$\text{calculated } t = \frac{(\bar{x}_1 - \bar{x}_2)}{\sqrt{\left(\frac{s_1^{\,2}}{n_1}\right) + \left(\frac{s_2^{\,2}}{n_2}\right)}}$$

6. Your analysis: ______________________

____

Name ______________________________

10.8 New Car Buyer Survey (B) - Comparison of Mean Differences

A recent survey of purchasers of new automobiles compared motivations between those buying domestic and foreign automobiles. Among the questions asked were the rated importance (1 = not very important, 7 = very important) of each of the following factors in the buying decision:

1. workmanship
2. handling
3. interior comfort

The results of the survey are shown below:

	Sample Size	Importance of: Workmanship		Handling		Interior Comfort	
		Mean	(Std.Dev.)	Mean	(Std.Dev.)	Mean	(Std.Dev.)
Domestic Car Buyers	376	6.04	(1.13)	5.90	(1.29)	5.64	(1.33)
Foreign Car Buyers	344	6.45	(0.86)	6.21	(1.05)	5.66	(1.32)
TOTAL	720						

Consider first the importance of workmanship.

1. State the research question concerning the difference between car buyers regarding the importance of workmanship.

2. What are the null and alternative hypotheses?

   null hypothesis: ______________________________

   alternative hypothesis: ______________________________

3. Compare the significance of the differences in mean importance. Test at the 95% level of confidence.

formula: $$t = \frac{(\overline{x}_1 - \overline{x}_2)}{\sqrt{\left(\frac{s_1^2}{n_1}\right)+\left(\frac{s_2^2}{n_2}\right)}}$$

calculated t ______________________________

critical t at 95 percent level ______________________________

your analysis: ______________________________

____

4. Repeat the same analysis for the importance of handling and interior comfort and write a concluding comment concerning the differences between domestic and import car buyers.

Handling

Interior Comfort

CHAPTER 11

REPORTING RESEARCH RESULTS

The research report is the finished product of the research study. There is no definitive style or format for such reports. Undoubtedly your textbook will provide you with some suggested guidelines. Some important points to consider are: 1) write to a particular audience in the appropriate language, 2) keep your report concise; 3) arrange the report in a logical order, and 4) summarize facts and draw conclusions from them. Often the report can be improved by reporting facts in tables and in charts.

11.1 San Diego Convention and Visitors Bureau (F)

Following is a portion of the results from one quarter of a previous year from the CONVIS visitor advertising survey.

Assume that you've just been hired as the marketing research assistant at CONVIS, reporting to Ronni Hawthorne, the director of visitor marketing. As an initial task Ms. Hawthorne has asked you to analyze the results of the advertising survey for this quarter. She would like you to prepare a brief report which summarizes the major findings. Specifically, she would like the report to tell her what kinds of visitors have been attracted by the advertising program, what these visitors do in San Diego and how much they spend.

Prepare a brief report for Ms. Hawthorne. For important statistics, you may want to show the results in tables of your own design or through the use of bar charts or pie diagrams.

1. HOW MANY NIGHTS IN TOTAL WERE YOU AWAY FROM HOME?

	(N)	Relative Percent	Adjusted Percent
Daytrip	2	0.4	0.4
1 Night	1	0.2	0.2
2-3 Nights	23	4.7	4.8
4-7 Nights	103	20.9	21.4
8-14 Nights	205	41.7	42.5
15-28 Nights	121	24.6	25.1
1-2 Months	23	4.7	4.8
2-4 Months	4	0.8	0.8
No Answer	10	2.0	____
	492	100.0	100.0

2. HOW MANY NIGHTS WERE YOU IN SAN DIEGO?

	(N)	Relative Percent	Adjusted Percent
Daytrip	32	6.5	6.6
1 Night	18	3.7	3.7
2-3 Nights	144	29.3	29.8
4-7 Nights	191	38.8	39.5
8-14 Nights	74	15.0	15.3
15-28 Nights	21	4.3	4.3
1-2 Months	2	0.4	0.4
2-4 Months	1	0.2	0.2
No Response	9	1.8	____
	492	100.0	100.0

3. WHAT WAS YOUR PRIMARY DESTINATION?

	(N)	Relative Percent	Adjusted Percent
San Diego	312	63.4	65.0
Los Angeles/ Anaheim	45	9.2	9.4
Other Southern California	15	3.1	3.1
Other California City	43	8.7	9.0
California in General	31	6.3	6.5
Mexico	1	0.2	0.2
Other Western State	9	1.8	1.9
Western United States	9	1.8	1.9
Other	8	1.6	1.7
No Answer	12	2.4	
	492	100.0	100.0

4. WHAT OTHER AREAS DID YOU VISIT ON YOUR TRIP?

	Number Visiting	Percent
Areas in San Diego County	304	61.8
Tijuana/Baja California	190	38.6
Anaheim-Disneyland	217	44.1
Los Angeles	248	50.4
Other California City	190	38.6
Arizona	86	17.5
Nevada	96	19.5
Other Western State	59	12.0

(Base = 492 Respondents)

5. MODE OF TRANSPORTATION USED TO ARRIVE IN SAN DIEGO

	(N)	Relative Percent	Adjusted Percent
Private automobile	163	33.1	34.0
Rental automoble	77	15.7	16.0
Air	195	39.6	40.6
Motor home - R.V.	16	3.3	3.3
Train	11	2.2	2.3
Bus	15	3.1	3.1
Other	3	0.6	0.6
No Response	12	2.4	
	492	100.0	100.0

6. MODE OF TRANSPORTATION USED IN SAN DIEGO

	Number Using	Percent
Private automobile	223	45.3
Rental automobile	174	35.4
R.V.-Van	23	4.7
Public bus	54	11.0
Taxi	28	5.7
Other Transporation	23	4.7

(Base = 492 respondents)

7. WHAT TYPE OF LODGING DID YOU OCCUPY?

	(N)	Relative Percent	Adjusted Percent
Daytrip	17	3.5	3.6
Hotel-motel	336	68.3	70.7
Private home	84	17.1	17.7
R.V.-camper park	18	3.7	3.8
Rental-condo-apartment	13	2.6	2.7
Other	7	1.4	1.5
No answer	17	3.5	
	492	100.0	100.0

8a. ABOUT HOW MUCH MONEY WOULD YOU ESTIMATE YOU SPENT IN A TYPICAL DAY IN SAN DIEGO?

	(N)	Relative Percent	Adjusted Percent
$ 0-25	52	10.6	11.5
$ 26-50	107	21.7	23.7
$ 51-75	100	20.3	22.2
$ 76-100	118	24.0	26.3
$101-125	16	3.3	3.5
$126-150	41	8.3	9.1
$151-175	4	0.8	0.8
$176-200	9	1.8	2.0
$201-225	1	0.2	0.2
$226-250	1	0.2	0.2
$251-275	0	0.0	0.0
$276-300	1	0.2	0.2
$301-325	0	0.0	0.0
$326-350	0	0.0	0.0
$351-375	0	0.0	0.0
$376-400	0	0.0	0.0
$401-425	0	0.0	0.0
$426-450	0	0.0	0.0
$451-500	0	0.0	0.0
No response	42	8.5	
	492	100.0	100.0

Mean value = $77.56 (450)

8b. HOW MUCH DO YOU ESTIMATE YOU SPENT DURING YOUR TOTAL VISIT IN SAN DIEGO?

	(N)	Relative Percent	Adjusted Percent
$ 0-100	45	9.1	9.6
$ 101-200	87	17.7	18.7
$ 201-300	89	18.1	19.2
$ 301-400	58	11.8	12.5
$ 401-500	50	10.2	10.8
$ 501-600	20	4.1	4.3
$ 601-700	21	4.3	4.5
$ 701-800	21	4.3	4.5
$ 801-900	8	1.6	1.7
$ 901-1000	21	4.3	4.6
$1001-1500	29	5.9	6.2
$1501-2000	5	1.0	1.0
$2001-2500	3	0.6	0.6
$2501-3000	1	0.2	0.2
$3001-3500	1	0.2	0.2
$4000+	2	0.4	0.4
No response	31	6.3	
	492	100.0	100.0

(Mean value = $493.27

9. WHAT ATTRACTIONS DID YOU VISIT WHILE IN SAN DIEGO?

	Number Visiting	Relative Percent
Zoo/Museum	375	76.2
Sea World	296	60.2
Wild Animal Park	143	29.1
Cabrillo Monument	136	27.6
Coronado	195	39.6
La Jolla	233	47.4
East County/Mountains	59	12.0
Balboa Park	274	55.7
Missions	112	22.8
Beaches	285	57.9
Harbor Area	309	63.0
Mission Bay	241	49.0
Old Town	266	54.1
Downtown San Diego	252	51.2
Others	69	14.0

(Base = 492 respondents)

10. WHEN PLANNING YOUR TRIP, DID YOU USE TRAVEL AGENT OR AUTO CLUB?

	(N)	Percent
Travel agent	209	42.5
Auto Club	68	13.8
Neither/No response	215	43.7
	492	100.0

AGENT BOOKED AIRLINES:

	(N)	Percent
Yes	198	40.2
No/No Response	294	59.8
	492	100.0

AGENT BOOKED HOTEL/MOTEL:

	(N)	Percent
Yes	138	28.0
No/No response	354	72.0
	492	100.0

AGENT BOOKED ATTRACTIONS:

	(N)	Percent
Yes	68	13.8
No/No response	424	86.2
	492	100.0

AGENT BOOKED TOUR PACKAGE:

	(N)	Percent
Yes	55	11.2
No/No response	437	88.8
	492	100.0

11. HOW FAR IN ADVANCE DID YOU PLAN THIS TRIP?

	(N)	Relative Percent	Adjusted Percent
1-3 weeks	21	4.3	4.5
4-7 weeks	65	13.2	13.8
2-3 months	188	38.2	39.9
4-6 months	157	31.9	33.3
7-9 months	12	2.4	2.5
10-12 months	26	5.3	5.5
12 + months	2	0.4	0.4
No response	21	4.3	
	492	100.0	100.0

12. WHEN WERE YOU IN SAN DIEGO?

	(N)	Relative Percent	Adjusted Percent
January-February	2	0.4	0.4
March-April	13	2.6	2.8
May-June	187	38.0	39.7
July-August	264	53.7	56.1
September-October	3	0.6	0.6
November-December	1	0.2	0.2
No response	1	0.2	
	492	100.0	100.0

13. HAVE YOU BEEN TO SAN DIEGO BEFORE?

	(N)	Relative Percent	Adjusted Percent
No/First time	268	54.5	56.3
Once	73	14.8	15.3
2 times	36	7.3	7.6
3 times	31	6.3	6.5
4 times	14	2.8	2.9
5 times	9	1.8	1.9
6 times	8	1.6	1.7
7 times	2	0.4	0.4
8 times or more	35	7.1	7.4
No response	16	3.3	
	492	100.0	100.0

14a. HOW IMPORTANT WERE THE FOLLOWING IN YOUR DECISION TO VISIT SAN DIEGO?

	Very Important	Somewhat Important	Not Too Important	No Response
Climate	250(50.8%)	144(29.3%)	61(12.4%)	37(7.5%)
Cost of travel	95(19.3%)	166(33.7%)	150(30.5%)	81(16.5%)
Family oriented	171(34.8%)	80(16.3%)	170(34.6%)	71(14.4%)
Educational/ historical	103(20.9%)	193(39.2%)	110(22.4%)	86(17.5%)
Familiarity with area	94(19.1%)	122(24.8%)	178(36.2%)	98(19.9%)
Advertising	72(14.6%)	129(26.2%)	176(35.8%)	115(23.4%)

14b. WHERE WAS ADVERTISING SEEN?

	(N)	Relative Percent	Adjusted Percent
Sunset	28	5.7	14.0
Reader's Digest	3	0.6	1.5
Good Housekeeping	3	0.6	1.5
travel magazine	24	4.9	12.0
golf magazine	2	0.4	1.0
other or general magazine	83	16.9	41.5
local newspaper	29	5.9	14.5
brochure or pamphlet	11	2.2	5.5
other	17	3.5	8.5
No response	292	59.3	
	492	100.0	100.0

15a. HOW MANY PEOPLE INCLUDING YOURSELF CAME TO SAN DIEGO IN YOUR GROUP?

	(N)	Relative Percent	Adjusted Percent
Alone	40	8.1	8.6
2	187	38.0	40.1
3	73	14.8	15.7
4	74	15.0	15.9
5	34	6.9	7.3
6	20	4.1	4.3
7	11	2.2	2.4
8	3	0.6	0.6
9 or more	24	4.9	5.2
No response	26	5.3	
	492	100.0	100.0

15b. WERE YOU TRAVELING WITH FRIENDS OR RELATIVES?

	(N)	Relative Percent	Adjusted Percent
Friends	100	20.3	23.4
Relatives	267	54.3	61.4
Alone	66	13.4	15.2
No response	59	12.0	
	492	100.0	100.0

16. HOW MANY VISITORS WERE UNDER 18?

	(N)	Relative Percent	Adjusted Percent
1 or alone	79	16.1	36.9
2	84	17.1	39.3
3	31	6.3	14.5
4	8	1.6	3.7
5	7	1.4	3.3
6	1	0.2	1.5
7	1	0.2	0.5
8	1	0.2	0.5
9	2	0.4	0.9
No response	278	56.5	
	492	100.0	100.0

HOW MANY VISITORS WERE OVER 18?

	(N)	Relative Percent	Adjusted Percent
1 or alone	49	10.0	11.1
2	275	55.9	62.1
3	49	10.0	11.1
4	44	8.9	9.9
5	8	1.6	1.8
6	5	1.0	1.1
7	2	0.4	0.5
8	1	0.2	0.2
9 or more	10	2.0	2.3
No response	49	10.0	
	492	100.0	100.0

17. WHICH BEST DESCRIBES YOUR ANNUAL HOUSEHOLD INCOME?

	(N)	Relative Percent	Adjusted Percent
less than $5,000	6	1.2	1.3
$5,000-$9,999	20	4.1	4.4
$10,000-$14,999	61	12.4	13.4
$15,000-$19,999	68	13.8	15.0
$20,000-$24,999	100	20.3	22.0
$25,000 or more	199	40.4	43.8
No response	38	7.7	
	492	100.0	100.0

18. WHICH BEST DESCRIBES YOUR HOUSEHOLD?

	(N)	Relative Percent	Adjusted Percent
head of household under 45, not married	47	9.6	10.2
head under 45, married, no children	57	11.6	12.4
head married, youngest child under 6	46	9.3	10.0
head married, youngest child over 6	135	27.4	29.3
head over 45, married older children, none at home	109	22.2	23.6
head over 45, not married	35	7.1	7.6
single parent, other household type	32	6.5	6.9
no response	31	6.3	
	492	100.0	100.0

19. WHAT ARE YOUR FAVORITE MAGAZINES?

	First Mention	Second Mention	Third Mention	Fourth Mention	Total Mentions	Pct. Total
Sunset	37	15	7	11	70	(3.5)
Time	54	33	22	13	122	(6.2)
Newsweek	13	20	13	13	59	(3.0)
Reader's Digest	28	20	20	19	87	(4.4)
New Yorker	6	10	2	2	20	(1.0)
Good Housekeeping	29	21	25	8	83	(4.2)
Better Homes & Gardens	9	21	14	14	58	(2.9)
Ladies Home Journal	3	5	9	4	21	(1.1)
Family Circle	2	5	8	11	26	(1.3)
Smithsonian	3	5	3	2	13	(0.7)
National Geographic	42	30	27	11	110	(5.6)
Forbes	2	3	2	2	9	(0.5)
Fortune	1	0	1	1	3	(0.2)
Life	2	0	4	5	11	(0.6)
Playboy	4	6	10	8	28	(1.4)
Macleans	0	0	0	0	0	(0.0)
Prevention	1	1	0	1	3	(0.1)
Sports Illustrated	8	10	8	5	31	(1.6)
Popular Mechanics	1	1	1	2	5	(0.3)
People	21	11	9	10	51	(2.6)
U.S. News	10	12	6	1	29	(1.5)
travel magazines	33	18	20	10	81	(4.1)
golf magazines	0	1	3	0	4	(0.2)
other magazines	138	177	147	141	603	(30.6)
no response	45	67	131	198	441	(22.4)
					1968	100.0

11.2 San Diego Convention and Visitors Bureau (G)

If you have access to a computerized data analysis program, conduct your own marketing research analysis and prepare a short report of the results. A data file based on 200 cases is found in Appendix A. A sample S.P.S.S. (a widely used statistical package) computer program is found in Appendix B.

Below are some research issues or questions which might yield some ideas for your research project.

1. What is the consumer profile of the first time visitor?

2. Are there any major differences between visitors who arrive by automobile compared to those who arrive by other modes of transportation?

3. What major segments of visitors exist and how can they be defined?

4. What role does the travel agent play in influencing trip behavior?

5. What is the profile of the heavy spender? What are the motivations and visit behaviors of the heavy spender? What types of advertising (content and media) would be effective in reaching this visitor?

6. What is the consumer profile of those visiting a specific attraction (such as Sea World)? What other attractions did they visit?

APPENDIX A

CONVIS DATA FILE

1	2	3	4	5	6	7	8	9	10	11	12	13	14	15	16	17	18	19	20	21	22	23	24	25	26	27	28	29	30	31	32	33	34	35	36	37	38	39	40	41	42	43	44	45	46	47	48	49	50	51	52	53	54	55	56	57	58	59	60	61	62	63	64	65	66	67	68	69	70	71	72	73	74	75	76	77	78	79	80
	7	2	0		5	3	1	1			1	1				2		2							6	0		2	0	0		1		1		1	1				1	1			1	1	1	1			3	3	1	2	1	1	2	2	3		4	1		4	6	6	1	1	2	4	1	5			2				
	7	2	1		6	4	1	1	1				1			1	1						2		7	5		3	2	5	1	1			1	1			1				1	3							3	4	3	3	2	1	2	2	1	7	2	1		2	6	6	1	1	2	4	2	4	2	4	2				
	7	2	3		6	4	2	1		1	1	1				2		1					2	1	0	0		5	0	0	1	1		1		1				1			9			3					4	4		3	1	1	3		3		2	1		2	6	2	1	1	2	2					2				
	7	2	4		6	3	5				1				1	3		1					2	1	2	0		2	4	0				1	1	1			1	1	1		1		1	1	1	1			3	4	2	4						7	4	1				5	1	1	2	2		2	1	4	2				
	7	2	5		4	4	1	1			1					3		1					6					7	2	0	1	1	1		1	1		1		1	1	1	1	1		3					3	3	3	2	1	1	1	1	1		2			2	6	3	2	4	2	4		6	2	2					
	7	2	6		5	5	1			1	1					3		1					3	1	0	0	1	0	0	0	1	1				1		1		1		1		1		3					3	4	9	2	2	3	1			6	5		3	2	3	4	2	0	2	1		3	2	4	2				
	7	2	7		5	3	1						1			3		1					2	1	2	5		3	5	0					1				1	1	1		1	1		3					4	4	9	1	3			2			2			2	6	5	2	4	2	4	1	1	1	5	1				
	7	2	8		5	4	1	1			1			1		3		1					2		4	0		1	5	0	1	1	1	1		1		1	1	1	1	1	1	1		1	1	1			3	4	9	3	1	1	1	2	2		2			2	5		2	4	2	4		7			1				
	7	2	9		4	1	4	1				1				2		1					2		7	5			7	5							1						1	1		3					4	2	9	3	2	1	2	1	1		2	1		2	2	1	2	4	2	4	1	1	2	4	1				
	7	3	0		4	4	1	1	1							1	1						2	1	0	0		5	0	0					1	1				1	1				1	3					2	2	8	3	1	1	1	1	1	6	3	1	1	2	6	1	2	4	2	4		2	1	5	2				
	7	3	1		6	1	8						1	1	1	3		4	1				1								1	1					1	1			1		1	1		2				1	4		9	1	2	1	3	1	2	8	2	1		2	3	1	2	4	2	2	2	4	2	4	1				
	7	3	2		6	4	4	1	1		1	1				3		1					2		5	0	1	0	0	0	1				1	1	1	1		1	1		1			1	1				4	2	9	3	2				2	5	2	1		2		1	2	3	2	3	2	3	2	4	2				
	7	3	3		5	4	2		1		1	1		1		2		1					2		6	0		7	0	0					1	1		1			1	1				1	1				3	2	1	3	2	2	2	2	2		2	1		2	5	1	2	4	2	4	2	4							
	7	3	4		5	5	1	1	1	1	1					1							3		5	0		6	7	5	1						1			1	1		1	1		1	1		1		3	2	9	3	2	2	2	1	2		2	1		1	6		2	4	2	4	2	4	2	4	2				
	7	3	5		6	3	8	1	1	1	1	1	1	1	1	1	1						2		3	0			6	3	1	1	1					1				1	1			3					4	3	9	1	2	1	2	1	2	6	3	1		3	2	1	2	4	2	4		6		7	1				
	7	3	6		5	4	1				1					3		1					2		7	5		8	0	0									1	1	1		1	1		1	1				3	3	9	3	1	1	2	2	2		2	1	1	2	6	6	2	2	2	4		2	1	3	2				
	7	3	7		7	4	1	1		1	1	1	1	1	1	1	1						2	1	0	0	1	0	0	0				1	1	1	1	1	1	1	1	1	1	1	1	2		1	1		3	3	8	3	2	2	3	3	2	6	3	1		3	6	6	2	2	2	4	1	2	2	4	2				
	7	3	8		6	3	1	1	1	1	1	1	1	1	1	4			1				4		4	0		2	0	0		1								1	1	1			1	2						3	1	2	2	3	3	3	3	4	9	1	3	6	5	4	2	2	2	2					1				
	7	4	0		5	4	1	1				1		1		3	1							1	0	0		5	0	0	1								1	1				1		1	1	1			5	4	9	3							2	1		2	3	1	2	4	2	4	2	4	2	4	1				
	7	4	1		5	1	4				1	1				6						1	1		5	0			5	0		1	1							1				1		1					3	4	9	3	3	2	2				2	1		2	3		2	4	2	4	2	4	2	4	1				
	7	4	2		3	3	1	1								1	1						2		4	5		1	5	0	1	1			1				1	1	1	1		1		3					1	4	8	3	3	1	1	1	1		2	1		2	3	1	2	4	2	1	2	4	2	4					
	7	4	3		3	3	1	1								3	1					1	2	1	0	0		3	0	0		1				1				1	1			1		2	1				4	4	1	3	1	1	1	1	1		9	1			6	6	2	2	2	4		7		2	2				
	7	4	4		5	5	1	1	1		1	1				3		1					2		5	0		9	0	0	1	1				1	1		1	1		1		1	1	1	1				2	4	1	2	2	1	1	2	2	7	4	1		4	5	1	2	4	2	4	2	4	2	4					
8	7	0			7	1	1	1		1			1		1	1	1						6		4	0	1	2	0	0	1	1		1		1		1		1	1					3					4	4	3	2	2	2	3	2	1		4	2	2	2	5	3		2	1	1	2	4		1					
2	6	9			6	4	1	1			1					3		1					2		7	5		3	0	0																3					2	2	1	3	1	1	1	2			2	2		2	5	6	2	1	1	2	2	4		8					

1	2	3	4	5	6	7	8	9	10	11	12	13	14	15	16	17	18	19	20	21	22	23	24	25	26	27	28	29	30	31	32	33	34	35	36	37	38	39	40	41	42	43	44	45	46	47	48	49	50	51	52	53	54	55	56	57	58	59	60	61	62	63	64	65	66	67	68	69	70	71	72	73	74	75	76	77	78	79	80
	1	9	1		3	3	1				1	1				3		1					2		5	0		1	5	0	1			1		1		1		1	1	1	1	1		3					1	2	9	3	1	1	1	1	1		2	1		2	6	7		2	1	5	2	4	2	4	2				
	6	5	0		5	3	1	1			1	1				2		1					2		6	0		2	0	0		1		1		1	1				1	1			1	1	1	1			3	3	1	2	1	1	2	2	3		4	1		4	6	6	1	1	2	4	1	5			2				
	9	3	1		5	3	5	1	1	1	1	1				2		1					2		7	5		2	2	5	1			1		1		1			1		1	1		1	1	1	1	1	3	4	9	2	1	1	2	1	2	4	2	1		2	3		1	7	2	2					2				
	6	1	0		5	5	1		1				1			1	1						2		6	0		6	0	0	1	1		1	1	1				1	1	1		1		1		1			3	3	9	3	2						2			2	5	4	2	4	2	4	1	5							
	9	3	8		5	4	1	1			1			1		3							2		4	0		1	5	0	1	1	1	1		1		1	1	1	1	1	1	1		1	1	1			3	4	9	3	1	1	1	2	2		2			2	5		2	4	2	4		7			1				
	1	8	6		5	5	1	1	1	1	1	1				3	1						3		2	0		2	0	0	1	1	1		1	1	1	1	1	1	1	1	1	1		1	1					2	9	2	3	3	1	1	1		2	1		2	1	1	2	4	2	4	1	4			2				
	6	0	2		6	1	8						1	1	1	3			1				4								1	1	1				1	1			1		1	1		2				1	4		9	1	2	1	3	1	2	8	2	1		2	3	1	2	4	2	2	2	4	2	4	1				
	1	1	1		6	4	4	1	1		1	1				3		1					2		5	0	1	0	0	0	1				1	1	1	1		1	1		1			1	1				4	2	9	3	2				2	5	2	1		2		1	2	3	2	3	2	3	2	4	2				
	6	4	3		5	1	2	1	1	1	1	1				6				1			1		1	5			1	5					1	1		1					1			1	1	1		1	4	3	9	1	1	1	3	1	2		4	1		4	3	4	2	4	2	4		6	2	4	1				
	7	6	1		5	4	1				1					3		1					2		7	5		8	0	0									1	1	1		1	1		1	1				3	3	9	3	1	1	2	2	2		2	1	1	2	6	6	2	2	2	4		2	1	3	2				
	5	6	9		5	5	1	1								3							2		9	0		9	0	0	1	1	1	1	1	1		1			1		1	1	1	1	1	1		1	3	3	9	2			3		2	7	9	1		9	5	1	2	4	2	4	2	4	2	4	1				
	8	4	8		4	4	1	1								1	1						3		7	5		5	0	0	1	1		1	1			1		1	1		1			1			1		2	4	3	3				3			2	1		2	3	1	2	0	2	1	2	4		3					
	5	4	0		6	4	4	1	1	1	1	1				3				1					2	0		2	0	0	1	1	1					1		1		1		1		3					6	4	9	3	3	2	2	2	1		2	1	2		4	4	2	4	2	4		4	2	0	1				
	9	1	8		4	3	1									3		1					3		6	5		2	0	0		1					1			1	1			1		3					3	4	2	1	2	3	1	2	1	6	2	1		2	3	7	2	2	2	4									
	5	6	8		4	3	6	1	1	1	1	1				1	1						2	1	0	0		2	5	0	1									1	1			1	1						2	4	5	3	1	1	2	3	3	7	2	1		2	5	6	2	2	2	4	1	5		1	2				
	1	8	2		6	5	1	1	1					1		1	1						2		6	5		7	0	0	1				1	1		1		1			1			2		1	1		3	2	2	3	1	1	2		3	6	1	3		1	6	6	1	8	2	4		2			3				
	2	2	0		4	3	4					1				3						1	2		6	0		2	0	0	1	1						1			1				1	3					3	1	9								1	3		1	3	5		6	2	2	2	4		8	1				
	4	0	7		5	2	1	1				1				3		1					2	1	0	0		4	5	0	1	1		1		1		1				1				1					2		4	3				3			2	3		2	5	5		4	2	1		6		8	1				
	1	7	2		3	3	1	1								3		1					2		7	5		1	5	5	1	1	1	1				1			1					3					2		9	2	2	3	3	2	1		1	3		1	3	7	2	4	2	4	2	4	2	4	3				
	2	0	7		6	3	5	1			1	1				2		1					2		7	5		2	0	0					1	1				1						1	1	1			2	2	1	3	1	1	1	2	1		1	3		1	6	1	1	2	2	4		2	2	4	2				
	5	0	3		6	6	1	1	1	1						3	1						3		2	5		8	0	0	1	1	1	1	1	1		1	1	1	1	1	1			1	1				3	4	1	3		3					2	2		2	2	5	1	1							2				
	5	8	7		5	5	1	1				1				3	1						3		2	0		2	0	0			1	1	1	1	1	1	1	1	1	1	1	1		2	1				3	4	9	3		3	3	1	1		2			2	3	5		3		4					2				
		4	1		5	4	1			1	1		1			1	1						2		8	0		3	5	0	1	1			1					1		1		1		1		1			4	3	1	3	1	3	2	2	2	1	7	1	3	4	4	4		1		7					2				
		4	9		6	4	1					1				2		1					2		7	5		3	7	5	1					1	1	1			1			1	1						3	1	9	2	1		2				1	3		1	5	5		2		5					2				
		2	4		5	4	1					1				3		1					2	1	0	0		7	0	0	1		1	1	1	1		1	1		1	1	1			1	1				3	3	1									3		1	6	6	2	4		5					2				

1	2	3	4	5	6	7	8	9	10	11	12	13	14	15	16	17	18	19	20	21	22	23	24	25	26	27	28	29	30	31	32	33	34	35	36	37	38	39	40	41	42	43	44	45	46	47	48	49	50	51	52	53	54	55	56	57	58	59	60	61	62	63	64	65	66	67	68	69	70	71	72	73	74	75	76	77	78	79	80
	1	3	8		5	5	1									3	1						2		4	0		4	0	0	1	1		1	1	1		1			1	1	1			1					4	6	9	2	2	1	1	1	2		2	2		2	3										1				
		7	2		7	4	9			1	1	1		1	1	4	1						4					4	0	0		1			1	1		1					1	1					1		3	1	2	3	1	3	3	2	2	1	6	1	1	5	4	4		6		1					1				
	3	9	1		3	3	1	1								3					1		2		6	0		3	0	0	1		1													2				1	3	2	2					2	3	1	2	1		2	4	7	2	4		1	2	2			1				
	1	9	7		4	4	1									3				1	1		2	1	0	0		7	0	0	1	1								1	1		1	1		1	1	1				2	9	3	1	3	3	1	3	3	4	2	2	2	6	4		7		6					1				
			9		5	5	1	1		1						3	1						3		2	5		3	5	0	1		1	1		1			1	1	1					1	1				2	3	9	3	3	3		2	3	6		2	2	2	6	5	2	4		6	2	4			1				
	9	4	3		5	5	1	1	1	1	1	1				3		1				1			5	5		7	0	0	1					1				1		1	1	1		3					4	4	9	1	2	3					2	2	1	1	4	7		2		7					1				
		4	7		5	5	1									3	1						3		2	5		2	0	0	1				1			1		1	1			1		1	1				2	3	9	3		3					1	3			4	5	2	4	2	4					1				
	1	4	9		4	4	1	1	1							3		1					2		9	0		8	0	0	1			1	1	1		1			1		1	1		3					3	2	9	2	3	3					2	2		2	6	5		5	2	4					1				
	9	4	6		4	4	1	1								3				1	1		5		2	0					1	1				1		1		1		1				3					3	4	3	2	2	1	2	2	1		2	2		2	4	2	2	4	2	4		1			1				
	9	9	8		5	5	1	1	1	1	1					3	1						3		7	5					1	1	1		1	1		1		1	1		1	1		3					5	4	9	3	3	2	2	2	3		2	2		2	6	2		3	2	4	2	4			1				
	7	4	7		5	3	1	1	1	1	1					1	1						2		6	5		2	0	0					1	1		1		1	1	1	1			2		1	1	1	4	3	1	3	1	1	2	2	1		2	3	1	2		2		2	2	4		7		4	1				
	1	9	3		5	4	1			1	1					2		1					2	1	0	0		5	0	0	1	1									1		1			1	1	1	1	1	4	3	9	3	2	3	1	1	1		4	3	2	2	5	3		2	2	0	2	7		6	3				
	3	2	7		4	4	1		1	1			1			1	1						2	2	0	0		8	0	0	1	1	1			1		1	1	1	1	1	1	1		2		1	1		1		1	3	1	1	3	1	3	6	3	2	1	2	6	4	2	2	2	4		1		4	2				
		2	4		6	5	1	1			1	1	1	1		1	1						5		9	0	1	0	0	0	1	1				1				1		1	1	1		2			1		3	1	1	3		3	2	3			2	2		2	6	5		3	2	0		4		6					
	7	3	9		5	4	1		1	1	1	1				4		1					3								1	1	1		1			1		1		1	1	1		2								1	1	2	2	3	1		5	2	3		3	3	2	4	2	4	2	4		4	2				
			1		5	4	1	1		1	1	1				2		1					2		7	5		3	4	0	1		1		1	1		1		1	1	1	1	1	1	1	1	1			3		9	3	1	1	1	1	1		2	2		2	6	2	2	4	2	4	2	4		5	1				
	2	9	4		4	4	1	1	1							1			1				4		4	0		2	5	0	1	1				1		1		1	1		1			2					3	3	9	2	3	1	3	2	3	1	3	2	1	2	6	5	1	1		1		4		6					
	5	5	0		5	5	1	1	1	1			1			3				1			2					7	5	0	1	1	1		1			1			1	1	1	1		1	1				5	3	9	3	3	2	3	3	2	3	3	2		3	3	6		6		4		7		9	1				
	7	1	3		4	4	1	1		1	1	1				2	1						2	1	5	0		7	0	0	1	1			1			1	1	1	1			1		1	1				6	3	2	2	1	3	3	3	1		3	2	1	2	6	4	2	1		3	2	4		2					
	8	8	3		4	4	1		1	1						1	1						2	1	3	5		6	0	0	1		1					1			1					2		1			2	4	9	1	2	3	2	1	1	6	5	2	2	3	6	4		2		7	1	1		9					
	6	0	8		5	4	1						1	1		3		1					2	1	7	0		6	0	0	1	1			1	1		1		1	1	1	1			1	1	1			3	4	9	3	1	1	2	2	3	6	2	2		1	6	2		8		6	2	4		9					
	8	8	7		5	4	1		1	1	1					1	1						2		6	5		2	7	5	1	1									1	1		1		3					3	4	3	2	3	2	2	2	1	6	4	2	2	2	6	4		6		4		7		9	1				
	1	5	7		5	5	1	1			1					3	1						2		2	2		2	0	0	1			1		1	1	1		1	1	1		1	1	1	1				2	2	9	3	1	1	1	1	1		1	3		1	3	4	2	4		2	2	0		3	1				
	5	3	9		4	4	1	1		1	1	1				3				1			2		6	0		4	5	0	1		1	1	1	1		1	1	1	1	1	1	1		1	1		1	1	2	4	9	2	2	1	2	2	2		2	3		2	5	2	2	4		9		4		6	1				
	8	0	8		5	5	1	1								3		1					2	1	0	0	1	0	0	0	1		1		1	1		1			1		1	1	1						3	4	1	3	2	1	2	2	1		2	3		2	6	5		4		3		1		1	2				

1	2	3	4	5	6	7	8	9	10	11	12	13	14	15	16	17	18	19	20	21	22	23	24	25	26	27	28	29	30	31	32	33	34	35	36	37	38	39	40
	4	1	7		3	3	1	1								1	1						2		4	0		1	2	5						1			
	2	3	8		5	4	1	1	1				1		1	1							2		5	0		2	0	0	1	1	1						
	8	5	7		7	3	9				1	1				2		1					2	1	0	0		3	0	0									
	9	4	4		6	4	9				1	1				3				1	1		2		5	5		3	2	5	1	1							
	6	0	9		4	4	1	1	1		1	1				1	1						2	1	0	0		4	0	0		1			1	1			
	3	4	2		4	4	1	1			1	1				3				1			2		3	0		5	5	0	1	1							
	5	3	7		4	4	1							1		1	1						2		3	5		2	5	0	1			1	1	1		1	1
	8	2	7		5	1	2			1	1	1				2							1		2	5			2	5		1							1
	4	1	0		5	1	1	1	1	1						3	1						2		4	0	1	0	0	0	1	1				1		1	1
		1	7		4	4	1	1		1	1					1	1						2	1	3	0		4	0	0	1	1	1	1		1		1	
	1	8	7		5	3	6	1		1	1					3	1	1			1		3					2	0	0	1		1			1		1	
	2	4	1		6	5	1		1			1				3		1					2	1	5	0	3	5	0	0		1			1	1	1	1	
	1	5	5		5	4	1	1			1			1		3		1					2	1	5	0		6	5	0	1				1			1	
	7	5	0		3	3	1	1								3				1	1		2		7	5		1	5	0			1						
	9	1	5		4	3	1	1		1	1	1				6						1	6					3	0	0	1								
	9	3	7		5	4	1	1			1					2	1						3		7	5		8	0	0	1	1							
	9	2	9		4	4	1		1							3		1					2	1	5	0		7	5	0	1				1	1		1	
	8	0	2		5	4	1			1						2		1					2		8	0		5	0	0						1			
	9	7	0		5	3	4				1	1				2		1					2		7	5		1	5	0	1				1	1			
	2	1	4		4	3	1	1	1			1				1	1						3	1	0	0		4	0	0	1				1	1			
	8	7	4		5	4	1	1								1	1						2		6	2		4	3	0	1	1				1		1	
	1	1	9		5	4	1			1				1		3		1					2	1	2	5	1	0	0	0	1							1	
		4	3		5	1	2		1	1	1			1		6							2	1	5	0		3	0	0	1								1
	5	9	2		6	3	1	1		1	1		1			1	1						4		5	0		1	5	0			1			1			
	9	0	3		6	4	1	1	1	1		1				3		1					2		7	5		3	0	0	1	1			1	1		1	

41	42	43	44	45	46	47	48	49	50	51	52	53	54	55	56	57	58	59	60	61	62	63	64	65	66	67	68	69	70	71	72	73	74	75	76	77	78	79	80
	1	1	1	1		3					3	2	8	2	2	1	2	3	1		2	2		2	6	4	2	4		7		1		4					
1	1		1	1		1				1	3	2	1	2	2	2	2	2	2		6	2	2	4	3	5	2	4		4		7		8	2				
1						3					4	3	8	3	1	3	3	3	1		2	2		2	6	5	2	4		1		4		2	2				
	1	1		1		1	1	1			3	4	1	3			2			7	2	1		1	3	6		2	2	1	2	4			1				
1	1	1		1		3					4	3	8	3	3	1	1	3	2		2			2	3	2	1	3	2	4	2	2	2	4	2				
	1			1	1	1	1	1			3	3	9	3	3			3			2			2	3	5		6		7		4		8	2				
1			1	1	1	2					4	6	1								1			2	5	2	2	2		7		2		3	1				
						3					3	4	9	3	1	1	3	1			2	1		2	3	4	2	4		2	2	4		3	1				
1	1	1		1	1	3					3	2	9	2	1	2	2	1	1		1	3		1	2		2	4		3	2	4		4	1				
	1		1	1		3					3	1	9	3	1	2	3	3	3	4	4	1		4	6	5		2	2	1	2	2	2	4	2				
			1		1	1				1	3	2	3	2	1	3	3				8	1		8	5	5		5	2	4	2	4	2	4	2				
1	1	1	1	1	1	1	1	1			3	2	9	3							6	1		6	6	5		6	2	3		2	2	4	3				
			1			1	1	1			2	2	9	3	1	1	2	1	1		2	1		2	6	1		1	2	4	1	5	2	4	2				
				1		1	1	1			3	3	1	2	2	1	3	2	1		1	1	1	2	5	6		7	2	4	1	0		5	1				
						3					4	4	2	3	1	3	3	2	1	6	9	1	9	8	5	4		1	2	4		4	1	0	1				
1	1	1	1			1	1				4	4	9	2		3					4	2	2	2	6	4		3	1	7	2	4			1				
	1	1	1			1	1	1			3	4	9	3	2	2	1	1	2	4	3	2	1	2	6	4	2	2	1	1		3	1	8	2				
1	1			1		1	1				4	4	3								3	2	1	2	6	3		2	1	1	2	4			2				
	1		1		1	1	1	1			3	4	9	3	1	1	1	2	3		2	2		2	6	2		7	1	8					1				
1		1	1			3					1	2	9	3		3					2			2	6	5		1	2	4		8			1				
1	1			1		3					2	4	8	3	2	2	2	3	3	8	2			2	4	5		2	2	0		4							
1	1					1	1	1			3	2	9	3	1	1	1	1	2		2	2		2	6	2		4	1	1	1	3		2	2				
			1			3					4	3	9	2	2	3	3	2	3		4	2	1	3	6	4	1	1	1		2	4	2	4	1				
	1	1	1			3					4	3	1	1	1	3	2	1	1		5	2	2	3	4	4		6	1	1	2	4		4	1				
1		1		1		1	1	1	1	1	3	3	9	3	1	2	1	1	3	6	4	2	2	2	6	4	2	1	1	1		2		4	2				

```
         1111111111222222222233333333334444444444555555555566666666667777777777
12345678901234567890123456789012345678901234567890123456789012345678901234567890
  94 221        11     2 95 150 11            3    269223322 422263 21518212
 541 6351 111   3 1    2140 40011 1 1 11  11  11   4493232117422254 418    2
 457 62   111 1111     2 45  60111111     11   3    629333333 22 262241124 11
  74 513  1 1   11     1 35  351    1         1 1     8333 3  523264 118 724
  30 69511 11 1 3 1    2125 5001   111 111111 2    21932332  421364 311 4222
 599 431 1  1   2 1    2 95 300       1  1   111   3 8221311 22 2 4 212224
 411 43911111   3 1    2 65 20011         1 1  111 429321211 22 242 614 4  1
 154 7331 11111111     2100 30011 1 1 1111 1  3    329211212422 265241113242
 597 62411111   2 1    3 30  401    1 1 1          3492313 2921 241241124  1
  98 541   11   3 1    2125 20011     1111   1 11  31931321  533264 711 1242
  19 4411       3 1    2100 700111 1     1 1111  111421331211 23 265 218 1 7
 297 5471       3    1122 80 3501111 1 1 11111  111 33931 3 3413  2722112424
 988 64511111   2 1    2100 50011 111 11111 1 111  449311212823 2622418 6242
 368 532  111   2 1    2100 20011   1  11    1 3   5293211137321264241 8 724
  37 5311    11 3 1    2 70 3001 11    1 11111 211  2112111212  2 5 11122
 181 439   11   2 1    2 95 200 1 11     11   111  329111221 41 464 7112 4243
 299 33         11     2450150011   11 1  1    1 1 338311121 411463 11524
 375 421   11   4   1  4 75 1001         11  3     32523332396 4244201824242
 293 4411       3 1  112 75 3501 11    1 111  11   639          64241821 4
  26 5411111    3     12 55 425111111111  1111 11  319       21 2412014 4241
 439 5511       3 1    2 50 550111   111    111 3  2293232   22 262 12424
  91 441        2 1    2100 60011111111 11 1 12 1  211331211 42 462 324 1
 436 661111   1 3 1    2100250011  1 1  11  11 1111412333232742 465 32024
 646 651  1     3 1    3 45100011  11   1  11  111  6313 3    523264242424
 997 532  111   5   11 2 10 10011 1 1 1   1   111  449211311 22 221 62424
```

1	2	3	4	5	6	7	8	9	10	11	12	13	14	15	16	17	18	19	20	21	22	23	24	25	26	27	28	29	30	31	32	33	34	35	36	37	38	39	40	41	42	43	44	45	46	47	48	49	50	51	52	53	54	55	56	57	58	59	60	61	62	63	64	65	66	67	68	69	70	71	72	73	74	75	76	77	78	79	80
	3	9	6		4	9	1		1	1						3		1					2		7	5		4	5	0	1	1		1	1	1		1	1	1	1		1	1		1	1	1		1	2	2	1	3	2	1	1	1	1		2			2	5	5		4	1	1					1				
	6	1	6		5	3	1	1	1							3		1					2	1	5	0	1	2	0	0	1	1			1	1		1	1	1	1	1	1	1		2	1				4	4	2	3	2	1	2	2	1		3	2		3	4	2													
	8	9	0		5	3	8	1								3		1					2		5	5		1	5	0	1			1		1				1	1	1	1	1		1	1	1			3	4	9	2	2	1	2	2	2	6	4	1		4	4	6	1	1		7									
	6	5	5		5	5	1	1	1							3	1						3	1	0	0	1	0	0	0				1	1			1		1		1				3					4	3	9	2	2	1	1	1	1		1	3		1	3	7	2	4		6	2	4							
		9	3		5	1	2	1		1	1	1				4			1				2	0	6	0			6	0	1					1		1				1	1			3					3	1	2	2	1	2	2	2	2	6	4	2	2	2	5	3		1		7									
		3	1		4	4	1	1	1							3	1						3		2	5		2	0	0	1				1	1		1		1	1			1		1	1				2	3	1	2	2	1	2	2	1		2	2		2	6	5		4		6									
	2	9	8		4	4	1	1	1							3		1			1		2		9	0		4	5	0	1	1	1			1		1		1	1		1	1		3					4	3	9	3	2	1	2				2	3	1	2	6	4	1	6	2	4		2							
	5	5	6		5	4	1	1	1		1	1		1		2		1					2		7	5		3	5	0	1				1			1	1		1	1	1	1		1	1	1		1	3	3	1							9	4	1		4	6	5													
	9	2	6		5	1	2			1	1					2		1					1		6	0			6	0	1				1			1			1		1			1	1	1			4	4	9	2	1	1	3	2	1	4	3		1	2	4	7	2	2											
	4	2	2		5	5	1		1				1	1		1	1						5		5	0		5	0	0	1	1			1			1		1	1					3					2	2	9	3		3					2	3		2	6	5		2		1	1								
	4	0	2		5	5	1	1								3							2		7	5	1	2	0	0	1	1	1	1		1		1		1	1	1	1			1	1				3	2	5	3	1	2	2	3			2	2		2		5													
	5	3	2		5	4	1		1	1				1		1	1						3		2	0			8	5	1							1		1		1		1							3	3	8	2	3	2	2	3	2	1	2	2		2	6	2													
	9	0	8			1	2				1			1		1	1							1	0	0		1	0	0	1											1									3	4	9		3	3				7	6	2	3	3	3	3		4											
	2	0	9		6	5	1			1	1		1	1		4	1						4		2	0		2	5	0	1			1		1				1	1	1	1	1	1	3					3	2	2	3	1	3	1	2	3		2	2		2	5	5	2	4		1	2	4			2				
	3	0	6		5	3	1			1	1					1	1						2		6	0		2	5	0	1	1										1				3					4	2	1	2	1	3	1	1	1	6	3	2		3	5	4		1		4					2				
	2	8	0		3	3	1	1								1	1						2		7	5		2	0	0	1	1	1													3					3	3	9	2	3	3	2	1	1		6	2	2	4	4	3		1		2					2				
	8	1	1		5	4	1				1					1	1						2	1	0	0		5	0	0	1	1	1					1		1	1	1		1							6	4	8	3	2	2	2	2	2	9	4	2	2	2	6	5	2	4		4	2	2			2				
	6	4	1		4	4	1		1	1		1				3				1	1		2		3	5		4	2	0	1				1	1					1	1	1	1		1	1	1		1	2	4	4	3	2	1	1	2	2	4	1	3		1	3	6	2	2	2	4					2				
	4	4	7		5	5	1	1	1		1	1				3		1					2		9	0	1	2	0	0	1		1	1	1	1	1	1	1	1	1	1	1	1		1	1				3	2	1	3	2	1	1	2			2	2		2	6	2		2	2	4					2				
	5	7	7		6	3	7				1	1		1		2		1					2	1	5	0		3	2	0	1					1				1	1	1				2	1				4	3	9	1	1	1					4	2	1	3	6	9	1	1	2	4					2				
	7	1	5		5	3	1	1	1							3	1						2		7	5		2	2	5	1			1	1	1	1	1		1	1		1	1		1	1				3	3	9	2	1	2					2	2		2	6	5		4	2	1					2				
	9	9	4		4	4	1		1							1	1						2		8	0		3	6	0	1					1				1		1				3					3	4	3	3	3	3		3	3	6	7	2	5	2	6	3	1	1	2	4	2	4			2				
	5	1	8		6	2	8			1	1	1	1	1	1	2		1					2					1	7	5	1							1			1					1	1			1	4	4	9	1	1	2	1	1	2	9	6	2	2	4	5	5	4	1	1	2	4				2				
	2	3	0		4	4	1									1	1						2	1	0	0		5	0	0	1	1				1		1		1	1		1			3					2	2	1	1	1	3	2	1	1		3	2	1	2	6	6	3								3				
	2	2	8		4	4	1	1								1	1						2		7	5		3	0	0	1	1	1					1		1	1					3					4	2	2					3			2	2		2	4	4	5		1	2	4				3				

1	2	3	4	5	6	7	8	9	10	11	12	13	14	15	16	17	18	19	20	21	22	23	24	25	26	27	28	29	30	31	32	33	34	35	36	37	38	39	40
	2	4	3		5	4	1		1			1				2		1					2		4	5		5	0	0	1	1	1			1		1	
		4	2		6	5	1	1	1	1	1	1				3		1					2		5	0		5	0	0	1	1		1		1		1	
	9	6	6		6	1	3	1	1	1	1			1		1	1						1		6	0		2	5	0		1		1				1	1
	8	8	6		5	5	1		1							3					1		2	1	0	0	1	0	0	0	1								
	5	5	4		6	3	7	1	1	1	1	1		1		2		1					2		5	0		2	2	5	1						1		
	5	5	5		5	5	1					1				3	1						3		5	0	1	0	0	0	1	1							
	8	1	7		6	6	1	1								1	1						5		7	5	2	5	0	0	1	1							
			7		4	1	1		1	1	1					3				1	1		2		6	5		2	0	0	1	1			1				
			8		5	4	1	1			1			1		3		1					2		8	0		4	0	0	1	1	1					1	
	8	3	6		5	3	2			1	1	1				2		1					2		7	9		3	0	0	1	1	1						
	7	5	3		5	4	1			1	1		1		1	1	1						2		7	0		2	7	5	1			1		1		1	
		2	1		5	5	1	1			1	1				1	1						2		7	0		8	0	0	1	1	1			1			
	8	0	9		5	5	1	1	1															1	0	0		8	0	0	1	1	1	1	1			1	1
	8	4	9		6	4	3	1		1	1	1				2		1					2	1	0	0		7	0	0	1	1					1	1	
	9	2	4		6	3	8	1		1						2		1					2		3	5		1	1	0	1	1				1			
	8	5	3		4	3	2			1	1					2		1					2		3	5		2	5	0	1	1				1			
	1	9	1		6	5	1	1	1							3		1					3		5	0		8	3	5	1		1	1		1	1	1	
	1	2	9		4	4	1	1								3						1	2		7	0		3	0	0					1				
		5	2		4	3	1			1						2		1					2		7	5		2	2	5	1	1			1				1
	1	1	0		3	3	1									1	1						2	1	0	0		2	0	0	1	1	1						
	5	9	1		6	9	1		1				1	1	1	1	1						2	1	2	5		7	0	0	1	1			1			1	
	5	8	9		5	3	1			1	1			1		2		1					2		4	0			8	5		1							
	8	2	1		7	3	5	1		1	1	1	1	1	1	1	1						3		1	0			3	0	1	1		1					
		4	8		5	4	1				1	1				3						1	2	1	0	0		5	0	0	1								
	8	4	0		5	5	1	1		1						3					1		2		4	0		3	5	0	1	1	1	1	1				1

41	42	43	44	45	46	47	48	49	50	51	52	53	54	55	56	57	58	59	60	61	62	63	64	65	66	67	68	69	70	71	72	73	74	75	76	77	78	79	80
	1	1	1			1	1	1			3	2	1	2	3		2	3	1	1	2	2		2	6	4		1	2	4		2			3				
1	1	1	1	1	1	1	1				3	6	9	2	3	1	2	1	1	7	2	2		2	5	1	1	6	2	4	2	4	2	4	1				
		1	1			3					4	4	9	3	1	3	2	2	2	6	7	2	4	3		4	2	4	2	0	2	4	2	4	1				
	1		1			1	1				4	4	9	3	1	1	3	1	1		2	2		2	5	1	2	4	2	4	2	4	2	4	1				
	1			1		1	1	1	1		4	4	9	3	2	1	1	1	1		4	2		4	4	2	2	4	2	2	2	4	2	4					
1			1		1	1					3	4	1	2	2	3		2		7	4	2	2	2	6	4		2	2	4	1	8	2	4	2				
1	1	1	1								4	4	8	3	3	3	2	3	2		7	2	2	5	6	4	2	4											
	1					3					2	1	9				2	3																					
1	1					3					3	2	9	3	3	3	2	1	1																				
	1					3					4	4	1	2	1	2	1	1	2	6																			
1	1			1		3					3	3	4	2	2	3	2	3	1	6	3	2	1	2	5	4		3		2	1	8	2	4	2				
	1		1			2		1			3	6	9	2	1	2	2	1	1	1	3	2		3	6	4	1	1		1	2	4	2	4	2				
1	1		1								5	4	9	3	1		2	2	2	9	2	2		2	4	5	2	4		2		8	2	2	2				
1	1	1		1		3					6	4	2	3	1	1	1	2	1	6	2	2		2	6	2	2	0		7	2	1	2	4					
1	1		1	1		1	1	1			4	4	2	3	1	1	2	2	1	6	2	2		2	4	1		5		2	2	4	2	0					
1		1	1	1	1	3					3	4	9	3	2	3	2	1	1		3	2	1	2	4	2	2	0		8		6	2	4					
1	1	1	1	1	1	1	1				3	2	9	3		3					2	2		2	6	5		2		6		8	2	3					
	1		1	1							3	2	5	2	2	3	1	3	1	7	2	2		2	6	5	2	1		2	1	1	2	4	2				
			1			3					1	1	9	2	2	2	1	1	2	1	3	2	1	2	5	3		7		1	2	4	2	4					
						3					2	2	8	3	2	2	2	2	2	9	2	2		2	6	5		3		2		4	2	0	2				
1						3					4	3	3	3	2	3	2	3	2	6	6	2	3	3	4	4	1	1		7	2	4	2	4	2				
			1	1		3					3	3	9	2	1	1	2	1			4	2	2	2	5	4	2	4		2	2	4	2	0	2				
						2			1	1	4	4	9	1	1	1	2	1	2	6	3	1		3	3	1	2	4		6	2		2	4					
1						3					3	3	9	3							9	3		9	6		2	4		3	2	4	2	4	1				
	1	1	1	1							3	3	9	3			3		3	7	1	3		1	4	6		8		2	2	2	2	4	1				

1	2	3	4	5	6	7	8	9	10	11	12	13	14	15	16	17	18	19	20	21	22	23	24	25	26	27	28	29	30	31	32	33	34	35	36	37	38	39	40	41	42	43	44	45	46	47	48	49	50	51	52	53	54	55	56	57	58	59	60	61	62	63	64	65	66	67	68	69	70	71	72	73	74	75	76	77	78	79	80
	6	5	6		5	5	1	1								3	1						3		2	0		3	0	0			1			1				1	1	1		1		3					3	3	2	3	1	3	1	2	2			3			5	6	2	4		5		8	2	2	1				
		6	9		6	3	9	1			1		1		1	5				1			2		3	5		1	0	0	1		1		1			1	1	1			1			3					3	6	6	2	2	1	3	3	2		1	3		1	3	6		1		4	2	2	2		2				
		7	0		6	4	2	1	1	1						1	1						2	1	0	0		5	0	0	1					1			1			1	1			3					4	1	9	3	1	1	2		3	9	2	2		2	6	2		2		4	1	1	2		2				
	4	3	0		5	4	4	1	1		1					3				1			2		4	5		2	1	5					1	1				1				1		3					1	2	3	2	3	1	2	3	2	6	1	3		1	5	1	2	2	2	4	2	4	2	4	2				
		4	9		5	1	5	1	1	1	1	1				5		1					2					2	5	0	1			1	1			1			1	1				2		1	1		2	3	9	2	2	1	1	1	2	8	2	3		2	6	2	2	4	2	4		7	2	4					
	9	2	8		5	5	1	1	1	1						3				1	1		2	1	5	0	1	4	0	0	1	1						1		1	1	1		1		1	1				3	4	2	3	2	3	3	3			3	1	1	2	4	4		4		2	2	4	2	4	2				
	7	2	2		6	4	1	1		1	1	1				2	1						2		5	0		1	5	0	1	1				1				1	1	1	1			1	1	1			4	3	9	2	3	1	3	1	1		2	1		2	3	4	1	1		2		7	2	4	1				
	1	9	4		5	4	1	1		1		1				3				1	1		3					4	0	0	1			1					1	1	1		1	1		1	1		1		3	2	9	3		3		3			2			2	6	5	2			5		4	2	4	2				
	4	5	3		5	5	1	1	1			1	1	1		3	1						3		4	0		4	0	0	1	1	1	1	1	1		1			1	1	1	1	1	1	1			1	3	2	5	3	3	3	2	3	3		2	1				5	2	4		2	1	8	2	0	1				
	3	9	5		5	5	1		1		1	1				3		1					2	2	0	0	2	2	0	0	1	1				1	1	1		1	1	1	1	1		1	1	1	1		2	2	4	3	2	1	1	1	1	6	4	1		4	6	6	2	1		4		7	2	4	1				
	2	1	7		5	4	1	1	1		1	1			1	2					1	1	2	2	0	0	1	2	0	0	1				1			1			1	1				1	1	1	1		3	2	9	3	2	1	2	1	2	6	9	1		9	6	4	2	4		7	2	4	2	4	3				
	9	4	5		4	3	2			1						3							2								1	1						1			1		1			1				1	3	2	4	3	2	1	3	2	2		2	2	1	1	4		1	1	2	4	2	4	1	7	1				
		1	6		6	4	1	1	1				1		1	1	1						2	1	5	0	1	3	0	0	1	1					1	1		1	1	1		1					1		3	3	8	2	1	3	3	2	3	5	4	2	2	2	6	4	2	1	2	3	2	4	1	9					
	5	1	2		5	2	3		1	1	1					3	1						2		4	0			6	5	1	1														1	1				3	4	1	2	2	3	2	1	1	6	6	2	2	4	6	4		2	2	4	2	4	1	5	2				
	8	1	5		5	5	1	1	1	1						3				1	1		2		6	0		5	0	0	1		1	1		1		1			1		1	1		1		1			2	4	9	2	3	1	3	3	3		4	2		4	4	5	2	4	2	4	1	5	1	4	2				
	1	6	4		5	3	1		1	1	1	1				3		1					2	1	0	0		3	0	0		1	1						1		1		1	1		1				1	1	1		2			2	2			3			3	5	5		9		7	2	4	2	4	2				
	5	3	4		5	5	1	1	1	1	1			1		6				1			2	1	5	0		3	5	0		1			1						1	1	1			1	1				5		1	3	2	3	1	2	2		9	1	5	4	4	4		4		2	1	8	2	4	2				
		4	8		4	3	1	1								3							2	1	0	0		2	5	0	1	1						1			1					1	1	1			1	1	9								4	2	2	2	3	4	2	4	2	4	1	1	1	9					
	2	3	3		8	7	1	1	1		1					3	1			1			2		2	5		7	0	0	1	1	1	1		1		1	1	1	1	1	1		1	1					4	2	5	3	1	2		3		6	3	2		2	4	7	2	4	2	4		4	1	1	1				
		8	6		6	4	1	1							1	3		1					2	1	0	0		7	0	0	1	1		1		1	1	1	1	1	1	1				1	1				3	1	3	3	1	1	1	2	1	1	2	2		2	6	5		1	2	4	2	4	1	3	1				
	4	2	0		5	1	1	1	1							3	1						2		4	0		4	0	0	1	1	1			1	1	1		1	1	1	1	1		2	1				4	2	9	2	2	3	2	2	2	6	3	2		3	2	5	1	6	2	4	1	4	1	1					
		2	2		5	3	8			1			1			2		1					2	1	0	0		3	5	0	1	1			1	1					1					3					2	1	9	2	2	2	2	1	1		5	2	3	2	6	4		2		5	2	0	1	3	2				
	2	8	2		2	2	2			1		1				1	1						2		8	5			9	0		1												1							3	3	8	2	3	3	2	2	2	8	6	2	4	2	5	3	2	4		3		1	1	2					
	8	2	5		5	3	5			1	1	1		1		2		1					2		7	5		1	7	5	1	1						1		1	1			1	1	3					4	4	9	3	1	1	2	1	1	6	2	2		2	6	2	1	8		6	2	4	1	5	2				
	6	1	9		4	4	1			1	1					3						1	2		3	0		2	0	0	1							1						1		1	1				3	4	1	3	1	1	2	3	1		1	3		1	2	1	2	4	2	4	2	4	1	5	2				

APPENDIX B

SPSS PROGRAM FOR CONVIS SURVEY

```
RUN NAME          VISITOR SURVEY
FILE NAME         CONVENTION/VISITORS BUREAU
VARIABLE LIST     V1 TO V62
INPUT MEDIUM      CARD
N OF CASES        200
INPUT FORMAT      FIXED (5X,19F1.0,F3.0,F4.0,36F1.0,4F2.0,F1.0)
VAR LABELS        V1 NIGHTS AWAY FROM HOME TOTAL/
                  V2 NIGHTS IN SAN DIEGO/
                  V3 PRIMARY DESTINATION/
                  V4 VISIT SAN DIEGO COUNTY/
                  V5 VISIT TIJUANA-BAJA/
                  V6 VISIT ANAHEIM-DISNEYLAND/
                  V7 VISIT LOS ANGELES/
                  V8 VISIT OTHER CALIFORNIA CITY/
                  V9 VISIT ARIZONA/
                  V10 VISIT NEVADA/
                  V11 VISIT OTHER WESTERN STATE
                  V12 ARRIVAL TRANSPORTATION/
                  V13 USED PRIVATE AUTO IN SAN DIEGO/
                  V14 USED RENTAL AUTO IN SAN DIEGO/
                  V15 USED RV-VAN IN SAN DIEGO/
                  V16 USED PUBLIC BUS IN SAN DIEGO/
                  V17 USED TAXI IN SAN DIEGO/
                  V18 USED OTHER TRANSPORTATION IN SAN DIEGO/
                  V19 TYPE OF LODGING USED/
                  V20 DAILY EXPENDITURE IN SAN DIEGO/
                  V21 TOTAL EXPENDITURE IN SAN DIEGO/
                  V22 VISITED ZOO-MUSEUM/
                  V23 VISITED SEA WORLD/
                  V24 VISITED WILD ANIMAL PARK/
                  V25 VISITED CABRILLO MONUMENT/
                  V26 VISITED CORONADO/
                  V27 VISITED LA JOLLA/
                  V28 VISITED EAST COUNTY/
                  V29 VISITED BALBOA PARK/
                  V30 VISITED MISSIONS/
                  V31 VISITED BEACHES/
                  V32 VISITED HARBOR AREA/
                  V33 VISITED MISSION BAY/
                  V34 VISITED OLD TOWN/
                  V35 VISITED DOWNTOWN/
                  V36 VISITED OTHERS/
                  V37 USE OF AGENT/
                  V38 AGENT BOOKED AIRLINES/
                  V39 AGENT BOOKED HOTEL-MOTEL/
                  V40 AGENT BOOKED ATTRACTIONS/
                  V41 AGENT BOOKED TOUR PACKAGE/
                  V42 WHEN TRIP PLANNED/
                  V43 WHEN IN SAN DIEGO/
                  V44 VISITED SAN DIEGO BEFORE/
                  V45 IMPORTANCE OF CLIMATE/
                  V46 IMPORTANCE OF COST OF TRAVEL/
                  V47 IMPORTANCE OF FAMILY ORIENTATION/
                  V48 IMPORTANCE OF EDUCATIONAL-HISTORICAL ASPECTS/
```

```
                V49 IMPORTANCE OF FAMILIARITY WITH AREA/
                V51 WHERE AD SEEN/
                V52 TOTAL VISITORS/
                V53 TRAVELING COMPANIONS/
                V54 NUMBER UNDER 18/
                V55 NUMBER OVER 18/
                V56 ANNUAL HOUSEHOLD INCOME/
                V57 FAMILY STATUS/
                V58 FAVORITE MAGAZINE A/
                V59 FAVORITE MAGAZINE B/
                V60 FAVORITE MAGAZINE C/
                V61 FAVORITE MAGAZINE D/
                V62 SEX OF RESPONDENT/
VALUE LABELS    V1 TO V2 (1)DAYTRIP(2) 1 NIGHT(3)2-3 NIGHTS(4)4-7
                NIGHTS(5) 8-14 NIGHTS(6) 15-28 NIGHTS(7)1-2
                MONTHS(8)2-4 MONTHS(9) 4+ MONTHS/
                V3 (1)SAN DIEGO(2)LA-ANAHEIM(3)OTHER SOUTHERN
                CAL(4)OTHER CAL CITY(5)CAL IN GENERAL
                (6)MEXICO(7)OTHER WESTERN STATE(8)WESTERN
                US(9)OTHER/
                V4 TO V11 (1)YES/
                V12 (1)PRIVATE AUTO(2)RENTAL AUTO(3)AIR(4)MOTOR
                HOME-RV(5)TRAIN(6)BUS(7)OTHER/
                V13 TO V18 (1)YES/
                V19 (1)DAYTRIP(2)HOTEL-MOTEL(3)PRIVATE HOME(4)RV-
                CAMPER PARK(5)RENTAL-CONDO-APT(6)OTHER/
                V22 TO V36 (1)YES/
                V37 (1)USED TRAVEL AGENT(2)USED AUTO CLUB(3)USED
                NEITHER/
                V38 TO V41 (1)YES/
                V42 (1)1-3 WEEKS(2)4-7 WEEKS(3)2-3 MONTHS(4)4-6
                MONTHS(5)7-9 MONTHS(6)10-12 MONTHS(7)12+ MONTHS/
                V43 (1)JAN-FEB(2)MAR-APR(3)MAY-JUN(4)JUL-
                AUG(5)SEP-OCT(6)NOV-DEC/
                V44 (1)ONCE(2)2 TIMES(3)3 TIMES(4)4 TIMES (5)5
                TIMES(6)6 TIMES(7)7 TIMES(8)8 TIMES(9)NO-FIRST
                TIME/
                V45 TO V50 (1)NOT TOO IMPORTANT(2)SOMEWHAT
                IMPORTANT(3)VERY IMPORTANT/
                V51 (1)SUNSET(2)READERS DIGEST(3)GOOD
                HOUSEKEEPING(4)TRAVEL MAG(5)GOLF MAG(6)OTHER OR
                GENERAL MAG(7)LOCAL NEWPAPER(8)BROCHURE OR
                PAMPHLET(9)OTHER/
                V52 (1)ALONE (9)NINE/
                V53 (1)FRIENDS(2)RELATIVES(3)ALONE/
                V54 TO V55 (1)ONE OR ALONE(9)NINE/
                V56 (1)LESS THAN 5,000(2)5,000-9,999(3)10,000-
                14,999(4)15,000-19,999(5)20,000-24,999(6)25,000
                OR MORE/
                V57 (1)HEAD OF HOUSEHOLD UNDER 45, NOT MARRIED
                (2)HEAD UNDER 45, MARRIED, NO CHILDREN (3)HEAD
                MARRIED, YOUNGEST CHILD UNDER 6 (4)HEAD MARRIED,
                YOUNGEST CHILD OVER 6 (5) HEAD OVER 45, MARRIED,
                OLDER CHILDREN, NONE AT HOME (6) HEAD OVER 45,
```

```
                NOT MARRIED (7)SINGLE PARENT, OTHER/
                V58 TO V61 (1)SUNSET(2)TIME(3)NEWSWEEK(4)READERS
                DIGEST(5)NEW YORKER(6)GOOD HOUSEKEEPING(7)BETTER
                HOMES & GARDENS(8)LADIES HOME JOURNAL(9)FAMILY
                CIRCLE(10)SMITHSONIAN(11)NATIONAL GEOGRAPHIC
                (12)FORBES(13)FORTUNE(14)LIFE(15)PLAYBOY
                (16)MACLEANS(17)PREVENTION(18)SPORTS ILLUSTRATED
                (19)POPULAR MECHANICS(20)PEOPLE(21)US NEWS
                (22)TRAVEL MAGS(23)GOLF MAGS(24)OTHER MAGS/
                V62 (1)FEMALE(2)MALE(3)CANNOT TELL
READ INPUT DATA
FREQUENCIES     GENERAL = ALL
STATISTICS      ALL
FINISH
```